Writing Logically,
Thinking Critically

"Our _real_ first line of defense, wouldn't you agree, is our capacity to reason."

Writing Logically, Thinking Critically

THIRD EDITION

Sheila Cooper
Rosemary Patton

New York   Boston   San Francisco
London   Toronto   Sydney   Tokyo   Singapore   Madrid
Mexico City   Munich   Paris   Cape Town   Hong Kong   Montreal

Acquisitions Editor: Lynn M. Huddon
Marketing Manager: Carlise Paulson
Supplements Editor: Donna Campion
Production Manager: Mark Naccarelli
Project Coordination, Text Design, and Electronic Page Makeup: Nesbitt Graphics, Inc.
Cover Designer/Manager: Nancy Danahy
Cover Image: *Ocean Park, No. 79,* 1975 by Richard Diebenkorn (American, 1922–1993). Photo by
Graydon Wood, 1993. Philadelphia Museum of Art: Purchased with a grant from the National
Endowment for the Arts and funds contributed by private donors.
Photo Researcher: Photosearch, Inc.
Print Buyer: Roy Pickering
Printer and Binder: R.R. Donnelley & Sons Company
Cover Printer: Coral Graphic Services, Inc.

For permission to use copyrighted material, grateful acknowledgment is made to the copyright
holders on pp. 251-252, which are hereby made part of this copyright page.

Library of Congress Cataloging-in-Publication Data

Cooper, Sheila, 1946–
    Writing logically, thinking critically / Sheila Cooper, Rosemary Patton.--3rd ed.
        p. cm.
    Includes index.
    ISBN 0-321-07237-5 (alk. paper)
        1. English language--Rhetoric. 2. Critical thinking. 3. Academic writing. 4. Logic. I.
Patton, Rosemary. II. Title.

PE1408.C5485 2000
808'.042--dc21   00-030458

Please visit our website at http://www.awl.com/englishpages

ISBN 0-321-07237-5

2345678910—DOH—03 02 01

He who will not reason, is a bigot; he who cannot, is a fool; and he who dares not, is a slave.

—LORD BYRON

A mind that is stretched to a new idea never returns to its original dimension.

—OLIVER WENDELL HOLMES

The vital habits of democracy: the ability to follow an argument, grasp the point of view of another, expand the boundaries of understanding, debate the alternative purposes that might be pursued.

—JOHN DEWEY

BRIEF CONTENTS

DETAILED CONTENTS

CHAPTER 8

The Language of Argument—Style 205

CHAPTER 9

Research and Documentation 226

PREFACE

We agree and embrace the corollary, good thinking is essential for good writing. More and more, experts admit that in this age of ever-expanding information and changing careers, knowledge of facts alone will not serve. As futurist Heidi Toffler puts it, "Teach people how to think. There are no facts. Everything is open to interpretation." And long ago in 1914, Herbert Croly recognized the importance of thinking critically when he described the purpose of his new magazine, *The New Republic,* as "less to inform or entertain its readers than to start little insurrections in the realm of their convictions." With this third edition, we continue to promote such views, presenting writing skills as inextricably linked to logical thinking.

Writing Logically, Thinking Critically is designed as the central text in a course devoted to composition with an emphasis on argumentation or in a course combining writing and critical thinking. For independent readers interested in sharpening the logic and fluency of their prose, *Writing Logically* offers many practical strategies.

We expect instructors to change the sequence of chapters to suit the particular needs of a given class, to pick and choose as occasion demands. For many, the emphasis will fall on writing, for others, the exercises in logic will be valuable as well. We do not, as readers will notice, provide a reference of correct grammar and usage, but we do include sections on strengthening style at the sentence level. Handbooks on these topics abound.

Content Changes

This new edition has given us the opportunity to update examples and exercises for relevancy and to add some fresh cartoons. In response to helpful suggestions from those who have used the second edition, we have expanded material on revision, coherence, thesis statements, critical reading, and research and documentation. We have rearranged, combined, and divided chapters in order to streamline the sequence of instruction.

We have expanded Chapter 1, "Thinking and Writing—A Critical Connection," with more on the media, audience and purpose, and the writing process. We have extended Chapter 2, "Inference—Critical Thought," by adding an essay about responsible reporting of facts in journalism. We have also added Ernest Hemingway's short story, *Hills Like White Elephants.* Where literature is a major component of a composition class, this chapter can serve as a platform on which to build further readings. In Chapter 4, "Written Argument," we have expanded our discussion of the thesis and the revision process and provided strategies for promoting coherence.

We offer a few words here to help those of you already familiar with the text to find old topics or identify additions. We have kept the number of chapters at nine but have combined the former Chapters 5, 6, and 7 on deduction and induction to form one chapter, Chapter 7, "Deductive and Inductive Argument." Chapter 6, "Fallacious Arguments," retains much the same content as the old Chapter 8. We and many other users of the text continue to find that work on fallacies rewards students' efforts by making them more critical readers of the appeals, political and commercial, that surround them. The former Chapter 9, "Language: Meaning and Style," is divided in two. The first part now appears as Chapter 5, "The Language of Argument—Definition," an obvious extension of the instruction in written argument found in Chapter 4. The second section of the old Chapter 9 remains near the conclusion of the text as Chapter 8, "The Language of Argument—Style," appropriate for revising and polishing drafts. Some may want to refer to this chapter throughout the semester in connection with some or all writing assignments. We have upgraded and expanded the former appendix on research and documentation to a full new chapter—Chapter 9. This chapter, in addition to an enlarged discussion of how to develop and research a topic, now focuses on the ever-expanding role of the Internet in the research students do.

As before, we assume that *Writing Logically, Thinking Critically* will be most effective in classes where the students have already completed an introductory semester or quarter of composition. However, many find the book works well as the foundation text in first-year writing classes. Some secondary school instructors have been enthusiastic about its success in their advanced composition classes.

Pedagogy

We include a number of collaborative activities to encourage an interactive approach to learning. Most of the exercises and assignments can, in fact, be approached collaboratively. Writing assignments and exercises invite a broad range of responses that should cover the demands of writing across a diverse curriculum. The sequence of chapters as well as that of exercises and writing assignments can be changed to suit individual needs. At the request of several instructors who have used the book, we have eliminated answers to selected examples.

An Instructor's Manual is available for teachers who are using *Writing Logically, Thinking Critically*.

Acknowledgments

Once again, we owe many debts of gratitude. We continue to be grateful to our students, a few of whom are represented here and to whom we dedicate this text. They have helped us test, shape, and reflect upon the material, and, with their enthusiasm and their questions have inspired us to grow with them in the rewarding enterprise of writing logically and thinking critically. We are now also indebted to those instructors who have commented on our book and helped us improve it. Our debt to colleague William Robinson remains.

We would like to thank the following reviewers, whose comments and suggestions enabled us to make this a better book:

Hilayne E. Cavanaugh, Bridgewater Community College
Janel Davis, Saddleback College
Karl L. Edwards, Ricks College
Pamela Gold, University of Central Oklahoma
Margaret Langhans, Orange Coast College
Nancy Malone, Diablo Valley College
Mariann Maris, University of Wisconsin-Milwaukee
Alison McNeal, Slippery Rock University
JoAnna Stephens Mink, Minnesota State University
Troy Myers, California State University, Long Beach
Stephen D. Powell, TCU

Sheila Cooper
Rosemary Patton

CHAPTER 1

Thinking and Writing— A Critical Connection

It is doubtful whether a man [or woman?] ever brings his faculties to bear with their full force on a subject until he writes upon it.
—CICERO

For more than 2000 years, thinkers and writers have commented on the close relationship between thinking and writing. It would hardly seem debatable that to write well we need to think clearly. And the evidence is strong for concluding that writing about ideas can help to clarify them. Taking this notion a step further, many would argue that the act of writing can create ideas, can lead writers to discover what they think. Language, according to many scholars, can give birth to thought, and written language provides a way to refine our thoughts since, unlike speech, it can be manipulated until it accurately reflects our thinking.

Thinking Made Visible

Consider writing then as thinking made visible, as thinking in slow motion, a process whereby we can inspect and reflect on what we are thinking about. As novelist E. M. Forster put it, "How can I tell what I think till I see what I've said?" Roger Traynor, a former Chief Justice of the California Supreme Court, agreed when he spoke of writing and the law:

> I have not found a better test for the solution of a case than in its articulation in *writing*, which is *thinking at its hardest*.

Discourse doesn't simply convey thought; it also forges it. Language is a two-way street, both expressing and generating ideas.

Writing and thinking, when taken seriously, are not easy—a reality that led painter and critic Sir Joshua Reynolds to comment, "There is no expedient to which we will not resort to avoid the real labor of thinking." And many writers have groaned over the pain of writing. New York writer Fran Lebowitz takes an extreme position on the subject: "Writing is torture. It is very hard work. It's not coal mining, but it's work."

After visiting the Galapagos Islands in the 1830s, evolutionist Charles Darwin wrote to his sister from his ship, the *Beagle*, about the special challenge of reasoning on paper, the kind of writing we emphasize in this book.

> I am just now beginning to discover the difficulty of expressing one's ideas on paper. As long as it consists solely of description it is pretty easy; but where reasoning comes into play, to make a proper connection, a clearness and a moderate fluency, is to me a difficulty of which I had no idea.

The Power of Writing Persuasively

But, while writing and thinking may be difficult, mastery and success in both can be well worth the effort. We live in an increasingly complex society where clear writing is often essential. If we are not able to articulate a request, a complaint, or an endorsement in precise, forceful language, we may find ourselves settling for less than we need or deserve or giving to others the right to impose their decisions on us. If we can't write a persuasive application, the job or graduate school position may go to someone else. Linguist Robin Lakoff, in her book, *Talking Power: The Politics of Language,* puts it this way:

> In a meritocracy such as ours, we believe that those who best demonstrate the ability to think and persuade should have the lion's share of power. Articulateness according to the rules goes a long way; and its possessors are assumed to possess intelligence and virtue as inseparable concomitants. People who say things right, who plead their cases well, will be listened to and their suggestions acted upon. They will make the money, win the offices, find love, get all the goodies their society has to give.

Our Multicultural Society

It should be noted, however, that in a multicultural society such as ours, there are those who question our singular admiration for persuasive rhetoric, who look to less confrontational means of exploring issues and resolving differences. Seen through the eyes of a Japanese visitor, Yoshimi Ishikawa, who came here at age 18 and spent two years working and observing, the United States is a surprisingly violent nation. In his book, *Strawberry Road,* he claims that "the violent impression that America makes on foreigners is a result not just of its high crime rate but also of the one-sided nature of conversation here." But he too concludes that "the power to persuade and be eloquent are weapons one needs to survive in America." Whether a virtue or a weapon, the power of persuasion is seen as an asset in America today. As you will discover in *Writing Logically, Thinking Critically,* we are inclined to share both Lakoff's and Ishikawa's views and recognize that if we are to embrace the multiplicity of views represented in our culture we must avoid dogmatic, one-sided advocacy.

Critical Thinking

If, as we maintain, there is a strong relationship between thinking clearly and writing well—if one skill strengthens the other—then integrating the two as a course of study makes sense. But what do we mean by "thinking clearly"? Poets and engineers, marketing experts and philosophers would find any number of differing applications for such a broad term. For our purposes, we have found it helpful to narrow our focus and concentrate on the phrase **critical thinking.** This term has assumed a central position in both academic and public life and is variously defined today.

EXERCISE 1A

Defining Critical Thinking

Before you read further in this chapter, put this book aside, take a piece of paper, and write a few sentences discussing what you think the phrase *critical thinking* means. If you do this in class, you may want to compare notes with other students.

Critical Thinking as Self-Defense

In most contexts today the term **critical** means censorious or faultfinding, but it comes to us from the Greek *kriticos* and Latin *criticus*, meaning able to discern or separate. It is this sense of critical that we have in mind—discerning or discriminating thought characterized by careful analysis and judgment. As student Denise Selleck described it: "Thinking critically is the ability to understand a concept fully, taking in different sides of an issue or idea while not being swayed by the propaganda or other fraudulent methods used to promote it." She recognizes the importance of an open mind and the element of self-defense implicit in critical thinking.

As society and the kinds of work it demands have changed over the past few decades, so has the need for particular job skills. Today, in the information age, people have to know how to think, to think critically and creatively, if they are going to succeed. There are no certainties. We are surrounded by facts, all of which are open to interpretation. Such interpretation requires complex critical thought. And if our democracy is to endure, we all have a moral responsibility to engage in deliberate, critical thinking. How else can we make informed decisions about political candidates and issues?

In his novel, *I Married a Communist,* Philip Roth describes a memorable high school English teacher who taught his students the liberating power of critical thinking. "Cri-ti-cal thinking," Mr. Ringold said, using his knuckles to rap out each of the syllables on his desk top—"there is the ultimate subversion." Critical thinking was his route to opening up young minds and making them strong, by demanding that they question the world around them and recognize the power critical thinking could give them.

Advertising and the media, with which we are confronted every day, require careful critical scrutiny if we are to protect ourselves from false claims, questionable judgments, and confusing or deceptive argument. The cigarette industry, for example, has been particularly persistent in its efforts to entice potential smokers. In the early 1990s, the Philip Morris Company ran what were called by *Newsweek* the "smokeless cigarette" ads, a series showing celebrated public figures endorsing the Bill of Rights, part of the U.S. Constitution. Nowhere did the actual product—cigarettes—appear, either in print or image. These ads were designed for people like you—literate adults. The creators of such ads expected you to apply limited critical thinking at one level—to make the necessary connections—but to suspend such thinking at a crucial point in their seduction.

More recently, the manufacturers of Camel cigarettes had significant success promoting their product among teenagers when they draped billboards and filled their magazine ads with a lively animal character they named Joe Camel. He always looked cheerful, even cool. In the interest of juvenile health, Joe Camel was outlawed in 1998 but not before he had worked his insidious magic on many young people.

As advertising invades ever-increasing corners of our lives, we can be hard-pressed to distinguish information from promotion. Names of public buildings reflect their corporate sponsors. The new baseball stadium in one city was named PacBell Park for Pacific Bell, and you can probably name others in your community. When we go to the movies, we can't tell which is a preview, which an ad for some unrelated product. School textbooks carry advertising as companies reach for young minds. The Public Broadcasting Service, which used to be the one source of advertising-free television, now carries as much advertising as some of its commercial rivals. Television infomercials push new products even as they masquerade as objective information. And our computers, when connected to the Internet, bombard us with an ever-increasing array of products and services for sale.

Even news reporting in reputable newspapers requires intelligent evaluation. Two different papers reporting on a Supreme Court decision illustrate how a message can vary according to the way an editor construes the story. Here's how *The New York Times* opened its article on one of Chief Justice Rehnquist's opinions:

High Court Upholds Buffer Zone of 15 Feet at Abortion Clinics

BY LINDA GREENHOUSE

Washington, Feb. 19—The Supreme Court today upheld a lower court's order keeping demonstrators at least 15 feet away from the doorways and driveways of clinics in upstate New York that were the targets of blockages and boisterous protests in the early 1990s. The decision reaffirmed the Court's broadly protective approach toward maintaining access for patients entering abortion clinics. . . .

On the same date, the *San Francisco Chronicle*, relying on the *Los Angeles Times*, reported:

Abortion Foes Entitled to Confront Patients
Supreme Court Says It's Free Speech

BY DAVID G. SAVAGE
Los Angeles Times

Washington—Abortion protesters have a free-speech right to confront pregnant women on the sidewalks outside clinics and to urge them vehemently not to go ahead with the procedure, the Supreme Court ruled yesterday.

The 8–1 decision calls into doubt a wave of new city ordinances and judges' orders that have barred persistent protesters from confronting and harassing doctors, nurses and patients outside clinics. . . .

The Supreme Court opinion was long and contained a number of different judgments on various parts of the case. The two papers chose to emphasize very different features with startlingly different effects. Later in each article, the other issues emerged, but who can tell how far a reader will go in the morning paper? Headlines and lead paragraphs can be misleading or emphasize only one element in a complex story.

We cannot be vigilant enough in our efforts to defend ourselves from those who would deliberately manipulate us for personal gain or those who may innocently be choosing and packaging our news for us.

EXERCISE 1B

Scrutinizing the Media

1. What connection do you think the Philip Morris Company wanted you to make between the Bill of Rights and smoking their cigarettes?

2. Explain why an animal like Joe Camel might be so effective in selling cigarettes. If you are not familiar with this cartoon character, look back at magazines from the mid 1990s to find a picture of the famous animal.

3. Find an up-to-date example of an advertisement in print media that seduces the reader by indirect means and explain the methods the advertiser uses.

4. What conclusions might you draw about the writers who presented the two differing slants on the abortion clinic rulings quoted above?

5. Look for a single news story that is reported in different ways. You may watch several TV news broadcasts on the same evening and note differences in emphasis. Network news programs may differ from those

on cable television or Public Broadcasting Service. Summarize the story and describe how different sources presented the same facts.

An Open Mind—Examining Your World View

Another definition of critical thinking that also captures the spirit we hope to foster in this book comes from Richard Paul of Sonoma State University: "the disposition to think clearly and accurately in order to be fair." Like the earlier definition by student Denise Selleck, Paul's suggests the importance of developing an open mind, of listening attentively to the views of others.

It is, however, equally important to be aware of where our views come from. Cultures, subgroups within those cultures, and families within these groups tend to share what is called a **world view,** a set of assumptions about the world and the behavior of people in it. Without acknowledging that we hold such views, we may harbor prejudices about groups that cloud our thinking and restrict fair judgment. Many of these attitudes grow from the contexts of our lives that we take for granted—the opinions of parents and friends, our ethnic and religious backgrounds. Questioning our personal world view can be one of the most challenging steps in our growth as critical thinkers.

Where does the weakness in Jennifer's defense lie?

Profile of a Critical Thinker

If we examine the implications of Denise Selleck and Richard Paul's definitions, we can begin to formulate a profile of how a critical thinker might behave. Critical thinkers question their own beliefs and the sources of these beliefs as well as the beliefs of others. They also formulate well-reasoned arguments to support their beliefs, recognize the possibility of change in their beliefs, and express their beliefs in clear, coherent language. As a consequence, critical thinkers stand a better chance of being both fair and reliable in the conclusions they reach and the actions they take and will find themselves better protected from those who seek to take advantage of them.

Sometimes a successful critical thinker must be able to hold two or more opposing views on an issue at once. For example, raising tuition at your college could be the only way to ensure current levels of instruction. Paradoxically, doing so could mean that you and other students would be unable to stay in school. Reconciling such conflicts, thinking through the issues to discover alternatives, can represent a difficult but important accomplishment of critical thinking.

EXERCISE 1C

Your Own World View

Try a little self-analysis. Rate yourself according to the following checklist to discover how closely your critical thinking conforms to Paul's definition:

> Do you automatically dismiss positions opposed to your own?
>
> Do you take your own beliefs for granted without recognizing the need for support?
>
> Do you deny that your beliefs could change?
>
> Do you accept public information without question?
>
> Do you recognize that some assumptions based on your world view need to be critically evaluated?

After you have rated yourself, compare notes with a small group of your classmates and, with their help, start to create a description of your own world view. This will not be an easy task, but don't be discouraged or feel threatened. Putting such views into writing or even formulating what you think can be a challenge. There is no right or wrong answer here: just a critical exploration of your thoughts discussed with your peers.

This exercise may take the form of discussion or note taking and list making or a short written report of your findings.

Reason, Intuition, and Imagination

The heart has its reasons which reason knows nothing of.

—BLAISE PASCAL

Critical thinking can involve more than logical analysis. The creative imagination adds another dimension. We don't see sharp lines drawn between reason and imagination or rational analysis and intuition but rather an interplay between them. Intuition, imagination, and creativity as well as logic are ways of knowing. Our theory of critical thinking welcomes originality, encourages personal opinion, and considers paradox and ambiguity to be central to thinking and writing well, reflecting the world as we know it. The great French philosopher, Blaise Pascal, quoted above, declared that there were two extravagances: "to exclude reason and to admit only reason." Contemporary biologist Richard Dawkins, supporting this view, claims that scientists must also be poets and thinks that poets are well served by a knowledge of science. Poet John Ciardi found reason inadequate for explaining the natural world:

> Who could believe an ant in theory.
> A giraffe in blueprint?
> Ten thousand doctors of what's possible
> Could reason half the jungle out of being.

Sometimes a **metaphor** (a figure of speech that imaginatively implies a comparison between one object and another) can carry, through images and associations, an understanding beyond what explicit reasoning can convey. Writer Zora Neale Hurston, in her autobiography, *Dust Tracks on a Road*, remembers the persuasive power of a mentor's argument for honesty: "Truth is a letter from courage." The image contributes to the point she is making.

Audience and Purpose

A major distinction between writing outside the classroom and writing for a class lies in the audience to whom we write, what novelist and essayist Virginia Woolf refered to as "the face beneath the page." Job-related writing tasks, for example, include a designated audience and a real purpose. An employee may write to a superior requesting a raise or to another company proposing a cooperative venture. Readers of a newspaper often express their opinions in persuasive letters to the editor, and many a college student has depended on familiarity with the audience and careful manipulation of circumstance to explain a poor grade to parents. But in a class, students are asked to write papers for the teacher to critique and grade, usually with no specified purpose beyond successfully completing an assignment. Teachers cannot remove themselves from the role of ultimate audience, but for most of the major writing assignments in this text we have suggested an additional audience to lend some authenticity to each project.

Although different academic disciplines require variations in format, all good writing of an explanatory or persuasive nature is built on a balance between three essential elements: knowledge of the subject or argument, an identified audience, and a clearly defined purpose. The task of thinking through an argument, the audience, and the purpose for the writing introduces a significant critical thinking component to an assignment. Only when you take a conscious rhetorical stance toward your writing, can you have an appropriate voice and give power to what you write. The goal for you, therefore, is to define your subject or argument, identify your audience, determine your purpose in writing to this particular audience, and thus establish a tone that fits the writing task. You will be aiming for a balance between you, the writer, and the audience you are hoping to inform or persuade.

For example, suppose you have found that the college preparation provided by your high school was clearly inadequate. You have decided to take steps to remedy the situation. You will have to write letters to several different people explaining your concerns, citing supporting examples, and suggesting possible solutions. You know the issues and your purpose is clear: explaining a problem and calling for action. But the tone of your letters will vary according to your audience. The language you choose and the emphasis of your argument will be different when you direct your argument to a classmate for support; to your high school principal and teachers expressing your concerns; and to local, state, and national political representatives asking for help in the improvement of secondary education. For more on the relationship between writer and audience, see the section on *Rogerian Strategy* in Chapter 4.

WRITING ASSIGNMENT 1

Considering Your Audience

Choose any public issue that disturbs you—be it small or large, campus, community, or cosmic—and write *two* short papers (one-and-a-half to two pages *each*) expressing your concern.

1. In the first version, direct your writing to someone connected to, perhaps responsible for, the problem you are concerned about. Your purpose here is to communicate your concern or displeasure and possibly persuade the person responsible to take appropriate action.

2. In the second version, address an individual who is in no way connected to the problem you are disturbed about. Your purpose here is to explain the situation and to inform your reader of something he may know nothing about and is not necessarily in a position to change.

Label the two papers at the top (*1*) and (*2*) and clearly identify each audience.

Writing as a Process

Where do you begin when faced with a writing assignment? Many students turn to the five-paragraph essay format—introduction, three supporting paragraphs, and conclusion—and choose material that will fit easily into this preconceived mold. Writers rely on this formula because they fear that without it they will produce an incoherent essay. They assume that if they follow it, their writing will at least be organized. Even inexperienced writers must learn to let go of this "safety net" because although it may save them from anxiety and a disorganized essay, it can also determine the content of the essay; if an idea does not fit easily into the mold, the writer must discard it. This rigid structure prevents writers from exploring their topic, from following thoughts that may lead to interesting insights, and from allowing the material, the content, to find the shape that best suits it.

The most common misconception that student writers have is that a good writer is one who sits at his desk and produces in one sitting a polished, mechanically correct, cohesive piece of writing. If students are unable to do this, they conclude that they cannot write and approach all writing tasks with dread and apprehension. As a first step toward improving their writing, students must discard this myth and replace it with a realistic picture of how writers write. Hemingway, in Paris in the 1920s writing his first collection of short stories, *In Our Time,* spent whole mornings on single paragraphs. French novelist Gustave Flaubert, who wrote *Madame Bovary,* would spend a day finding *le mot juste,* the right word. While no one expects students, whose goal it is to produce a competent essay or report rather than a literary masterpiece, to spend this kind of time on their writing, students must realize that writing is a complex intellectual act, that it involves many separate tasks, and that the mind is simply not able to handle all of these tasks at once. It is unrealistic to expect that it should.

As writer Henry Miller saw it, "Writing, like life itself, is a voyage of discovery." Let's look at the distinct tasks involved in the act of writing a paper, in this voyage of discovery:

Generating ideas

Focusing a topic

Establishing a thesis

Organizing the essay

Organizing paragraphs

Providing transitions between sentences and paragraphs

Polishing sentences for fluency

Choosing appropriate diction (word choice)

Correcting grammar, usage, spelling, and punctuation

Each of these tasks could, of course, be broken down further. What is the solution to this problem, this mental overload that writing forces on us? The answer is that it must be done in stages.

Writing is a process that breaks down into roughly three stages—creating, shaping, and correcting. A common error students make is to focus their energy on what should be the last stage (correcting) at the beginning, when the focus should be on the creative stage of the writing process. The effect of this misplaced attention is to inhibit creative thinking. It is essential that the writer give ample time to the first stage, to generating ideas, to following impulsive thoughts even if they may initially appear unrelated or irrelevant. At this stage a writer must allow himself to experience confusion, to be comfortable with chaos; he must learn to trust the writing process, to realize that out of this chaos a logical train of thought will gradually emerge. Most important of all, writers must learn to suspend all criticism as they explore their topic and their thinking.

Strategies for Generating Ideas

Two concrete methods for beginning this exploration of your topic are brainstorming and freewriting, one or both of which you may already be familiar with.

To **brainstorm,** simply put the topic of the writing assignment at the top of a blank piece of paper or your screen. Then jot down words or phrases that come to mind as you think about this topic—as many words as possible even if you are not sure they relate directly to the topic. After brainstorming, look at your list: Circle ideas that you want to develop, draw lines through those that are decidedly unrelated or uninteresting, and draw arrows or make lists of ideas that are connected to one another. At this point you should be able to go to the next stage, organizing your essay either by writing an outline or simply by listing main points that you want to develop into paragraphs. Brainstorming is particularly effective with two or more people.

In **freewriting,** you begin by writing your topic on a blank sheet, but instead of jotting down words and phrases, you write continuously, using sentences. These sentences do not have to be mechanically correct, nor do they have to be connected. The only rule of freewriting is that you may not stop writing; you may not put down your pen or leave the keyboard for a set length of time. After freewriting for five to ten minutes if writing by hand, or longer if using a computer, read over your freewriting, circling ideas that you find interesting or insightful. Now you may do another freewriting on the idea or ideas you have circled, or you may try to formulate a thesis or list ideas you want to develop.

Both of these methods have two things in common. They are relatively painless ways to begin the writing process, and they allow you to circumvent your own worst enemy, your self-criticism, the voice that says, "That's not right," "That's not what I mean," "This doesn't make sense." Critical evaluation of your writing is necessary but inappropriate and self-defeating if you are critical at the beginning. In addition, freewriting may offer surprising access to ideas you never knew you had.

EXERCISE 1D

Generating Ideas

1. Choose an issue that is currently causing concern on your campus or in your community. Following the process discussed above, brainstorm as many ideas as possible on this topic. If others in your class agree on a shared topic, brainstorm together in groups of three or four, with one person acting as scribe or note-taker. After ten or fifteen minutes, go through your list of ideas and put them into some form of organized sequence that could later help give shape to a paper on the issue. Remember that you may have to discard some details that don't seem relevant. None of your points will be adequately developed yet.

2. As an alternative to brainstorming or as a follow-up, take a separate sheet of paper and freewrite for ten minutes on the issue. Then, in

preparation for a paper, read over your writing and circle or underline ideas that would contribute to an essay.

These steps are offered here as practice for Writing Assignment 1. We suggest you try them on assignments throughout this text. If, in this exercise,
you have identified a different topic but one that interests you, keep these
preliminary steps. They may fit a longer paper later.

The First Draft

After exploring your topic in this way and examining your data if you have
done research, you will have a sense of what you want to say and will be
ready for a first draft. If your paper requires research, consult Chapter 9,
"*Research and Documentation*," both before you start the process and
again later when you are ready for the "polishing" stage discussed below.

Successful writer Anne Lamott, in her book about writing, *Bird by
Bird: Some Instructions on Writing and Life*, discusses the role of first
drafts. Her advice grew out of her own experience as a writer and from
writing classes she has taught. The title refers to a family story in which her
brother, when 10 years old, was overwhelmed by a school report on birds
that had been assigned three months earlier and was now due. Their father, a professional writer, put his arm around his almost weeping son and
counseled, "Bird by bird, buddy. Just take it bird by bird." Good advice for
writing and for life. See if you can start treating your first drafts as what
Lamott calls "the child's draft" in the excerpt from her book which follows.

Now, practically even better news than that of short assignments is the idea of
shitty first drafts. All good writers write them. This is how they end up with
good second drafts and terrific third drafts. People tend to look at successful
writers, writers who are getting their books published and maybe even doing
well financially, and think that they sit down at their desks every morning feeling like a million dollars, feeling great about who they are and how much talent
they have and what a great story they have to tell; that they take in a few deep
breaths, push back their sleeves, roll their necks a few times to get all the cricks
out, and dive in, typing fully formed passages as fast as a court reporter. But
this is just the fantasy of the uninitiated. I know some very great writers, writers
you love who write beautifully and have made a great deal of money, and not
one of them sits down routinely feeling wildly enthusiastic and confident. Not
one of them writes elegant first drafts. All right, one of them does, but we do
not like her very much. We do not think that she has a rich inner life or that
God likes her or can even stand her. (Although when I mentioned this to my
priest friend Tom, he said you can safely assume you've created God in your
own image when it turns out that God hates all the same people you do.)

Very few writers really know what they are doing until they've done it. Nor do they go about their business feeling dewy and thrilled. They do not type a few stiff warm-up sentences and then find themselves bounding along like huskies across the snow. One writer I know tells me that he sits down every morning and says to himself nicely, "It's not like you don't have a choice, because you do—you can either type or kill yourself." We all often feel like we are pulling teeth, even those writers whose prose ends up being the most natural and fluid. The right words and sentences just do not come pouring out like ticker tape most of the time. Now, Muriel Spark is said to have felt that she was taking dictation from God every morning—sitting there, one supposes, plugged into a Dictaphone, typing away, humming. But this is a very hostile and aggressive position. One might hope for bad things to rain down on a person like this.

For me and most of the other writers I know, writing is not rapturous. In fact, the only way I can get anything written at all is to write really, really shitty first drafts.

The first draft is the child's draft, where you let it all pour out and then let it romp all over the place, knowing that no one is going to see it and that you can shape it later. You just let this childlike part of you channel whatever voices and visions come through and onto the page. If one of the characters wants to say, "Well, so what, Mr. Poopy Pants?," you let her. No one is going to see it. If the kid wants to get into really sentimental, weepy, emotional territory, you let him. Just get it all down on paper, because there may be something great in those six crazy pages that you would never have gotten to by more rational, grown-up means. There may be something in the very last line of the very last paragraph on page six that you just love, that is so beautiful or wild that you now know what you're supposed to be writing about, more or less, or in what direction you might go—but there was no way to get to this without first getting through the first five and a half pages.

The Time to Be Critical

In agreement with Anne Lamott, teacher and writer Donald Murray, in an essay on revision entitled "The Maker's Eye," points out a key difference between student writers and professional writers:

> When students complete a first draft, they consider the job of writing done—and their teachers too often agree. When professional writers complete a first draft, they usually feel that they are at the start of the writing process. When a draft is completed, the job of writing can begin.

The time to be critical arrives when you have a complete draft. Now is the time to read with a critical mind, trusting your instinct that if a word, a sentence, or a passage seems unclear or awkward to you, your reader will most likely stumble over the same word, sentence, or passage. You are ready to reshape your first draft, adding and deleting ideas, refining your thesis, polishing sentences for fluency, and finally writing another draft. Writer

Zora Neale Hurston described the process as "rubbing your paragraphs with a soft cloth."

Hurston didn't have the advantage of a word processor with which to move words, sentences, and paragraphs around freely. Sometimes the writing of the first draft will tell you when you need to do a little more research, expand your explanation of a point, or check some of your facts to be sure of your evidence. Computers make it relatively easy to revise your work and make repeated drafts.

Finally, you will be ready to check your spelling (in the dictionary or with a computer spell check) and your punctuation (in an English handbook; to date, computer grammar checks have been disappointing) and to read your essay aloud to yourself or to a friend, always ready to write another draft if it becomes necessary.

Every stage in the writing process is important, and each must be given its due. To slight one is to limit the success of the final product. There are exceptions of course. Some writers are able to compress some of these steps, to generate and organize ideas before ever putting pen to paper. But for most of us, successful writing results from an extended writing process that is continually recursive.

A caution: The danger in the way we have described the writing process is that we make it seem as though it progresses in three neat steps, that it proceeds in a linear fashion from prewriting to writing to rewriting and correction. In fact, this process is messy. You may be editing the final draft when you decide to add a completely new paragraph, an idea that didn't exist in any of the previous drafts. Nevertheless, if you realize that writing involves many separate tasks, that it is chaotic and unpredictable, you will not be defeated before you begin by criticizing yourself for having to do what all writers do—struggle to find your way, to express your thoughts so that you and your reader understand them.

In the following poem, Richard Wilbur describes this struggle.

THE WRITER

In her room at the prow of the house
Where light breaks, and the windows are tossed with linden,
My daughter is writing a story.

I pause in the stairwell, hearing
From her shut door a commotion of typewriter-keys
Like a chain hauled over a gunwale.

Young as she is, the stuff
Of her life is a great cargo, and some of it heavy:
I wish her a lucky passage.

But now it is she who pauses,
As if to reject my thought and its easy figure.
A stillness greatens, in which

The whole house seems to be thinking,
And then she is at it again with a bunched clamor
Of strokes, and again is silent.

I remember the dazed starling
Which was trapped in that very room, two years ago;
How we stole in, lifted a sash

And retreated, not to affright it;
And how for a helpless hour, through the crack of the door,
We watched the sleek, wild, dark

And iridescent creature
Batter against the brilliance, drop like a glove
To the hard floor, or the desk-top,

And wait then, humped and bloody,
For the wits to try it again; and how our spirits
Rose when, suddenly sure,

It lifted off from a chair-back,
Beating a smooth course for the right window
And clearing the sill of the world

It is always a matter, my darling,
Of life or death, as I had forgotten. I wish
What I wished you before, but harder.

EXERCISE 1E

Understanding Metaphor

Consider this poem for a few minutes. To what two things does Wilbur compare the writing process? What do these metaphors say about his view of the writing process? Identify and explain a metaphor that describes your own writing process.

As pointed out on page 9, metaphors can provide a vivid means of probing and revealing ideas. The creative thinking we do when we compare one thing to another can lead to new understanding. When we think creatively about our writing process, we are likely to *see* our writing in fresh and in-structive ways.

"I was on the cutting edge. I pushed the envelope. I did the heavy lifting. I was the rainmaker. Then I ran out of metaphors."

One Writer's Process

Let us add to Lamott's suggestions and Wilbur's poem a description of the writing process that produced this section of Chapter 1.

> ### Day 1:
> I spent two hours at the computer writing on the topic, "writing as a process." During this freewriting, my goal was to say everything I could think of on this subject that was important for students to know. Most of the paragraphs were focused on one point, but there were no transitions between sentences and paragraphs, and most of the sentences were only an approximation of the ideas I was trying to express. As I typed, I jotted down ideas which I wanted to include but which at the moment were interrupting the idea I was currently working on. I gave no thought to punctuation or spelling. Getting ideas on paper was my top priority.

Day 2:

I printed a copy of the three pages of freewriting I had done the previous day and spent three hours revising: eliminating, adding, and moving passages; providing transitions; and rephrasing most of the sentences.

Day 3:

I spent one hour polishing my sentences but made no major additions or deletions in the content.

Day 4:

I spent one last hour on a final review of my sentences, revising only a few of them. I checked my spelling with the help of a computer program, which indeed turned up several misspellings.

As you can see, it took a total of seven hours to write three single-spaced, typed pages that will take most readers ten minutes to read. And still I was not finished. The next step was to give this draft to my coauthor, who made further revisions. In Chapter 8, you will find an entire Writing Assignment devoted to revising one of the essays you considered finished. As Donald Murray notes in his essay on revision, "Most readers underestimate the amount of rewriting it usually takes to produce spontaneous reading." But we can take heart from novelist Kurt Vonnegut: "This is what I find most encouraging about the writing trades: They allow mediocre people who are patient and industrious to revise their stupidity, to edit themselves into something like intelligence."

WRITING ASSIGNMENT 2

Your Writing Process

Write an essay in which you discuss your writing experiences and yourself as a writer. Describe in some detail your writing process, what you consider your strengths and weaknesses as a writer, and conclude with your thoughts about the value of writing well.

Audience

Your primary audience for this assignment is your instructor, but you will also be an audience as you write your way to an understanding of yourself as a writer.

Purpose

To inform your instructor about your writing experiences and to gain insight into your individual writing process.

He or She?

You will notice that in our references to a writer or a student in this text, we alternate between female and male designations. This reflects not arbitrary choice but one of the ways writers today resolve the problem posed by the lack of a gender-neutral pronoun for the third person singular. This deficiency in our language reflects more than a simple inconvenience. The way we use language—the choices we make, the emphasis we place—suggests a broad range of personal and community attitudes, a world view, conscious and subliminal. A world described only in terms of masculine references assumes a world dominated by men. It is not surprising that as women began to share the public worlds of business, politics, medicine, art, and sport, the universal *he, him, his,* without the balance of *she, her, hers,* presented a bruising contradiction and a linguistic dilemma for writers and public speakers. Women were no longer willing to seem invisible.

Attempts to invent a new singular pronoun comparable to the helpful plural "they" to solve this problem have so far failed. In the meantime we are left with a number of choices. We must choose carefully on the basis of audience, purpose, circumstance, context, and, ultimately, personal inclination, all the time recognizing the implications of our choice.

Often we can use a plural noun to which the all-purpose plural pronouns—they, their, them—refer:

> *Writers* need to be aware of *their* audience when choosing language.

But when the noun we are referring to is singular, we have various choices:

> *Each* writer must consider the audience when revising *his or her* [*his/her*] paper.
> First, *he or she* [*she/he, s/he*] must decide how much background information the particular audience will need.
> First, *he* must decide how much background information the particular audience will need. [This represents the traditional use of "he" as a referent for both males and females.]
> First, *she* must decide how much background information the particular audience will need. [This choice redresses centuries of exclusion.]

Or we can sometimes drop the pronoun:

> Each writer must consider the audience when revising a paper. [A simplification of " . . . when revising his/her paper."]

Many readers object to the awkwardness that multiple pronouns create in the flow of a sentence. But others are offended by the implicit sexism of relying exclusively on the third person masculine pronoun [*he, him, his*].

"You'll just love the way he handles."

The crucial point is to be sensitive to the audience and aware of the power of language, while at the same time observing conventions of written English as closely as possible.

What You Can Expect from This Book

More Than One Approach

We explore a variety of strategies for expanding both writing and thinking skills, emphasizing the symbiotic relationship between them. We propose no formulas, no quick solutions. Rather, we view the development of each as a process that can take different turns for different people according to the occasion for writing. Reflecting our views on this diversity, the writing assignments throughout this book aim to avoid rigid adherence to form. Contrary to the advice of many writing texts, assignments in real life are not limited to prescribed numbers of paragraphs or a required sequence of parts. Essays or reports, whether explanatory or persuasive, should be designed to communicate a writer's ideas in such a way that the writer's purpose is clear and logical and satisfies the needs of a particular audience or discipline.

Collaboration

With your instructor, you can work out collaborative approaches to many exercises and writing assignments. You will find that the more opportunities you have to work with classmates, the clearer your thinking is likely to become, and the more likely it will be that the assignments reflect the writing and problem solving you will encounter in all academic disciplines and in the working world. Writing in the workplace more often than not requires collaboration with others. (This text, written by two authors, represents an example of such a collaboration.)

Sharpening Sentence Skills

Throughout many of the chapters, you will find practice in sentence-building skills, simple review for some of you, new strategies for others. Ideas tend to travel in sentences, and the greater the fluency of your sentences, the better equipped you will be to express complex reasoning in cohesive, logical prose. This is not a handbook of grammar and usage, but rather a carefully sequenced selection of rhetorical strategies selected to complement particular topics and issues. The logical relationships between ideas in a sentence and techniques for creating coherence come in Chapters 3 and 4. More on coherence and sentence development with appositives, verbal modifiers, and parallel structure comes in Chapter 8, as do other refinements of style such as sentence focus with concrete subjects and active verbs. These sentence skills may also be addressed on an individual basis as the need arises, not necessarily in the sequence given.

Enjoying the Challenge of Thinking and Writing

In his poem *The Four Quartets*, T. S. Eliot writes of the "intolerable wrestle / With words and meaning." But before you conclude that this whole enterprise is to be a bleak struggle, let us assure you that our goal is quite the contrary. Systematic thinking can be an exciting adventure. Polishing your prose to convey your ideas precisely and logically can be enormously satisfying. Writer Isaac Asimov expresses such an outlook well:

> Thinking is the activity I love best, and writing to me is simply thinking through my fingers.

Our expectations are broad and flexible. What we ask is that you reflect on your ideas, support your opinions, and practice writing about them with care. We hope to foster fair and independent thinking, a capacity for empathy, and the ability to advocate your own ideas logically and fluently.

KEY TERMS

brainstorming   unrestrained, spontaneous generation of ideas

critical thinking   discerning or discriminating thought characterized by fairness, openmindedness

freewriting   unrestrained, spontaneous, continuous generation of complete sentences for a set length of time

metaphor   figure of speech that imaginatively implies a comparison between one object and another

world view   a set of assumptions about the world and the behavior of people in it

CHAPTER 2

Inference—Critical Thought

Question

What do you infer from this cartoon?

Answer

As the evidence suggests, someone, we don't know who, jumped on his or her pogo stick and out the window of a very tall apartment building, meeting a gruesome fate. Though we do not see this unfortunate event, we see the opened box labeled "POGO STICK" and the marks of the stick on the floor leading to the broken window. On the basis of these observations, we infer what must have happened. But it is important to note, however, that we do not see an individual on a pogo stick jumping through a window; instead, we see evidence indicating that this is the case. We make an inference.

What Is an Inference?

An inference is a conclusion about the unknown made on the basis of the known. We see a car beside us on the freeway with several new and old dents; we infer that the driver must be a bad one. A close friend hasn't called in several weeks and doesn't return our calls when we leave messages; we infer that she is angry with us. Much of our thinking, whether about casual observations or personal relationships, involves making inferences. Indeed, entire careers are based on the ability to make logical inferences. In *Snow Falling on Cedars,* a contemporary novel by David Guterson, a coroner describes his job.

> It's my job to infer. Look, if a night watchman is struck over the head with a crowbar during the course of a robbery, the wounds you're going to see in his head will look like they were made with a crowbar. If they were made by a ball-peen hammer you can see that, too—a ball-peen leaves behind a crescent-shaped injury, a crowbar leaves, well, linear wounds with V-shaped ends. You get hit with a pistol butt, that's one thing; somebody hits you with a bottle, that's another. You fall off a motorcycle at 40 miles an hour and hit your head on gravel, the gravel will leave behind patterned abrasions that don't look like anything else. So yes, I infer from the deceased's wound that something narrow and flat caused his injury. To infer—it's what coroners do.

How Reliable Is an Inference?

The reliability of inferences covers an enormous range. Some inferences are credible, but inferences based on minimal evidence or on evidence that may support many different interpretations should be treated with skepticism. In fact, the strength of an inference can be tested by the number of different explanations we can draw from the same set of facts. The greater the number of possible interpretations, the less reliable the inference.

In the cartoon, given the marks made by the pogo stick and the broken window, we cannot arrive at any other inference but that the person on the pogo stick went out the window. But the inferences drawn in the other two cases are not as reliable. The driver of the dented car may not be the owner: She may have borrowed the car from a friend, or she may own the car but have recently bought it "as is." Our friend may not have called us for a number of reasons: a heavy work schedule, three term papers, a family crisis. She may not have received our messages. These alternate explanations weaken the reliability of the original inferences. Clearly, the more evidence we have to support our inferences and the fewer interpretations possible, the more we can trust their accuracy.

THE LANGUAGE OF INFERENCE

The verbs to infer and to imply are often confused, but they can be readily distinguished.

    to imply: To suggest, indicate indirectly, hint, intimate; what a writer, speaker, action, or object conveys.

    to infer: To arrive at a conclusion by reasoning from facts or evidence; what a reader, listener, or observer determines or concludes.

    A writer, speaker, action, or object implies something, and readers, listeners, or observers infer what that something is. A final distinction: Only *people* can make inferences; *anything* can imply meaning.

EXERCISE 2A

Interpreting a Cartoon

Quickly determine the message the following cartoon implies. What inferences do you draw from the evidence given? After writing a short response, compare your interpretation with those of others in the class. Are they the same?

TOLES COPYRIGHT © THE BUFFALO NEWS. REPRINTED WITH PERMISSION OF UNIVERSAL PRESS SYNDICATE. ALL RIGHTS RESERVED.

What Is a Fact?

We make inferences based on our own observations or on the observations of others as they are presented to us through speech or print. These observations often consist of **facts, information that can be verified.** Marks on the floor lead to a broken window. We see dents in the car. You have not spoken to your friend in several weeks. "A crowbar leaves linear wounds with V-shaped ends." Our own observations attest to the truth of these claims. But often we are dependent on others' observations about people, places, and events that we cannot directly observe. Take, for example, the claim that the last Americans left Vietnam in 1975. Few of us observed this action firsthand, but those who did reported it, and we trust the veracity of their reports. Books, newspapers, magazines, and television programs are filled with reports—facts—giving us information about the world that we are unable to gain from direct observation. If we doubt the truth of these claims, we usually can turn to other sources to verify or discredit them.

Facts come in a vast array of forms—statistics, names, events—and are distinguished by their ability to be verified. Confusion tends to grow less from the facts themselves than from the inferences we make based on a given set of facts. It is important, however, to think critically about our sources, including our own observations, in order to understand possible biases. Eyewitness reports and individual experiences, your own or those of others, can serve as valuable factual evidence. Whether or not evidence is accepted depends on how your audience views you as a witness or on their evaluation of a cited witness and the circumstances under which the report was made. The celebrated Japanese movie, *Roshomon,* in which four witnesses give different reports of the same crime, and numerous other tales, such as Lawrence Durrell's Alexandria Quartet or Ford Maddox Ford's *The Good Soldier,* illustrate how perceptions of the same event can vary.

Facts and Journalism

In "The Facts of Media Life," writer Max Frankel comments on the growing number of journalists, some of them well known, who have forgotten that verifiable facts are the foundation of good journalism.

The Facts of Media Life

In journalism, the highest truth is truth. Period.

The roster of fallen journalists grows apace: Stephen Glass, Mike Barnicle, Patricia Smith, James Hirsch, a whole team of CNN investigators. But the year's toll is proof not that many reporters often lie; it bespeaks a heroic battle by the news media to preserve the meaning of fact and the sanctity of quotation marks. Reporters have been losing their jobs for committing fiction, a crime that is no crime at all in too many other media venues, notably film and television docudramas.

While news teams root out the tellers of tall tales, the rest of our culture argues that a good yarn justifies cutting corners, imagining dialogue, inventing characters and otherwise torturing truth.

Barnicle was rightly fired by The Boston Globe for spinning sob stories around characters nowhere to be found. But he simply labored in the style of Truman Capote, who gained fame and wealth for the inventive conjecture and made-up conversations of "In Cold Blood," his "nonfiction novel." Glass and Smith were sacked for composing too-good-to-be-true plots. But Geoffrey Rush won an Academy Award for "Shine," his false depiction of David Helfgott as a pianist improbably driven mad by an abusive father reenacting Nazi brutalities.

The CNN producers were fired for believing too passionately that they had unearthed a wartime atrocity by American troops. But no one was punished for the atrocious slander committed by an MGM team in a movie called "Hoodlum," which showed Thomas E. Dewey, the three-term Governor of New York and Republican nominee for President in 1944 and 1948, taking bribes from mobsters whom in truth he had prosecuted fearlessly, at great personal risk.

Hirsch's unforgivable offense was to print a lie, albeit an inconsequential one: that The New York Times had no comment about the Barnicle affair. (It had commented that The Globe, its subsidiary, was editorially "autonomous.") But Random House sells "Midnight in the Garden of Good and Evil" as "all true" (and The Times has for nearly four years listed it as a "nonfiction" best seller) even though John Berendt, the author, acknowledges "rounding the corners" and inventing dialogue "to make a better narrative."

As for television, it routinely appropriates the personas of celebrities and crudely distorts their words, thoughts and features. Just the other night, I watched imposters trying to steal my treasured images of John and Robert Kennedy and Frank Sinatra, Sammy Davis Jr. and the rest of the Rat Pack.

What's wrong with a little mendacity—so goes the theory—to give a tale velocity?

It is unforgivably wrong to give fanciful stories the luster of fact, or to use facts to let fictions parade as truths. The authors of hybrid "factions" and "nonfiction novels" claim poetic license to distort and invent so as to serve a "higher truth" than—sneer—"mere journalism." But why then won't they create fictional names and characters and pursue their higher truths in imaginary plots? Why usurp the label of history while rejecting its disciplines?

The answer is that fiction and fact live in radically different emotional worlds and the fabricators greedily want the best of both. Fiction thrills by analogy, by the reader's knowledge that unreal plots can illuminate the deepest truths. Nonfiction excites by experience, by extending a reader's knowledge and understanding of reality. Why should not writers, editors, producers and publishers pretend, like carnival barkers, that fictions are facts? Because a reader who is lured into the House of Facts, poor sap, has paid to experience facts.

I have learned from Prof. Ben Yagoda that when Capote first submitted "In Cold Blood" to The New Yorker in 1965, its editor, William Shawn, repeatedly questioned the book's authenticity with a marginal note: "How know? d[iscuss]/w/author." Whatever the discussion, Capote escaped with his conjectures and fraudulent quotation marks. Though famous also for its fiction, Shawn's New Yorker pretended that Capote had satisfied their vaunted fact checkers.

Shawn was not called to account until 1984, when another of his writers, Alastair Reid, was discovered to have for many years routinely invented Spanish taverns and characters because, he said, "if one wants to write about Spain, the facts won't get you anywhere." Shawn defended the falsehoods with the fatuous remark that their author was "a man of utter integrity, and that's all I have to know." Watch out, Tina Brown, late of The New Yorker: the filmworthy manuscripts you seek for your new Disney magazine will encourage the maulers of fact to drown you in falsehoods.

Happily, journalism's infantry slogs on, struggling to distinguish fact from fiction. It wants to preserve the thrills of reality and believes that readers deserve the honesty implicit in Frank McCourt's refusal to put quotation marks around the reconstructed dialogue in his memoir of an Irish childhood, "Angela's Ashes."

It is a noble but uphill struggle. Admired intellectuals like Joyce Carol Oates have scoffed at the distinction, observing that all language tends by its nature to distort experience and that writing, being an art, "means artifice." But see how much she, too, values separating fact from fiction: Oates defeats her own defense of artifice with the supporting observation that Thoreau compressed two years into one in "Walden" and "lived a historical life very different from the . . . monastic life he presents in his book." How could she ever know in a world without fact?

Facts, unlike literature, do not promise truth. They only record what has been seen and heard somehow, by someone, subject to all the frailties and biases of their observers and interpreters. Yet they must be defended, particularly in a society that values freedom, because by definition, facts can be challenged, tested, cross-examined. Wrong facts and the truths derived from them are always correctable—with more facts. Fictional facts are forever counterfeit.

EXERCISE 2B

Questions for Discussion

1. What does Frankel mean by "the sanctity of quotations marks?"
2. Why did author Frank McCourt refuse to put quotation marks around the dialogue in his childhood memoir, *Angela's Ashes*?
3. What is Frankel's explanation for this outbreak of dishonesty among journalists?
4. Why is the phrase "nonfiction novel" an oxymoron (a figure of speech in which contradictory ideas are combined)?

What Is a Judgment?

When we infer that the individual on the pogo stick took one jump too many, we laugh but are unlikely to express approval or disapproval of the event. On the other hand, when we infer that the woman in the car in front of us is a poor driver, we express disapproval of her driving skills; we make a **judgment,** in this case a statement of disapproval. Or, when we infer from a friend's volunteer work with the homeless that she is an admirable person, we express our approval, i.e., make a favorable judgment. **A judgment is also an inference, but although many inferences are free of positive or negative connotation, such as "I think it's going to rain," a judgment always expresses the writer's or speaker's approval or disapproval.** In an attempt to mitigate disapproval of his client's behavior, one of Bill Clinton's lawyers asked that special prosecutor Ken Starr in his then not-yet-released report, refrain from interpreting facts: "Nothing . . . authorizes your office to prepare a 'report' to the House that purports to summarize and analyze evidence." In other words, he was asking Starr to make no inferences or express any judgments (though many would say the facts spoke for themselves).

Certain judgments are taken for granted, become part of a culture's shared belief system, and are unlikely to be challenged under most circumstances. For example, most of us would accept the following statements: "Taking the property of others is wrong" or "People who physically abuse children should be punished." But many judgments are not universally accepted without considerable well-reasoned support or may be rejected regardless of additional support and cogent reasoning. Frequently, a judgment is further complicated by potentially ambiguous language and even punctuation. Take for example the highly controversial wording of the Second Amendment to the Constitution:

Amendment II
A well-regulated militia, being necessary to the security of a free State, the right of the people to keep and bear arms, shall not be infringed.

Those in favor of gun control interpret this to mean that only "a well-regulated militia," not every individual, is guaranteed the right to bear arms. "Well-regulated" implies an official militia, not a private one free of government regulations. But those against gun control believe that the Second Amendment guarantees "the people," meaning all individuals, the right to bear arms.

To merit the right to be heard on this volatile issue, a person must provide considerable factual evidence and cogent reasoning.

THE FAR SIDE   By GARY LARSON

9-17   © 1985 Universal Press Syndicate

"Oh, what a cute little Siamese. ... Is he friendly?"

EXERCISE 2C

Distinguishing Between Facts, Inferences, and Judgments

Determine whether the following statements are facts (reports), inferences, or judgments and explain your reasoning. Note that some may include more than one, and some may be open to interpretation.

> *Example:* I heard on the morning news that the city subway system has ground to a halt this morning; many students will arrive late for class.
>
> "I heard on the morning news that the city subway system has ground to a halt this morning": *fact.* I did hear it and the information can be verified.
>
> "Many students will arrive late for class": *inference.* This is a conclusion drawn from the information about the breakdown of the subway.

1. Material on the Internet should not be censored by government or any other organization.

2. For sale: lovely three-bedroom house in forest setting, easy commute, a bargain at $325,000.

3. Forty-one percent of Californians who die are cremated—almost twice the national average of 21 percent.

4. Arnold has a drinking problem.

5. John Updike, reviewing Tom Wolfe's *A Man in Full,* concludes that the novel "amounts to entertainment, not literature."

6. After I took Richard Simmons' Vitamin Pills, the boss gave me a raise. Those pills sure did the trick.

7. Commuter—one who spends his life
   In riding to and from his wife;
   A man who shaves and takes a train
   And then rides back to shave again.
   —E. B. WHITE

EXERCISE 2D

Drawing Logical Inferences

Draw inferences from the following statistics and evaluate the relative reliability of your inferences.

N U M B E R S

$725 million Total fines the Justice Department levied on two of the world's largest drug companies for fixing vitamin prices

$1.4 billion Other antitrust fines collected by Justice since 1997

$95 million Annual budget for Justice's antitrust division

- -

$28.5 million Box-office receipts on the opening day of *Star Wars: Episode I*

$300 million Estimated cost to the economy of people's skipping work to see the movie

- -

77% Proportion of parents surveyed who say they would like to use a V-chip to block TV programs, if they had one

2 Number of nationwide electronics chain stores that stopped selling V-chip decoder boxes, for lack of interest

- -

3% Teenage girls in Fiji with eating disorders in 1995, before TV arrived

15% Fijian girls with eating disorders three years after the islands got TV

Sources: Washington *Post*, CNN, AP, L.A. *Times*, Kaiser Foundation

EXERCISE 2E

Solving Riddles

Use your inferential skills to solve these riddles by English poet John Cotton.

1.
Insubstantial I can fill lives,
Cathedrals, worlds.

I can haunt islands,
Raise passions
Or calm the madness of kings.
I've even fed the affectionate.
I can't be touched or seen,
But I can be noted.

2.
We are a crystal zoo,
Wielders of fortunes,
The top of our professions.
Like hard silver nails
Hammered into the dark
We make charts for mariners.

3.
I reveal your secrets.
I am your morning enemy,
Though I give reassurance of presence.
I can be magic,
or the judge in beauty contests.
Count Dracula has no use for me.
When you leave
I am left to my own reflections.

4.
My tensions and pressures
Are precise if transitory.
Iridescent, I can float
And catch small rainbows.
Beauties luxuriate in me.
I can inhabit ovens
Or sparkle in bottles.
I am filled with that
Which surrounds me.

5.
Containing nothing
I can bind people forever,

Or just hold a finger.
Without end or beginning
I go on to appear in fields,
Ensnare enemies,
Or in anothere guise
Carry in the air
Messages from tower to tower.

6.
Silent I invade cities,
Blur edges, confuse travelers,
My thumb smudging the light.
I drift from rivers
To loiter in the early morning fields,
Until Constable Sun
Moves me on.

—JOHN COTTON, *TIMES LITERARY SUPPLEMENT*

Now apply the same skills to these two poems by Sylvia Plath (1933–1963). What does each describe?

7.
I am silver and exact. I have no preconceptions.
Whatever I see I swallow immediately
Just as it is, unmisted by love or dislike.
I am not cruel, only truthful—
The eye of a little god, four-cornered.
Most of the time I mediate on the opposite wall.
It is pink, with speckles. I have looked at it so long
I think it is a part of my heart. But it flickers.
Faces and darkness separate us over and over.

Now I am a lake. A woman bends over me,
Searching my reaches for what she really is.
Then she turns to those liars, the candles or the moon.
I see her back, and reflect it faithfully.
She rewards me with tears and an agitation of hands.
I am important to her. She comes and goes.

Each morning it is her face that replaces the darkness.
In me she has drowned a young girl, and in me an old woman
Rises toward her day after day, like a terrible fish.

8.
I'm a riddle in nine syllables,
An elephant, a ponderous house,
A melon strolling on two tendrils.
O red fruit, ivory, fine timbers.
This loaf's big with its yeasty rising.
Money's new-minted in this fat purse.
I'm a means, a stage, a cow in calf.
I've eaten a bag of green apples,
Boarded the train there's no getting off.

APPLICATION TO WRITING

Achieving a Balance Between Inference and Facts

We need to distinguish inferences, facts, and judgments from one another to evaluate as fairly as possible the events in our world. Whether these events are personal or global, we need to be able to distinguish between facts, verifiable information that we can rely on, and inferences and judgments, which may or may not be reliable.

We also need to evaluate the reliability of our own inferences. Are there other interpretations of the facts? Have we considered all other possible interpretations? Do we need more information before drawing a conclusion? These are useful thinking skills that we need to practice, but how do these skills relate to writing? To answer that question, read the following paragraph and distinguish between statements of fact and inference.

A white player's life in the National Basketball Association is a reverse-image experience all but unique in American culture. Although fewer than 13 percent of United States citizens are African-American, about 80 percent of the N.B.A.'s players are. Of the 357 players on N.B.A. rosters, 290 were African-American, including several of mixed descent. Every one of the league's 20 leading scorers was black, and all but 2 of its leading rebounders. Not one N.B.A. teams has as many whites as blacks.

—ADAPTED FROM "THE LONELINESS OF BEING WHITE" BY BRUCE SCHOENFELD

This paragraph contains one inference while the remaining statements are factual, capable of verification. Notice that the facts support and convince us of the inference.

INFERENCE	FACTS

A white player's life in the ⟵────── National Basketball Association is a reverse-image experience all but unique in American culture.

Although fewer than 13 percent of United States citizens are African-American, about 80 percent of the N.B.A.'s players are.

Of the 357 players on N.B.A. rosters, 290 were African-American, including several of mixed descent.

Every one of the league's 20 leading scorers was black, and all but 2 of its 20 leading rebounders.

Not one N.B.A. team has as many whites as blacks.

Facts Only

Now, what I want is Facts. Teach these boys and girls nothing but Facts. Facts alone are wanted in life. Plant nothing else, and root out everything else. You can only form the minds of reasoning animals upon Facts: nothing else will ever be of any service to them. This is the principle on which I bring up my own children, and this is the principle on which I bring up these children. Stick to Facts, sir!

So says Thomas Gradgrind in Charles Dickens' novel *Hard Times*, an indictment against Victorian industrial society. Dickens knew that facts alone do not make for a good education nor for good writing. Expository writing frequently consists of a blend of inference and fact with the one supporting the other. If you were to write a paper consisting only of facts, it would be of no interest to the reader because reading facts that lead nowhere, that fail to support a conclusion, is like reading the telephone book. Jeff Jarvis, a book reviewer for *The New York Times Book Review*, comments on the dangers of this kind of writing:

Objectivity, in some quarters, means just the facts, ma'am—names, dates, and quotations dumped from a notebook onto the page. But facts alone, without perspective, do not tell a story. Facts alone, without a conclusion to hold them together, seem unglued. Facts alone force writers to use awkward transitions, unbending formats or simple chronologies to fend off disorganization.

A facts-only approach can also have serious consequences in our schools' textbooks. A recent report on public education cites such facts-only textbooks as one of the causes of students' lack of interest and poor achievement.

Elementary school children are stuck with insipid books that "belabor what is obvious" even to first graders. At the high school level, history—or "social studies"—texts are crammed with facts but omit human motivations or any sense of what events really meant.

Keep the danger of a facts-only approach in mind when you are assigned a research paper. Do not assume that teachers are looking exclusively for well-documented facts; they also want to see what you make of the data, what conclusions you draw, what criticisms and recommendations you offer. Do not fall into the trap of one eager young college freshman, Charles Renfrew, who, proud of his photographic memory, expected high praise from a distinguished philosophy professor for a paper on Descartes. He suffered disappointment but learned a lasting lesson when he read the comment: "Too much Descartes, not enough Renfrew." A photographic memory for factual information can be an asset, but your own inferences and judgments fully explained are also important.

Selecting Facts

Equally important when considering the facts you use in your papers is your selection of which facts to include and which to omit. When we omit relevant facts, we may be reflecting personal, political, or cultural biases and in the process distorting "reality." The omission of certain facts from accounts of historical events can have serious consequences, in small ways and large. Audre Lorde in her book, *Zami: A New Spelling of My Name*, illustrates this point eloquently.

I had spent four years at Hunter High School, with the most academically advanced and intellectually accurate education available for "preparing young women for college and career." I had been taught by some of the most highly considered historians in the country. Yet, I had never once heard the name mentioned of the first man to fall in the American revolution [Crispus Attucks], nor even been told that he was a Negro. What did that mean about the history I had learned?

Lorde is illustrating what others in recent decades have noted. For example, *Harvey Wasserman's History of the United States* and Frances Fitzgerald's *America Revised: History Schoolbooks in the Twentieth Century* explore the ways in which historians, through a systematic selection process, have distorted history. (Some would say Wasserman also distorts history in his efforts to right past wrongs.)

Inferences Only

It is possible to err in another direction as well; a paper consisting only of inferences and judgments would bore and antagonize readers as they search for the basis of our claims, the facts to support our opinions. If our writing is to be logical, convincing, and interesting, we must draw inferences and support them with relevant facts.

Reading Critically

Finally, distinguishing between facts, inferences, and judgments and evaluating their reliability allow us to analyze information, to read critically as writers, as consumers, as voters. Whether it is an article we find on the Internet, an auto salesperson, or a political candidate, we need to be able to separate facts from judgments and to ask that the judgments offered be supported by the facts. If we read or listen without these distinctions in mind, we are susceptible to false claims and invalid arguments, often with serious consequences for us as individuals and for society as a whole.

WRITING ASSIGNMENT 3

Analyzing a Recent Inference

Write a paragraph or two about a recent inference you've made. Include what facts the inference was based on and why you made it. Discuss with your classmates whether the inference was logical given the facts that led to it, whether others might have made a different inference from the same data, and why they might have done so.

Audience

Yourself and other members of the class.

Purpose

To think critically about your own thinking.

Reconstructing the Lost Tribe

> *Every language is also a special way of looking at the world and interpreting experience. Concealed in the structure of language are a whole set of unconscious assumptions about the world and the life in it.*
>
> —CLYDE KLUCKHOHN

With the above quotation in mind, imagine that a previously unknown civilization has been discovered and that linguistic anthropologists, after observing the civilization for a while, have delineated the following characteristics about the society's language:

Three words for terrain, designating "absolutely flat," "rolling," and "slightly hilly."

No word for ocean.

Dozens of terms for grains, including eight for wheat alone.

Several words for children, some of which translate as "wise small one," "innocent leader," and "little stargazer."

Seven terms to describe the stages of life up to puberty, only one term to describe life from puberty to death.

The word for sex translates as "to plant a wise one."

Terms for woman are synonymous with "wife and mother."

Terms for man are synonymous with "husband and father."

Twenty words for book.

No words for violent conflict or war.

Nine words for artist.

Terms for praise translate as "peacemaker" and "conciliator."

Words designating cow, pig, calf, and sheep but no terms for beef, pork, veal, leather, or mutton.

Several words for precipitation, most translating as "rain," only one meaning "snow."

Several words for leader but all are plural.

Four words meaning theater.

The Topic

Write an essay in which you characterize the society that uses this language.

As you analyze the characteristics of the language, you will be reconstructing a culture. Obviously, because the data are limited, you will have to make a few educated guesses and qualify conclusions carefully. ("Perhaps," "possibly," "one might conclude," "the evidence suggests," and similar hedges will be useful.)

The Approach

Examine and group the data; look for patterns.

Draw inferences, depending only on the data given.

Cite evidence to support these inferences—be sure to base all your conclusions on the linguistic evidence provided. Do not draw inferences that you don't support with specific examples. Be sure to use all the data. Explain your line of reasoning—how and why the data lead to the inferences you have made.

Don't simply write a narration or description based on the information. A narrative or story will only imply the conclusions you have arrived at from examining the data. This can be enjoyable to write and entertaining to read and certainly requires critical thinking, as does all good fiction. But your purpose here is to explain why you have made the inferences you have and to back up your inferences with facts drawn from the language list.

Consider giving a name to this tribe to help focus your sentences.

Audience and Purpose

You have a wide range of possibilities here; we leave the choice to you. Your paper may assume the form of a report, scholarly or simply informative, directed to any audience you choose. It may be a letter to a personal friend or fictional colleague. It may be a traditional essay for an audience unfamiliar with the assignment, explaining what the language tells us about the people who use or used it. What is crucial for success is that you, as the reporter-writer, assume that *you have not seen this tribe and have no first-hand evidence of it. You will also assume that your reader does not have a copy of this assignment;* it is up to you to cite all the specific evidence (the terms given in the list) to justify your inferences.

Making Inferences—Writing About Fiction

Many students are intimidated by assignments that require them to write about a poem, play, short story, or novel. What can they say about a piece of literature? Isn't there a right answer known to the author and the teacher but not to them?

Fiction is implicit. Writers of fiction—through character, plot, setting, theme, point of view, symbolism, irony, and imagery—imply meaning. Fiction is oblique. The work implies meaning; you infer what that meaning is. As you can see, interpreting literature requires critical thinking; it requires you to make inferences about the meaning of the work and to support these inferences with details from it as you have done with cartoons, statistics, and poems earlier in this chapter.

Reading is the making of meaning and the meaning we make depends on who we are—our sex, age, ethnicity, culture, and experience all influence our reading. Given the multiple interpretations possible, there is not a single right answer but only well-supported inferences that add up to a logical interpretation.

A final point: A critical essay is not a continuation of class discussion but a formal piece of writing that can stand on its own apart from the class. To accomplish this, you may think of your audience as one who is not familiar with the work you are writing about. This does not require you to retell every detail of the piece, but it ensures that you include the relevant details, the facts, on which your inferences are based rather than assume your reader knows them.

The next three assignments will give you ample opportunity to practice the skill of reading closely and thinking critically while making and supporting inferences about literature. The three stories, all quite short, on which the assignments are based are arranged in order of difficulty, so regardless of the one or more assignments chosen by your instructor, you may want to read all three stories and see how you do.

E X E R C I S E 2 F

Making Inferences About Fiction

Read "The Story of an Hour" by Kate Chopin [1850–1904] and answer the following question: Does Louise die "of joy" as her doctors suggest? Support your answer, your inference, with facts from the story.

The Story of an Hour

Knowing that Mrs. Mallard was afflicted with a heart trouble, great care was taken to break to her as gently as possible the news of her husband's death.

It was her sister Josephine who told her, in broken sentences; veiled hints that revealed in half concealing. Her husband's friend Richards was there, too, near her. It was he who had been in the newspaper office when intelligence of the railroad disaster was received, with Brently Mallard's name leading the list of "killed." He had only taken the time to assure himself of its truth by a second telegram, and had hastened to forestall any less careful, less tender friend in bearing the sad message.

She did not hear the story as many other women have heard the same, with a paralyzed inability to accept its significance. She wept at once, with sudden, wild abandonment, in her sister's arms. When the storm of grief had spent itself she went away to her room alone. She would have no one follow her.

There stood, facing the open window, a comfortable, roomy armchair. Into this she sank, pressed down by a physical exhaustion that haunted her body and seemed to reach into her soul.

She could see in the open square before her house the tops of trees that were all aquiver with the new spring life. The delicious breath of rain was in the air. In the street below a peddler was crying his wares. The notes of a distant song which some one was singing reached her faintly, and countless sparrows were twittering in the eaves.

There were patches of blue sky showing here and there through the clouds that had met and piled one above the other in the west facing her window.

She sat with her head thrown back upon the cushion of the chair, quite motionless, except when a sob came up into her throat and shook her, as a child who has cried herself to sleep continues to sob in its dreams.

She was young, with a fair, calm face, whose lines bespoke repression and even a certain strength. But now there was a dull stare in her eyes, whose gaze was fixed away off yonder on one of those patches of blue sky. It was not a glance of reflection, but rather indicated a suspension of intelligent thought.

There was something coming to her and she was waiting for it, fearfully. What was it? She did not know; it was too subtle and elusive to name. But she felt it, creeping out of the sky, reaching toward her through the sounds, the scents, the color that filled the air.

Now her bosom rose and fell tumultuously. She was beginning to recognize this thing that was approaching to possess her, and she was striving to beat it back with her will—as powerless as her two white slender hands would have been.

When she abandoned herself a little whispered word escaped her slightly parted lips. She said it over and over under her breath: "free, free,

free!" The vacant stare and the look of terror that had followed it went from her eyes. They stayed keen and bright. Her pulses beat fast, and the coursing blood warmed and relaxed every inch of her body.

She did not stop to ask if it were or were not a monstrous joy that held her. A clear and exalted perception enabled her to dismiss the suggestion as trivial.

She knew that she would weep again when she saw the kind, tender hands folded in death; the face that had never looked save with love upon her, fixed and gray and dead. But she saw beyond that bitter moment a long procession of years to come that would belong to her absolutely. And she opened and spread her arms out to them in welcome.

There would be no one to live for her during those coming years; she would live for herself. There would be no powerful will bending hers in that blind persistence with which men and women believe they have a right to impose a private will upon a fellow-creature. A kind intention or a cruel intention made the act seem no less a crime as she looked upon it in that brief moment of illumination.

And yet she had loved him—sometimes. Often she had not. What did it matter! What could love, the unsolved mystery, count for in face of this possession of self-assertion which she suddenly recognized as the strongest impulse of her being!

"Free! Body and soul free!" she kept whispering.

Josephine was kneeling before the closed door with her lips to the keyhole, imploring for admission. "Louise, open the door! I beg; open the door—you will make yourself ill. What are you doing, Louise? For heaven's sake open the door."

"Go away. I am not making myself ill." No; she was drinking in a very elixir of life through that open window.

Her fancy was running riot along those days ahead of her. Spring days, and summer days, and all sorts of days that would be her own. She breathed a quick prayer that life might be long. It was only yesterday she had thought with a shudder that life might be long.

She rose at length and opened the door to her sister's importunities. There was a feverish triumph in her eyes, and she carried herself unwittingly like a goddess of Victory. She clasped her sister's waist, and together they descended the stairs. Richards stood waiting for them at the bottom.

Some one was opening the front door with a latchkey. It was Brently Mallard who entered, a little travel-stained, composedly carrying his grip-sack and umbrella. He had been far from the scene of the accident, and did not even know there had been one. He stood amazed at Josephine's piercing cry; at Richards' quick motion to screen him from the view of his wife.

But Richards was too late.

When the doctors came they said she had died of heart disease—of joy that kills.

WRITING ASSIGNMENT 5

Interpreting Fiction

Read the short story, "Hostess," by Donald Mangum, and write an essay based on the inferences you make about the narrator. Include the facts on which these inferences are based and an explanation of why you made such inferences.

Audience

Someone who has not read the story.

Purpose

To characterize the hostess—what kind of woman is she?

Hostess

My husband was promoted to crew chief, and with the raise we moved into a double-wide, just up the drive. Half the park came to the house-warming. Well, Meg drank herself to tears and holed up on the toilet, poor thing. "Meg? Hon?" I said from the hall. "You going to live?" She groaned something. It was seeing R.L. with that tramp down in 18 that made her do this to herself. Now there was a whole line of beer drinkers doing the rain dance out in the hall, this being a single-bath unit. I was the hostess, and I had to do something. "Sweetheart," I said, knocking. "I'm going to put you a bowl on the floor in the utility room." The rest of the trailer was carpeted.

Dale, my husband, was in the kitchen with an egg in his hand, squeezing it for all he was worth. Veins stuck out everywhere on his arm. Paul and Eric were laughing. "What's going on in here?" I said.

Dale stopped squeezing and breathed. "I got to admit," he said, "I never knew that about eggs." I could have kicked him when he handed Paul five dollars. I found the bowl I was after, plus a blanket, and took care of Meg.

Then Hank and Boyce almost got into a fight over a remark Hank made about somebody named Linda. They had already squared off outside when it came out that Hank was talking about a Linda *Stillman,* when Boyce thought he meant a Linda *Faye.* Well, by that time everybody was ready for something, so the guys agreed to arm-wrestle. Hank won, but only because Boyce started laughing when Kathy Sueanne sat in Jason's supper and Jason got madder than Kathy Sueanne did because there wasn't any more potato salad left.

You won't believe who showed up then. R.L.! Said he was looking for Meg. "You think she wants to see you, R.L.?" I said. "After what you did to her with that trash Elaine?" So he said he'd only kissed Elaine a couple of times. "Or not even that," he said. "She was the one kissed *me.*"

"You know what you can kiss," I said. He stood there looking like some dog you'd just hauled off and kicked for no good reason. "Well, come on," I said, taking him by the shirt. I led him to the utility room to show him the condition he'd driven his darling to. I'm here to say, when R.L. saw that precious thing curled up in front of the hot-water heater he sank to his knees in shame. I just closed the door.

Back in the den, there was this Australian kangaroo giving birth on the television. The little baby kangaroo, which looked sort of like an anchovy with legs, had just made it out of its mama and was crawling around looking for her pouch. The man on the show said it had about ten minutes to get in there and find a teat or it would die. He said a lot of them don't make it. I got so wrought up watching that trembly little fellow that I started cheering him on. So did everyone else. Well, to everyone's relief, the little thing made it. Then Gus wanted to know why everyone over there always called each other Mike. Nobody had any idea.

Eric ate a whole bunch of dried cat food before figuring out what it was and that somebody had put it in the party dish as a joke. He tried to act like it didn't bother him, but he didn't stay too long after that. Melinda went out to her car for cigarettes, and a yellow jacket stung her behind the knee, so when she came in howling, Rod slapped this wad of chewing tobacco on the spot to draw out the poison, which made her howl even louder, till I washed it off and applied meat tenderizer and let her go lie in the guest bed for awhile.

That's when something strange happened. The phone started ringing, and I ran back to get it in Dale's and my bedroom, which was the closest to quiet in the trailer. I answered and just got this hollow sound at first, like you get with a bad connection over long-distance.

There was a mumble, then a woman's voice said, "She's gone." I didn't recognize the voice, but I was sure what "gone" meant by the way she said it. It meant someone had died. Then she said—and she almost screamed it—"Someone should have been here. Why weren't you and Clarence here?"

Now, I don't know a soul in this world named Clarence, and this was clearly a case of the wrong number. "Ma'am," I said as gently as I knew how.

"You'll have to talk louder," she said. "I can hardly hear you."

I curled my hand around my lips and the mouthpiece and said, "Ma'am, you have dialled the wrong number."

"Oh, God, I'm sorry," she said. "Oh dear God." And here is the strange thing. The woman did not hang up. She just kept saying, "Dear God" and crying.

I sat there listening to that woman and to all the happy noise coming from everywhere in the trailer and through the window from outside, and when she finally brought it down to a sniffle I said, "Honey, who was it that passed away?"

"My sister," she said. "My sister, Beatrice." And it was like saying the name started her to sobbing again.

"And none of your people are there?" I said.

"Just me," she said.

"Sweetheart, you listen to me," I said, trying to close the window for more quiet. Sweet Christ, I thought. Dear sweet Christ in Heaven. "Are you listening, angel? You should not be alone right now. You understand what I'm telling you?" I said, "Now, I am right here."

—DONALD MANGUM

WRITING ASSIGNMENT 6

Analyzing Fiction

One critic said of Ernest Hemingway (1899–1961) that his writing is like an iceberg—nine-tenths of it is beneath the surface. A writer having difficulty adapting one of Hemingway's novels for the screen complained that the novelist wrote in the white spaces between the lines. Hemingway's elliptical style stems, in part, from his frequent use of the objective point of view. A writer employing this point of view is like a video camera that only records what it sees and hears: It cannot comment or interpret or enter a character's mind. This point of view demands that the reader make inferences about the characters' behavior and motivations. Hemingway's "Hills Like White Elephants" is just such a story. After reading the story and answering the questions that follow it, write an essay about the conflict at the heart of this story.

Audience

Someone unfamiliar with the story.

Purpose

To infer the meaning of the story.

Hills Like White Elephants
ERNEST HEMINGWAY

The hills across the valley of the Ebro were long and white. On this side there was no shade and no trees and the station was between two lines of rails in the sun. Close against the side of the station there was the warm shadow of the building and a curtain, made of strings of bamboo beads, hung across the open door into the bar, to keep out flies. The American and the girl with him sat at a table in the shade, outside the building. It was very hot and the express from Barcelona would come in forty minutes. It stopped at this junction for two minutes and went on to Madrid.

"What should we drink?" the girl asked. She had taken off her hat and put it on the table.

"It's pretty hot," the man said.

"Let's drink beer."

"Dos cervezas," the man said into the curtain.

"Big ones?" a woman asked from the doorway.

"Yes. Two big ones."

The woman brought two glasses of beer and two felt pads. She put the felt pads and the beer glasses on the table and looked at the man and the girl. The girl was looking off at the line of hills. They were white in the sun and the country was brown and dray.

"They look like white elephants," she said.

"I've never seen one," the man drank his beer.

"No, you wouldn't have."

"I might have," the man said. "Just because you say I wouldn't have doesn't prove anything."

The girl look at the bead curtain. "They've painted something on it," she said. "What does it say?"

"Anis del Toro. It's a drink."

"Could we try it?"

The man called "Listen" through the curtain. The woman came out from the bar.

"Four reales."

"We want two Anis del Toro."

"With water?"

"Do you want it with water?"

"I don't know," the girl said. "Is it good with water?"

"It's all right."

"You want them with water?" asked the woman.

"Yes, with water."

"It tastes like licorice," the girl said and put the glass down.

"That's the way with everything."

"Yes," said the girl. "Everything tastes of licorice. Especially all the things you've waited so long for, like absinthe."

"Oh, cut it out."

"You started it," the girl said. "I was being amused. I was having a fine time."

"Well, let's try and have a fine time."

"All right. I was trying. I said the mountains looked like white elephants. Wasn't that bright?"

"That was bright."

"I wanted to try this new drink. That's all we do, isn't it—look at things and try new drinks?"

"I guess so."

The girl looked across at the hills.

"They're lovely hills," she said. "They don't really look like white elephants. I just meant the coloring of their skin through the trees."

"Should we have another drink?"

"All right."

The warm wind blew the bead curtain against the table.

"The beer's nice and cool," the man said.

"It's lovely," the girl said.

"It's really an awfully simple operation, Jig," the man said. "It's not really an operation at all."

The girl looked at the ground the table legs rested on.

"I know you wouldn't mind it, Jig. It's really not anything. It's just to let the air in."

The girl did not say anything.

"I'll go with you and I'll stay with you all the time. They just let the air in and then it's all perfectly natural."

"Then what will we do afterward?"

"We'll be fine afterward. Just like we were before."

"What makes you think so?"

"That's the only thing that bothers us. It's the only thing that's made us unhappy."

The girl looked at the bead curtain, put her hand out and took hold of two of the strings of beads.

"And you think then we'll be all right and be happy."

"I know we will. You don't have to be afraid. I've known lots of people that have done it."

"So have I," said the girl. "And afterward they were all so happy."

"Well," the man said, "if you don't want to you don't have to. I wouldn't have you do it if you didn't want to. But I know it's perfectly simple."

"And you really want to?"

"I think it's the best thing to do. But I don't want you to do it if you don't really want to."

"And if I do it you'll be happy and things will be like they were and you'll love me?"

"I love you now. You know I love you."

"I know. But if I do it, then it will be nice again if I say things are like white elephants, and you'll like it?"

"I'll love it. I love it now but I just can't think about it. You know how I get when I worry."

"If I do it you won't ever worry?"

"I won't worry about that because it's perfectly simple."

"Then I'll do it. Because I don't care about me."

"What do you mean?"

"I don't care about me."

"Well, I care about you."

"Oh, yes. But I don't care about me. And I'll do it and then everything will be fine."

"I don't want you to do it if you feel that way."

The girl stood up and walked to the end of the station. Across, on the other side, were fields of grain and trees along the banks of the Ebro. Far away, beyond the river, were mountains. The shadow of a cloud moved across the field of grain and she saw the river through the trees.

"And we could have all this," she said. "And we could have everything and every day we make it more impossible."

"What did you say?"

"I said we could have everything."

"We can have everything."

"No, we can't."

"We can have the whole world."

"No, we can't."

"We can go everywhere."

"No, we can't. It isn't ours any more."

"It's ours."

"No, it isn't. And once they take it away, you never get it back."

"But they haven't taken it away."

"We'll wait and see."

"Come on back in the shade," he said. "You mustn't feel that way."

"I don't feel any way," the girl said. "I just know things."

"I don't want you to do anything that you don't want to do——"

"Nor that isn't good for me," she said. "I know. Could we have another beer?"

"All right. But you've got to realize——"

"I realize," the girl said. "Can't we maybe stop talking?"

They sat down at the table and the girl looked across at the hills on the dry side of the valley and the man looked at her and at the table.

"You've got to realize," he said, "that I don't want you to do it if you don't want to. I'm perfectly willing to go through with it if it means anything to you."

"Doesn't it mean anything to you? We could get along."

"Of course it does. But I don't want anybody but you. I don't want any one else. And I know it's perfectly simple."

"Yes, you know it's perfectly simple."

"It's all right for you to say that, but I do know it."

"Would you do something for me now?"

"I'd do anything for you."

"Would you please please please please please please please stop talking?"

He did not say anything but looked at the bags against the wall of the station. There were labels on them from all the hotels where they had spent nights.

"But I don't want you to," he said, "I don't care anything about it."

"I'll scream," the girl said.

The woman came out through the curtains with two glasses of beer and put them down on the damp felt pads. "The train comes in five minutes," she said.

"What did she say?" asked the girl.

"That the train is coming in five minutes."

The girl smiled brightly at the woman, to thank her.

"I'd better take the bags over to the other side of the station," the man said. She smiled at him.

"All right. Then come back and we'll finish the beer."

He picked up the two heavy bags and carried them around the station to the other tracks. He looked up the tracks but could not see the train. Coming back, he walked through the barroom, where people waiting for the train were drinking. He drank an Anis at the bar and looked at the people. They were all waiting reasonably for the train. He went out through the bead curtain. She was sitting at the table and smiled at him.

"Do you feel better?" he asked.

"I feel fine," she said. "There's nothing wrong with me. I feel fine."

EXERCISE 2G

Questions for Discussion

1. What is "the awfully simple operation" the man refers to? How does he feel about it? How does Jig feel about it? Is the man sincere in everything he says?

2. Why do you think Hemingway gave the woman a name but not the man?

3. What do you know about their life together? What is the relevance of the woman's comments about absinthe?

4. What is the significance of Jig comparing the hills across the valley to white elephants? Why does Hemingway use that comparison for his title?

5. How is the conflict between the couple resolved?

EXERCISE 2H

Analyzing a Film

As a final exercise in making and supporting inferences, rent the 1999 John Sayles film, *Limbo*. The conclusion of the movie is open to interpretation; members of the audience are left to decide for themselves if the three individuals stranded on the island are rescued or murdered. What do you think? Write a short paper explaining your answer, citing as evidence specific details from the movie.

SUMMARY

In order to interpret the world around us and write effectively about it, we need to be able to distinguish facts, inferences, and judgments from one another and to evaluate the reliability of our inferences.

In written exposition and argument, and in the interpretation of literature, it is important to achieve a balance between fact and inference, to support our inferences with facts and reasoning.

KEY TERMS

Facts   information that can be verified.

Inference   a conclusion about something we don't know based on what we do know.

Judgment   an inference that expresses either approval or disapproval.

CHAPTER 3

The Structure of Argument

You always hurt the one you love!

When we offer our own views on an issue we are expressing an **opinion.** We all have them. We all should have them. But we should also recognize the difference between voicing an opinion and developing an argument. Someone might insist that using animals for medical research is wrong; a research physician might respond that this attitude is misguided. Both are expressing opinions. If they both stick to their guns but refuse to elaborate their positions, then each may simply dismiss the opponent's statement as "mere opinion," as nothing more than an emotional reaction. If, on the other hand, they start to offer reasons in support of their opinions, then they have moved the discussion to an argument. The critic might add that animals suffer pain in much the same way that humans do, and thus experiments inflict cruel suffering on the animals. The physician might respond that modern techniques have greatly reduced animal suffering and that such experiments are necessary for medical breakthroughs. They are now offering support for their opinions. Don't be afraid of your opinions. Just be prepared to defend them with good reasoning. Think of opinions as starting points for arguments.

In logic, an **argument** is not a fight but a rational piece of discourse, written or spoken, which attempts to persuade the reader or listener to believe something. For instance, we can attempt to persuade others to believe that cutting old timber will harm the environment or that a vote for a particular candidate will ensure a better city government. Though many arguments are concerned with political issues, arguments are not limited to such topics. We can argue about books, movies, restaurants, and cars, as well as about abstractions found in philosophical issues, to name just a few of the possibilities. Whenever we want to convince someone else of the "rightness" of our position by offering reasons for that position, we are presenting an argument.

Premises and Conclusions

The structure of all arguments, no matter what the subject, consists of two components: **premises** and **conclusions.** The **conclusion** is the key assertion that the other assertions support. These other assertions are the **premises,** reasons that support the conclusion.* For example:

> Because the poor spend proportionately more of their income on gambling than higher income groups and because gambling sends a "something for nothing" message that erodes the work ethic, government should take steps to contain and curtail the spread of gambling.

In this example, the conclusion—that government should take steps to contain and curtail the spread of gambling—is supported by two premises: that the poor spend proportionately more of their income on gambling than higher income groups and that gambling sends a message that erodes the work ethic. For a group of assertions to be an argument, the passage must contain both these elements—a conclusion and at least one premise.

Look at the following letter to the editor of a news magazine:

> I was horrified to read "Corporate Mind Control" and learn that some companies are training employees in New Age thinking, which is a blend of the occult, Eastern religions, and a smattering of Christianity. What they're dealing

---

*Throughout this book, we use the term premise in its contemporary, general sense, meaning a claim (or statement) that leads to a conclusion. We do not restrict its meaning to the classical definition—either one of the two propositions of a syllogism from which the conclusion is drawn. See syllogisms in Chapter 7.

with is dangerous—Krone Training will be disastrous to the company and the employee.

This writer thinks that she has written an argument against Krone Training, but her letter consists of a conclusion only, which is in essence that Krone Training is not a good idea. Because she fails to include any premises in support of her conclusion, she fails to present an argument and fails to convince anyone who did not already share her belief that Krone Training is "dangerous" and "disastrous." A conclusion repeated in different words may look like an argument but shouldn't deceive a careful reader. (See Chapter 6 for more on fallacious, or deceptive, arguments.) Can you formulate a premise that would transform the letter into an argument?

Distinguishing Between Premises and Conclusions

In order to evaluate the strength of an argument, we need to understand its structure, to distinguish between its premises and conclusion. **Joining words**—conjunctions and transitional words and phrases—indicate logical relationships between ideas and therefore often help us to make this distinction. Notice the radical change in meaning that results from the reversal of two clauses joined by the conjunction "because":

> I didn't drink because I had problems. I had problems because I drank.
>
> —BARNABY CONRAD

The use of joining words in argument is especially important because they indicate which assertions are being offered as premises and which are offered as conclusions. For example:

> Our government's decision to apply a similar tariff on luxury Japanese cars sold here was a just one *because* Japan imposed a prohibitive tariff on the sale of new American cars in their country.

> Japan imposed a prohibitive tariff on the sale of new American cars in their country, *so* our government's decision to apply a similar tariff on luxury Japanese cars sold here was a just one.

In the first example, "because" indicates a premise, a reason in support of the conclusion that the decision to impose a tariff on Japanese cars was a just one. In the second example, "so" indicates the conclusion. Both statements present essentially the same argument; the difference between the two sentences is rhetorical—a matter of style, not substance.

"Because" and "since" frequently introduce premises whereas "so," "therefore," "thus," "hence," and "consequently" often introduce conclusions.

conclusion because *premise*

premise therefore *conclusion*

Note: "and" as well as "but" often connects premises.

Standard Form

With the help of joining words and transitional phrases, we can analyze the structure of an argument and then put it into **standard form.** An argument in standard form is an argument reduced to its essence: its premises and conclusion. In other words, it is an outline of the argument. In the previous argument on gambling, each premise is indicated by the "because" that introduces it, the conclusion then following from these two premises. In standard form, the argument looks like this:

Premise 1 The poor spend proportionately more of their income on gambling than higher income groups.

Premise 2 Gambling sends a "something for nothing" message that erodes the work ethic.

∴ Government should take steps to contain and curtail the spread of gambling.

Note: ∴ is a symbol in logic meaning "therefore."

Read this argument about college grading policies taken from a *New York Times* editorial by Clifford Adelman, a senior research analyst with the Department of Education.

If there are 50 ways to leave your lover, there are almost as many ways to walk away from a college course without penalty. What are prospective employers to make of the following "grades" that I have seen on transcripts: W, WP, WI, WX, WM, WW, K, L, Q, X and Z. What does "Z" mean? "The student 'zeed out,'" one registrar told me. At another institution, I was told that it stood for "zapped." Despite the zap, I was informed, there was no penalty.

But there is a penalty. The time students lose by withdrawing is time they must recoup. All they have done is increase the cost of school to themselves, their families and, if at a public institution, to taxpayers.

This increasing volume of withdrawals and repeats does not bode well for students' future behavior in the workplace, where repeating tasks is costly.

Many employers agree that work habits and time-management skills are as important as the knowledge new employees bring. It wouldn't take much for schools to change their grading policies so that students would have to finish what they start.

Though this argument is three paragraphs long, in standard form it can be reduced to four sentences:

Premise 1 The time students lose by withdrawing is time they must recoup.

Premise 2 They increase the cost of school to themselves, their families and, if at a public institution, to taxpayers.

Premise 3 Work habits and time-management skills are as important as the knowledge new employees bring.

∴ Schools should change their grading policies so that students would have to finish what they start.

The first paragraph provides the reader with necessary background information because the writer can't assume that his readers will know the specifics of current college grading policies. The second paragraph contains two of his three premises while the final paragraph contains his third premise (and development of that premise) and his conclusion.

The conclusion of this argument—that schools should change their grading policy—is an inference, a judgment. Indeed, all conclusions are inferences. If they were facts we would not need to supply premises to support them; we would simply verify them by checking the source. In this argument, the first two premises are factual and the third is an inference, one which, on the basis of experience, most of us would be inclined to accept.

Examine the argument.

Baseball fans have long argued that the city should build a downtown baseball stadium. If the city doesn't build a new stadium the team may leave, and a major city deserves a major league team. Furthermore, downtown's summer weather is superior to the freezing wind of the present site, and public transportation to downtown would make the park more accessible.

In this example, four separate premises are offered for the conclusion.

Premise 1 If the city doesn't build a new stadium, the team may leave.

Premise 2 A major city deserves a major league team.

Premise 3 Downtown's summer weather is superior to the freezing wind of the present site.

Premise 4 Public transportation to downtown would make the park more accessible.

∴ The city should build a downtown baseball stadium.

EXERCISE 3A ⟋ ʜ૯ᴡ.

Reducing Simple Arguments to Standard Form

Put each of the following arguments into standard form by first circling the joining words and transitional phrases, then identifying the conclusion, and finally identifying the premises. List the premises, numbering each separate statement, and write the conclusion using the symbol ∴. Leave out the joining words and phrases, because standard form identifies premises and conclusions, but write each premise and the conclusion as a complete sentence.

Example: All politicians make promises they can't keep, and Jerry is nothing if not a politician. He will, therefore, make promises he can't keep.

1. All politicians make promises they can't keep.
2. Jerry is a politician.

   ∴ He will make promises he can't keep.

1. Because technical jobs are increasing more rapidly than other jobs, American high schools need to collaborate with industry in apprenticeship programs for those students who do not plan to attend college.

2. Because school vouchers would undermine public schools, permit discrimination, and transfer taxpayer money to those who need it least, private school parents, voters should not pass such legislation.

3. The student union building is ugly and uncomfortable. The preponderance of cement makes the building appear cold and gray both inside and out. Many of the rooms lack windows, so that one is left staring at the cement wall. The chairs are generally cheap and uncomfortable, while the poor lighting makes studying difficult, and the terrible acoustics make conversations almost impossible.

4. Abortion raises important moral questions, for abortion involves both a woman's right to privacy and the question of when life begins, and anything that involves personal rights and the onset of life raises serious moral questions.

5. Many biologists and gynecologists argue that life does not begin at conception. And the Supreme Court ruled in 1973 that to restrict a woman's right to have an abortion violates her right to privacy. These two facts lead us to believe that abortion should remain a woman's choice.

6. Capital punishment is not justified since with capital punishment, an innocent person might be executed, and no practice that might kill innocent people is justified.

7. Because some killers are beyond rehabilitation, society should have the right to execute those convicted of first-degree murder. More uniform implementation of the death penalty may serve as a deterrent, and victims' families are entitled to appropriate vengeance. Furthermore, the costs of maintaining a prisoner for life are too great, and no state guarantees that life imprisonment means no parole.

8. In his celebrated work *On Liberty,* a defense of freedom of speech, John Stuart Mill argues that "power can be rightfully exercised over any member of a civilized community" only to "prevent harm to others." Because he maintains that no opinion, no matter how disagreeable, can inflict harm, it follows that we don't have the right to suppress opinion.

9. Despite the controversy, we didn't need the movie rating NC–17 as we did not need the X rating before it. The R rating already protects children, and any further restriction of choice violates our freedom of expression guaranteed under the First Amendment. And as critics have pointed out, several R-rated films are more sexually explicit than some rated NC–17, making the distinction between the two ratings unclear as well as unnecessary.

10. S. Frederick Starr, former president of Oberlin College, argues in a controversial *New York Times* column that "colleges and universities should explore the possibility of a three-year baccalaureate." He claims that "higher education, private and public, is too expensive," with costs having risen 4.4 percent faster than inflation over a decade. He believes that a three-year degree would automatically reduce the cost to families and taxpayers by one-quarter and would provide several concrete educational benefits as well.

EXERCISE 3B

Reducing an Editorial to Standard Form

Put the argument presented in the following editorial into standard form.

Solves Surplus Problem

To the Editor:

   At last, someone else—Elizabeth Joseph (Op-Ed, May 23)—has put into words what I have been silently thinking for some time: Polygamy makes good sense.

Ms. Joseph writes from the perspective of a wife. I write from the perspective of a divorced working mother. How much more advantageous it would be for me to be part of a household such as Ms. Joseph describes, rather than to be juggling my many roles alone.

Nurit Karlin

If polygamy were legal, the problem—and I see it as a problem—of the surplus of extra women would disappear rapidly. No matter how many polemics there may be in favor of the free and single life-style, a divorced woman can feel extra in today's society, more so if she has children, which can isolate her from a full social life. How much easier to share the burdens—and the jobs.

When more women can rediscover the joys of sisterhood and co-wifehood (which are as old as the Bible), and overcome residual jealousy as a response to this type of situation, I think our society will have advanced considerably.

FRIEDA BRODSKY
BROOKLYN, NEW YORK

EXERCISE 3C

Creating a Political Handout

The following handout urges Californians to vote "no" on Proposition 174. This proposition (like other school voucher initiatives) would require the state to give parents vouchers to apply to their children's tuition if they choose private schools over public. This issue is currently being debated at the national level as well. As you will recognize, the content of this hand-

CARTOON COURTESY OF NURIT KARLIN/NYT PICTURES

out is essentially an argument in standard form: premises in support of a conclusion. Each premise is then developed and supported by a sentence or two.

After evaluating the effectiveness of this handout, create one of your own in support of or in opposition to a current political issue or campus issue. If the topic you choose is a ballot issue, refer to the Voter's Guide in your area for help in identifying the major premises. Pay special attention as well to the format and visual appeal of your document. Your computer program may allow you to add graphics to your design.

Five <u>Good</u> Reasons to Oppose the Vouchers Initiative

It provides no accountability.

- Though they would receive taxpayer dollars, the private and religious schools would be wholly unaccountable to the taxpayers—or to anyone other than their owners. Anyone who could recruit just 25 youngsters could open a "school." It would not need to be accredited, to hire credentialed teachers, or to meet the curriculum, health, and safety standards governing the public schools.

It undermines 'neighborhood' schools, making large tax hikes likely.

- The initiative would strip our public schools of 10 percent of their funding—even if not one student transferred to a private or religious school—to give vouchers to students currently in non-public schools. Either the public schools would be devastated—or hefty tax increases would be needed . . . not to improve education in the public schools, but to pay for subsidizing private, religious, and cult schools.

It permits discrimination.

- Private and religious schools could refuse admission to youngsters because of their religion, gender, I.Q., family income or ability to pay, disability, or any of dozens of other factors. In fact, they wouldn't even have to state a reason for rejecting a child.

It transfers taxpayer money to the rich.

- Rich parents already paying $7,000 to $9,000 or more in private school tuition would now gain $2,600 from the vouchers—a form of "Robin Hood in reverse."

It abandons public school students.

- The children left behind, in the public schools, would sit in classrooms that were even more crowded—and that had even less money, per student, for textbooks, science equipment, and other materials and supplies.

Vote No on Prop. 174

California Teachers Association/NEA • 1705 Murchison Drive • Burlingame, CA 94010

Ambiguous Argument Structure

Sometimes, the precise direction of an argument seems ambiguous; what is offered as conclusion and what is meant as supporting premise can be unclear. In such cases, it is important to look for what is most reasonable to believe, to give *the benefit of the doubt*. Try each assertion as the conclusion and see if the premises provide logical support for it, beginning with what seems most likely to be the intended conclusion.

Closely allied with the benefit of the doubt is the ancient methodologic principle known as **Occam's razor.** Named for William of Occam, the most influential philosopher of 14th-century Europe (immortalized a few years ago as William of Baskerville in Umberto Eco's novel, *The Name of the Rose*), this principle advocates economy in argument. As William of Occam put it, "What can be done with fewer assumptions is done in vain with more." In other words, the simplest line of reasoning is usually the best. Newspaper columnist Jon Carroll invoked Occam's razor when commenting on the O.J. Simpson trial: "I am not a juror; I am not required to maintain the presumption of innocence. I used Occam's razor, a tool that has served me well before. The simplest explanation is usually the true one; if a wife is killed, look to the husband."

Convoluted arguments, often those that sound the most impressive, can be difficult to unravel and rarely advance good reasoning. The ultimate question, however, when constructing an argument is always: What is enough? In the words of Toni Morrison, in her novel *Beloved,* "Everything depends on knowing how much, and good is knowing when to stop." But in most cases, our readers require more detailed support than we, as the advocates of a position, are likely to think necessary.

Argument and Explanation—Distinctions

As you elaborate support for premises in written argument, you often rely on explanation—of terminology, of background, of your reasoning—but you must not lose sight of your purpose, which is to persuade your reader of the wisdom of your position.

An **argument** is an attempt to establish a basis for belief, for the acceptability of your conclusion. In argument, you present reasons for your conclusion in order to convince someone of your point of view.

In **explanation,** on the other hand, you are clarifying why something has happened or why you hold a given opinion. Look at these examples:

I'm convinced he committed the crime because his fingerprints were on the murder weapon.

We are given a reason for believing that he committed the crime. We have an argument.

He committed the crime because he needed money.

We are given a reason why he committed the crime. We have an explanation.

What about these? Which illustrates argument, which explanation?

Don't go to that market because it's closed for renovation.

Don't go to that market because the prices are higher than anywhere else and the checkout lines are slow.

This distinction between explanation and argument may play a crucial role in your understanding of specific writing assignments and save you wasted effort on a false start. Is the instructor asking for an explanation, information on a particular subject or is he asking you to write an argument, to take and support a position? A written argument naturally includes explanation, information, but this material serves the purpose of convincing your reader of your point of view, which will be expressed in your thesis—the conclusion of your argument—and supported by premises. The following exercise should help to clarify further this important distinction.

EXERCISE 3D

Distinguishing Arguments from Explanations

The following two essays were both featured in the editorial section of *The New York Times;* one presents an argument whereas the other offers an explanation. Read them both carefully and decide which is which. Explain your answer with references to specific passages in both editorials.

A Threat to Student Privacy

The Orleans Parish School Board in Louisiana has ill-advisedly joined other educational institutions in considering broad student testing for drug abuse. The board is reviewing a program that would require random testing of all students involved in athletics and extracurricular activities, with voluntary testing for the rest of the student body.

The program was recommended to the board by the Orleans Parish District Attorney's office. Some board members have expressed concern over potential legal issues, as well they should. Testing on this scale clearly endangers students' Fourth Amendment rights, which guard against searches without probable cause. The District Attorney's office is also encouraging the use of hair tests, as opposed to more conventional urine sampling. But the reliability of hair tests has yet to be firmly established, and until it is, such tests should not be used. A false positive reading could have drastic effects on a child's life.

The public schools seem to have been inspired partly by the schoolwide drug testing in some private schools. But a key factor is the Supreme Court's 1995 decision upholding testing of student athletes. Justice Antonin Scalia's majority opinion argued that athletes were a distinct community because they had joined their teams on a voluntary basis and already had a "reduced expectation for privacy" in the locker-room atmosphere. He further argued that because school administrators served in loco parentis, students could not expect to enjoy the same privacy right as adults.

In a soundly reasoned dissent, Justice Sandra Day O'Connor argued that even random tests for athletes could be considered "blanket searches of mostly innocent students." She said that "suspicion based testing," invoking probable cause, would more effectively guard privacy rights. Nevertheless, the Scalia argument prevailed, raising fears among civil libertarians that it would someday open the door to schoolwide testing in public schools. In a subsequent case, the Seventh Circuit Court of Appeals ruled that an Indiana high school could require students involved in extracurricular activities to submit to random drug testing.

As for the tests themselves, there is general agreement that hair retains evidence of drug use for a longer period than urine. But scientists have raised questions, including whether the tests have a racial bias. False positives occur more frequently among minorities than among whites.

In many ways, students form a captive and vulnerable population. Justice O'Connor called the random testing of athletes a "mass, suspicionless search regime." Tests that applied to every student from the French club to the debate team would be an even broader threat to personal privacy. The Orleans board would be better advised to emulate school districts in Florida, New Jersey and Washington, which have chosen instead to build comprehensive drug education programs and trust between school administrators and students.

Women on the Soccer Field
Brazil Averts Its Eyes
By LARRY ROHTER

RIO DE JANEIRO

Across the United States right now, the Women's World Cup of soccer is the sports event of high summer, attracting stupendous crowds and frenzies of attention usually not seen there for any kind of soccer, or any women's sport, let alone both. Today Brazil meets the United States in the semifinals, but you would hardly know it from the coverage here in Rio.

While Sissi and Kátia (Brazilian soccer players use only one name) are heading toward their confrontation with Mia Hamm and Julie Foudy, Brazilian sports pages are focused almost entirely on the prospects of their men's soccer team winning the Copa America and the reasons why its coach, Wanderley Luxemburgo, left the top goal scorers Romário and Edmundo off the squad.

Soccer may be the king of sports here, but only the men's version of the game seems to wear the crown. Not one of this year's matches of the Brazilian national women's team has been televised live, sponsors have shied away from any association with the team, and hard-core fans who can recite the entire roster of the 1950 men's World Cup squad are hard-pressed to name even one of the current World Cup women.

"Unfortunately, women's soccer still doesn't have a chance in Brazil," Armando Nogueira, one of the country's leading sports commentators, said

"Jason, I'd like to let you play, but soccer is a girls' game."

when asked about the lack of interest here. "The best woman player in Brazil will never be as popular as the worst male player, and the main reason is that women have been idolized as delicate objects of desire, incapable of playing a physical-contact, body-to-body sport."

Renata Cordeiro, 29, is one of Brazil's new female sportscasters, working for the SporTV cable channel as a soccer specialist. She recalls that when she was a teen-ager, her best friend asked that soccer be added to their school's physical education curriculum. "Absolutely not," was the answer that came back. "Soccer is not an appropriate activity for girls."

Such attitudes can be encountered all over Latin America, where the passion for soccer is exceeded only by the deeply ingrained machismo that governs the social roles of daily life. And everything is accentuated in Brazil, which has won four men's World Cups, more than any other country. Since the days of Pelé, it has prided itself on grooming the world's best players and playing the most inventive and flashy version of the game.

"In Brazil, soccer has a strong gender demarcation that makes it a masculine domain par excellence," said Roberto da Matta, a prominent anthropologist and sociologist. "It is a sport that contains all of the various elements that are traditionally used to define masculinity: conflict, physical confrontation, guts, dominance, control and endurance."

APPLICATION TO WRITING

Argument Structure, Logical Essay Organization, and Revision

When we put arguments into standard form, we ask critical questions: Is this assertion the conclusion, the focus of the argument? Or is it a premise supporting the conclusion? Or does it support another premise? Asking and answering questions such as these sharpens our analytical skills and enables us to read more critically. But analyzing argument structure also has specific application to writing.

Standard form can provide an outline of the argument, an excellent aid in essay organization, one you can use either to plan your essay or to revise it. Such an outline states the thesis of the essay—the conclusion of the argument—and each premise signals a new point to be developed.

If you have thought out your argument carefully before you start writing, you will find that putting it in standard form can lead to a good working outline from which to proceed. Or you may find that you can impose standard form on your argument only when you have done some writing.

(Remember writing's power to actually generate ideas.) This kind of outlining is particularly helpful in the revision stage of your paper.

After writing a rough first draft of your argument, if time permits, put it away for a few hours. When you return to it, approach it as if you were not the writer but a reader. Set aside concerns of style, coherence, and mechanics; focus exclusively on the bones of the argument—the conclusion and the premises that support it. Write this skeleton of your draft in standard form. Now you are in an ideal position to evaluate the foundation of your argument—before proceeding to matters of development (well-supported premises), coherence, style, and mechanics. If the structure of your argument has problems—for example, information you initially saw as serving as a premise in your first draft, you now see does not directly support the conclusion—the time has come to repair any cracks you find in the foundation of your argument. This solid foundation makes the rest of the writing process less difficult and ultimately more successful.

Summaries

One way to explore an argument and reveal the important premises leading to a conclusion is to write a summary. Educator Mike Rose sees summarizing as an essential writing skill: "I [can't] imagine a more crucial skill than summarizing; we can't manage information, make crisp connections, or rebut arguments without it. The great syntheses and refutations are built on it."

Summaries come in many lengths, from one sentence to complete pages, depending on the purpose of the summary and the length of the piece to be summarized. Note, for example, the brief summaries at the conclusion of each chapter in this text.

A good summary is both complete and concise. To meet these conflicting goals, you must convey the essence of the whole piece without copying whole passages verbatim or emphasizing inappropriate features of the argument. Background information, detailed premise support, and narrative illustrations are usually omitted from summaries. Paraphrases of ideas—the author's meaning expressed in your own words—rather than direct quotations, except for a critically important phrase or two, are preferred. A summary should also be objective, excluding inferences and opinions. These are reserved for argument analysis.

Strategies for Writing a Summary

Read the piece you want to summarize carefully, identify the question at issue, and mark off the conclusion and important premises. A short summary sentence written in the margin beside each important premise and the conclusion(s) can be helpful. Now you are ready to write a first draft based on this outline. To ensure a smoothly written, coherent summary, in your second draft provide appropriate conjunctions and transitional phrases to join sentences and connect ideas (look ahead in this chapter for joining strategies). To ensure the conciseness that a summary demands, eliminate all "deadwood" from your sentences.

> SUMMARIES SHOULD BE OBJECTIVE, CONCISE, COMPLETE, COHERENT, AND WRITTEN IN YOUR OWN WORDS.

WRITING ASSIGNMENT 7

Constructing a Summary and Response

A. Read the following newspaper essay carefully, identify the question at issue, and sort out the various arguments offered.

B. Identify the conclusion to the argument Charlton Heston (a well-known actor, political conservative, and president of the National Rifle Association) presents and supply the key premises in its support. Standard form can help you here.

C. Now write a summary of the article (approximately 150–200 words). You may want to compare summaries with classmates.

D. Having read the article critically and organized your interpretation in writing, write a letter to the editor of the newspaper in which you express your opinion of Heston's article and your position on the issues he raises. Discuss the premises he presents, and if you think of others not mentioned in the article, include them. Letters to newspapers, like summaries, are usually compressed, so you will need to be economical and selective with words here, limiting yourself to between 300 and 400 words.

Audience

Readers of the daily newspaper who will need the key points of the original argument before they move on to your response.

Purpose

To present an insightful analysis of a complex argument in order to illuminate the issue for your readers.

Why U.S. Must Support the Arts
BY CHARLTON HESTON

Congress faces difficult issues this year in considering appropriations for the endowments for the arts and humanities. Cultural funding has never been easy or free of controversy.

The endowments have made mistakes. Some of the claims of politics in the humanities and lack of quality in the arts have been accurate. Some of the grants have been indefensible: a crucifix in a pot of urine, a self-portrait of a photographer with a bull-whip up his butt almost toppled the National Endowment for the Arts by themselves. The Smithsonian's original plans for the Enola Gay exhibit were equally appalling. It's crucial to prevent such blunders in the future.

But this does not, in my view, lead to the conclusion that the endowments should be defunded. I join with many conservatives in supporting their continuation.

Similar issues were raised in 1981 when Ronald Reagan asked me to cochair—along with Hanna Gray, then president of the University of Chicago—a task force on the arts and humanities.

The task force found "a clear public purpose in supporting the arts and humanities: preservation and advancement of America's cultural and intellectual heritage, the encouragement of creativity, the stimulation of quality in American education and the enhancement of our general well-being."

We also found that these public purposes are well-served by a diversity of sources of support, from the private, voluntary and governmental sectors. We found that endowments have helped stimulate private support, set standards and spur innovation—both in large and small institutions and in aiding individual scholars and artists.

Let me speak of my own experience. When I came back from overseas after World War II, my wife and I went to New York to make our livings. The American theater was then entirely concentrated in 50-some blocks of Manhattan. All the theaters were there, as were all the offices of agents, producers and designers. Most of the actors, directors, writers and producers lived there, too. All the plays done in America were conceived, cast and rehearsed there. If their Broadway runs were successful, they then toured the country in a dozen or so large cities, but the American theater was centered in Manhattan. I remember my wife did a national tour while I was on the West Coast making a movie. They played five weeks in Los Angeles in the only professional theater in the city. It was considered a phenomenal run.

Now, due in some part to the National Endowment for the Arts, there are major theaters in San Francisco, Chicago, Houston, Dallas, Seattle and many other cities, often with indigenous companies. The decentralization of the American theater is the most significant development since the death of vaudeville. The NEA deserves credit for that.

The NEA also created the American Film Institute, which I chaired for some years. Basically it serves film, generally recognized not only as the art form of the 20th Century, but the American art form. Its activities in many areas, perhaps most importantly in the archival preservation of American films, may in the long run prove to be their most important contribution.

The arts endowment's effort, seeded by federal tax dollars, helped to stimulate a vast opening up of American's heritage to its people. Conservatives generally agree that such a result is a "public good."

When we wrote our task force report in 1981, we had serious economic problems as a nation and major budgetary constraints. While the policies of those years essentially licked the high inflation of the '70s, I recognize we now have an even more serious problem in the federal budget deficit. I particularly sympathize with the very hard choices Congress faces. Let me be clearer; I fully understand that the endowments will have to share in budget cuts made in other areas.

Having said that, I also believe that the federal presence in supporting the arts and humanities can help with educating our young people in art, history, literature and the social sciences, just as the National Science Foundation helps with education in math and science. The arts and humanities are no less important than math and science. The national investment must not be abandoned. To do so would declare that these things so essential to our understanding of who we are as Americans don't really count. I know former Education Secretary Bill Bennet and former Labor Secretary Lynne Cheney don't believe that. They are correct to criticize endowment mistakes. These must be acknowledged and corrected. But it would be hurtful to the American tradition, and sharply out of the national character to repudiate the arts and the humanities. The United States would then be the only industrialized democracy that does not provide support for its culture.

This, we submit, is not what the American people want.

A great democracy like ours must neither abandon nor retreat from the world of ideas and culture. I urge Congress not to do this. The arts, the humanities, libraries and museums are part of the fabric of American life.

It has been said that the creation of the United States was the single most important political act in the history of mankind. I believe that. But for 40 years we've been wandering in the wilderness, in search of the promised land, as the Israelites followed Moses. I remember it well.

Now, even as they did, we have built a Golden Cow of entitlements in every area of our society. I know it is the job of Congress to dismantle this greedy creature; I applaud that undertaking. However, I beg Congress not to sweep away at the same time the immense good that's been done, at a very small cost, by these endowments. The humanities enrich the life of the American mind; art is the bread of our soul.

Logical Relationships Between Ideas— Joining Words

Joining words and transitional phrases are especially important in written argument because the strength of an argument is in part dependent on the clarity of the relationships between the premises and the conclusion. But their use and importance is not limited to argument. In a recent murder trial, the jury stopped its deliberations, asking the judge to clarify his instructions. "The questions dealt with subtle discrepancies between the jury instructions and other information given to the six-man, six-woman panel—for example, whether the word 'and' or the word 'or' was intended in several instances."

Whether we are analyzing jury instructions, describing our Aunt Frances, or telling of our narrow escape from an avalanche, these words are essential to conveying a logical sequence of thought. If logical connections are missing, the reader cannot follow the line of reasoning and either stops reading or supplies his own connections, which may not be the ones intended.

As an example of the kind of "choppy" or disjointed writing that results from the omission of logical connections, look at the following excerpt from former President Bill Clinton's Inaugural Address.

(1) When our Founders boldly declared America's independence to the world and our purpose to the Almighty, they knew that America to endure would have to change. (2) Not change for change's sake but change to preserve America's ideals—life, liberty, the pursuit of happiness. (3) Though we march to the music of our time, our mission is timeless. (4) Each generation of Americans must define what it means to be an American.

Although sentence 1 relates to sentence 2, sentences 3 and 4 fail to relate to these first two sentences or to each other. The result: a correct but incoherent paragraph. Joining words may not "fix" this paragraph—incoherence is sometimes the result of problems in organization that can't be remedied by the mere addition of joining words. But their use promotes coherence, showing your reader the logical connections between your ideas.

Joining words fall into three categories: coordinating conjunctions, subordinating conjunctions, and transition words.

Note that, while the list of coordinating conjunctions is complete, the other two lists are partial, featuring only the most commonly used words from both categories.

JOINING CHART

Logical relationship	Coordinating conjunctions	Subordinating conjunctions	Major transitions
Addition	and		also, moreover
Contrast and Concession	but yet	while whereas although though even though	however on the other hand
Cause	for	because since as	
Result Effect	so and so	so that in that in order that	therefore thus hence consequently
Condition		if unless provided that	

I love foreign films, *but* I have difficulty with subtitles.

I love foreign films *although* I have difficulty with subtitles.

I love foreign films; *however,* I have difficulty with subtitles.

Many of these words mean almost the same thing; they express the same logical connections between the ideas they join. For example, "but," "although," and "however" all express contrast, so we can join the following two ideas with any one of the three, and arrive at a similar, if not identical, meaning.

Choice of Joining Words

So what determines our choice? Notice that the two sentences joined by "but" and "although" are less formal in tone than the sentences joined by "however." We often find transition words such as "however," "moreover," "hence," and "consequently" in formal documents—legal briefs and contracts. In less formal writing, these words can be distracting, so the best writers use them sparingly. Try an "And" or a "But" instead of "Moreover" or "However" to open a sentence and save the transition words for major transitions.

On those occasions when we use transition words, it can often be effective for fluency to embed them within the clause rather than begin with them. For example:

Zoe loves foreign films and rarely sees American made movies; *however,* her roommate prefers American gangster films. ["However" begins the clause.]

Zoe loves foreign films and rarely sees American made movies; her roommate, *however,* prefers American gangster films. ["However" is embedded within the clause.]

A REVIEW: PUNCTUATION OF JOINING WORDS

Coordinating conjunctions—put a comma before the conjunction when it joins two independent clauses unless the clauses are short.

> The homeless are creating and living in unsanitary conditions all over America, so cities must provide housing for them.

Subordinating conjunctions—introductory subordinate clauses [clauses that begin with a subordinating conjunction] are usually followed by a comma.

> *Although* the homeless are creating and living in unsanitary conditions all over America, cities are not providing needed housing.

When a subordinate clause follows the main clause, the comma is usually omitted.

> Cities are not providing needed housing *even though* the homeless are creating and living in unsanitary conditions all over America.

Transition words—transitional words and phrases, because they do not join sentences but only connect ideas, should be preceded by a semicolon or a period when they come between two clauses.

> The homeless are creating and living in unsanitary conditions all over America; *therefore,* cities must provide adequate housing for them.

If, in the preceding example, a comma rather than a semicolon preceded "therefore," many readers would consider it a run-together sentence or comma splice.

When a transition word is embedded within a clause, it is usually set off with commas.

> The homeless are creating and living in unsanitary conditions all over America; cities, *therefore,* must provide adequate housing for them.

EXERCISE 3E

Joining Sentences for Logic and Fluency

Make this disjointed argument cohesive and logical by joining sentences with appropriate joining words. You don't need to change the sequence of sentences.

> Obstetricians perform too many Cesareans. They can schedule deliveries for their own convenience. They can avoid sleepless nights and canceled parties. They resort to Cesareans in any difficult delivery to protect themselves against malpractice suits. Cesareans involve larger fees and hospital bills than normal deliveries. Cesarean patients spend about twice as many days in the hospital as other mothers.
>
> The National Institutes of Health confirmed that doctors were performing many unnecessary Cesarean sections. They suggested ways to reduce their use. The recommendation was widely publicized. The obstetricians apparently failed to take note. In the 1980s, the operation was performed in 16.5 percent of United States' births. In the 1990s, 24.7 percent of the births were Cesareans.

Revising for Coherence

Joining words are one important tool available to writers to promote coherence—a logical flow—in their writing. Sentence focus, a consistent sentence subject that reflects the rhetorical subject (see Chapter 8, The Language of Argument—Style), is another. But since coherence comes from content as well as style, no textbook could specify every conceivable option available to writers. So a writer, when revising a draft, must keep his audience in mind, never forgetting to take his reader with him as he moves from sentence to sentence and paragraph to paragraph. The writer must be conscious of the separateness that exists between himself and his reader. The reader's only access to the mind of the writer is through the words on the page; the reader has no other access to the writer's thoughts.

Hidden Assumptions in Argument

Even when arguments appear to be well supported with premises, and where necessary, logical relationships are signaled with joining words, many real life arguments come to us incomplete, depending on **hidden assumptions,** unstated premises and conclusions. Sometimes a missing premise or conclusion is so obvious that we don't even recognize that it is unstated.

> The burglar had dark hair, so Tracey certainly wasn't the burglar. [Missing premise: Tracey does not have dark hair.]

> Ken is lazy and lazy people don't last long around here. [Missing conclusion: Ken won't last long around here.]

> Since I've sworn to put up with my tired VW until I can afford a BMW, I must resign myself to the bug for a while longer. [Missing premise: I can't afford a BMW now.]

Filling in the omitted assumptions here would seem unnecessarily pedantic or even insulting to our intelligence.

Literature, by its nature elliptical, depends on the reader to make plausible assumptions:

> Yon Cassius has a lean and hungry look; such men are dangerous.
> —SHAKESPEARE, *JULIUS CAESAR*

Shakespeare assumes his audience will automatically make the connection—Cassius is a dangerous man. But not all missing assumptions are as obvious or as acceptable. At the heart of critical thinking lies the ability to discern what a writer or speaker leaves **implicit**—unsaid—between the lines of what he has made **explicit**—what he has clearly stated.

Dear Abby's readers took her to task for a response she made to a man who complained that because he shared an apartment with a man, people thought he was gay. Abigail Van Buren called this rumor an "ugly accusation." The implicit assumption here is that homosexuality is ugly, an assumption many of her readers—both gay and straight—objected to. One reader asked, "If someone thought this man was Jewish, Catholic or African American—would you call that an 'ugly accusation?'" Van Buren apologized.

Law professor Patricia J. Williams, in *The Alchemy of Race and Rights*, examines the implicit assumptions that led to the death of a young black man in New York in the late 1980s. In this incident, three young black men left their stalled car in Queens and walked to Howard Beach looking for help, where they were surrounded by eight white teenagers who taunted them with racial epithets and chased them for approximately three miles, beating them severely along the way. One of the black men died, struck by a car as he tried to flee across a highway; another suffered permanent blindness in one eye.

During the course of the resultant trial, the community of Howard Beach supported the white teenagers, asking "What were they [the three black teenagers] doing here in the first place?" Examining this question, Williams finds six underlying assumptions:

Everyone who lives here is white.

No black could live here.

No one here has a black friend.

No white would employ a black here.

No black is permitted to shop here.

No black is ever up to any good.

These assumptions reveal the racism that led the white teenagers to behave as they did and the community to defend their brutality.

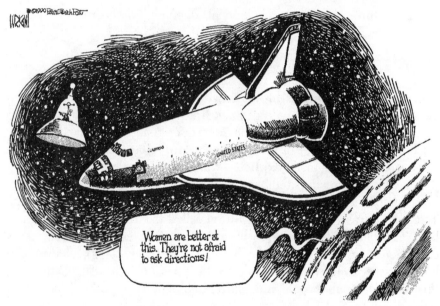

What unstated assumption does this cartoon depend on?

Dangers of Hidden Assumptions

Examine this seemingly straightforward argument:

John is Lisa's father, so clearly he is obligated to support her.

What's missing here? All fathers are obligated to support their daughters (or their children). But would everyone find this premise acceptable under all conditions? Probably not. What about the age factor? What about special circumstances: Lisa's mother has ample means while John is penniless and terminally ill? Or Lisa was legally adopted by another family, John being her birth father?

The danger with such incomplete arguments lies in more than one direction. A writer may leave his readers to supply their own assumptions, which may or may not coincide with those of the writer. If the issue is controversial, the risks of distorting an argument increase. Or, writers may deliberately conceal assumptions to hide an unsound, often misleading argument. Watch for these in advertising and politics. If you are on the alert for such deceptions, you are better able to evaluate what you read and hear and thus protect your own interests.

An example of a misleading argument:

> Echoing the arguments of the National Physicians for Social Responsibility and some public school districts, the Board of Education of a prominent Archdiocese refused to participate in a federal civil defense program that taught ways of preparing for nuclear war. They objected to instructions for teachers and students which recommended that "if there should be a nuclear flash, especially if you feel the warmth from it, take cover instantly in the best place you can find. If no cover is available, simply lie down on the ground and curl up." Their objections were leveled not at the specific suggestions but at the underlying unstated assumption: that nuclear war is survivable. In the words of the Board: "To teach children that nuclear war is a survivable disaster is to teach them that nuclear war is an acceptable political or moral option."

Hidden Assumptions and Standard Form

To help sort out the stated and unstated assertions in an argument, it can be illuminating to write out the argument in standard form. This means including the important hidden assumptions so the complete argument is before you and putting brackets around these assumptions to distinguish them from stated premises and conclusions.

Examples:

1. Harold is a politician so he's looking out for himself.
   a. [All politicians look out for themselves.]
   b. Harold is a politician.
      ∴ Harold is looking out for himself.
2. Products made from natural ingredients promote good health, so you should buy Brand X breads.
   a. Products made from natural ingredients promote good health.
   b. [Brand X breads are made from natural ingredients.]
      ∴ You should buy Brand X breads.
3. Products made from natural ingredients promote good health, and Brand X breads are made from natural ingredients.

a. Products made from natural ingredients promote good health.
b. Brand X breads are made from natural ingredients.
∴ [You should buy Brand X breads.]

EXERCISE 3F   *H.W.*

Identifying Hidden Assumptions

A. The following arguments are missing either a premise or a conclusion. Put them into standard form, adding the implicit premise or conclusion; then place brackets around the missing assumptions you have inserted. A word to the wise: As with all argument analysis, find the conclusion first and then look for what is offered in its support.

1. Maggie is a musician, so she won't understand the business end of the partnership.
2. Those who exercise regularly increase their chances of living into old age, so we can expect to see Anna around for a very long time.
3. I never see Loretta without a book; she must be highly intelligent.
4. "Most professional athletes don't have a college degree, and so have no idea how to handle the big salaries suddenly dumped in their laps." (Harry Edwards, college professor and financial consultant for professional athletes)
5. "I start with the assumption that all human beings sin. So all I'll say is that I've led a human life." (former Senate Majority Leader Newt Gingrich in response to reporters' questions concerning an extramarital relationship)
6. Having become so central a part of our culture, television cannot be without its redeeming features.
7. **CONVICTED:** U.S. Petty Officer 3/c **Mitchell T. Garraway, Jr.,** of premeditated murder in the stabbing of a superior officer. The military court must now decide his sentence; its options include the death penalty. The last execution carried out by the Navy took place in 1849. (*Newsweek*)
8. From a letter to *The Sacramento Bee* after an article reporting that a nursing mother had been evicted from a downtown department store cafeteria (thanks to Perry Weddle of Sacramento State University for this one):

   It was inhumane to deny this woman the right to nurse her baby in the cafeteria because she was simply performing a natural bodily function. (Where will this argument take you once you supply the suppressed assumption?)

B. The following article appeared in the news section of several major newspapers. Read it carefully and supply the hidden assumption it seems to be leading us to. Why would the writer choose to make this assumption implicit?

Robert Redford's Daughter Rescued

SALT LAKE CITY—Shauna Redford, daughter of actor Robert Redford, was rescued when her car plunged into a river, authorities said yesterday.

They said Redford was wearing a seatbelt and suffered only minor injuries in the accident Friday. Redford, 23, of Boulder, was rescued from her partially submerged auto by three other motorists, who saw her vehicle crash through a guardrail into the Jordan River, eight miles south of Salt Lake City.

The Utah Highway Patrol said the three rescuers released Redford's seatbelt, pulled her from the car and carried her to the riverbank.

She was held at a hospital overnight for observation and released.

Last summer, Sidney Wells, 22, a Colorado University student who had dated Shauna Redford, was shot and killed in Boulder. Police said the killing may have been drug related.

C. The Republican National Committee, referring to the then newly elected Democratic Speaker of the House, issued a three-page memorandum titled "Tom Foley: Out of the Liberal Closet." The memo went on to compare Foley's voting record with that of Representative Barney Frank, Democrat, of Massachusetts, openly homosexual, who was described in the memo as "the ultra-liberal representative from Massachusetts."

What **innuendo** (an indirect derogatory remark that is implicit rather than explicit) is the Republican National Committee making about former speaker of the house, Tom Foley?

D. Find one advertisement or political cartoon in print journalism that clearly depends for its message on one or more unstated assumptions. Clip or photocopy the ad, write out the principal argument including the missing assertions, and bring it to class to discuss with classmates.

Hidden Assumptions and Audience Awareness

As stated above, politicians and advertisers may deliberately suppress assumptions in order to manipulate the public. We will assume that we, as careful writers, do not share this goal and would not deliberately leave important assumptions unstated. At the same time, we don't want to bore our readers by spelling out unnecessary details. How do we determine what material to include, what to leave out?

George Lakoff and Mark Johnson, in their book *Metaphors We Live By*, point out that meaning is often dependent on context. They offer the following sentence as an example.

We need new sources of energy.

This assertion means one thing to a group of oil executives and quite another to an environmental group. The executives may assume the writer is referring to more offshore drilling, whereas the environmentalists may think the writer is referring to greater development of solar or other alternate sources of energy.

As writers, we must consider our audience carefully and understand the purpose for which we are writing. We make choices about which assumptions must be made explicit according to our knowledge of the reader. Are we writing for an audience predisposed to agree with us, or one that is opposed to our point of view? Are we writing for readers who are knowledgeable about the subject or ignorant? The answers to these questions help us to determine what material to include and what to omit.

A reviewer of the book *Murderers and Other Friends* criticizes the author, British writer John Mortimer, for making too many assumptions about his audience:

> Mortimer doesn't for a moment seem to believe that his new book will be read by anyone but old friends. He assumes we know Horace Rumpole and She Who Must Be Obeyed and that we've seen the television adaptations he has written of Evelyn Waugh's novel "Brideshead Revisited" and his own "Summer's Lease." He knows that we know about his father, the blind divorce lawyer, and the play he wrote about him, just as we know about his own years as a Queen's Counsel defending colorful riffraff in the Old Bailey. In short, he assumes we have not only read his autobiography but also have been paying close attention to "Mystery!" and "Masterpiece Theater."

You may find it helpful to have a friend, one who is unfamiliar with your topic, read a draft of your paper. Such a reader may help you spot assumptions that need clarification.

EXERCISE 3G

Identifying Your Reader

A common feature of many publications today is a section called "Personals." *The Nation* and *The New York Review of Books* (both probably in your library) and many local periodicals, including some campus papers, carry "Personals." What follows are four such ads, two from women who advertised in *Focus*, a public television magazine, and two from men who advertised in *The Daily Californian*, the University of California at Berkeley student newspaper. Form four groups and choose one of the following ads to analyze and respond to together.

From *The Daily Californian*

> **MALE UCB student**, 25, 6'1", interested in music, religion, literature, psychedelics, nature etc. seeks Lithuanian woman with beautiful soul—witty, pretty, intellectual, virtuous—for fun, friendship, maybe more.
>
> **ENGLISH/MUSIC major**, 25, would like to meet witty, intellectual, attractive female (pref. math/physics/other science major) for concerts, foreign films & after dinner activities.

From *Focus*

> **Sensual Blue-eyed Blonde**, successful entrepreneur, 30, 5'4", who is attractive, well traveled, well read, and has a great sense of humor, seeks a spiritual, self aware single white male, 30–45, 5'10" or taller, who is worldly but grounded, successful but sensitive, healthy but not fanatical and open to pursuing a long-term commitment. Note and photo appreciated.
>
> **Pretty Woman, International** travel, Ivy education, health career, would like to meet professional man, 35–50, for tennis, dancing, bear hugs and possible first-time family. Photo appreciated.

Your aim is to understand the writer of the ad, who will then become the audience for your response. Read the ad of your choice carefully. What kind of person is the writer? What can you infer about his or her character, personality, and values? What does the publication he or she chose to advertise in reveal about the writer? Read between the lines: What hidden assumptions are buried there?

After completing your analysis, as a group write a brief response informed by your knowledge of the writer of the ad. If time permits, reading these responses to the class might be entertaining.

WRITING ASSIGNMENT 8

A Letter of Application

Now, turn to the classified ads in any newspaper, select a job, and write a letter of application (a one-page cover letter). You need to consider your audience carefully in order to create a profile of your reader and a response that will appeal to him. Instead of a job in the classifieds, you may prefer to select an internship or a job on campus for this application.

Audience

A person who will be evaluating you for a position you particularly want.

Purpose

To present yourself as a desirable and qualified applicant for the position.

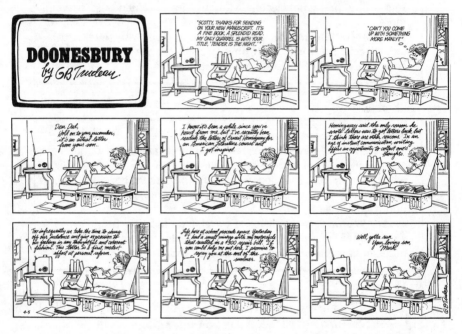

This writer has certainly considered his audience very carefully.

SUMMARY

In logic, the word argument has a special meaning, referring to rational discourse composed of premises and a conclusion rather than to a fight. It is useful to be able to recognize premises and conclusions in order to fully understand what an argument is proposing. Expressing arguments in standard form is a helpful strategy for understanding arguments.

Understanding the structure of arguments can be useful to writers when considering the organization of their written arguments.

The logical connections between assertions in argument can be signaled by conjunctions and traditional phrases to promote a logical flow of prose and ideas.

Arguments are frequently presented with some of the premises or the conclusion implied rather than stated. Sometimes such hidden assumptions are obvious, but in some instances they can be misleading and need to be made explicit. Recognizing hidden assumptions in argument is an important part of critical thinking.

KEY TERMS

Argument a rational piece of discourse, written or spoken, which attempts to persuade the reader or listener to believe something; composed of at least one premise in support of a conclusion.

Conclusion the key assertion in an argument, the statement which the other assertions support; the point one hopes to make when presenting an argument.

Explanation an attempt to clarify why something has happened or why you hold a given opinion.

Explicit clearly stated, distinctly expressed.

Hidden assumptions missing, unstated premises and conclusions in arguments; assertions that are necessary to recognize in order to fully understand an argument.

Implicit suggested so as to be understood but not plainly expressed.

Innuendo an indirect remark or reference, usually implying something derogatory.

Joining words words or phrases that indicate, or signal, the logical relationship between assertions in an argument. "Therefore" and its synonyms signal a conclusion; "because" and its synonyms signal a premise.

Occam's Razor a principle of argument that advocates ecomony, maintaining that the simplest line of reasoning is usually the best.

Opinion a provisional judgment or belief, requiring proof or support; a first step in developing an argument.

Premise a reason that supports the conclusion in an argument.

Standard form an argument reduced to its essence, its principal premises and conclusion listed in simple outline form, with premises numbered and conclusion stated at the end.

CHAPTER 4

Written Argument

If the cultivation of understanding consists in one thing more than in another, it is surely in learning the grounds of one's own opinions.

—JOHN STUART MILL

In the previous chapter, we focused on the structure of argument, distinguishing between premises and conclusions and reducing arguments to these two basic components. But how do we begin to write an argument?

Focusing Your Topic

A first critical step is to focus and refine the topic. At one time or another, we have all been part of heated political discussions between friends or family members. Grandfather states that taxes are too high under the current administration. Cousin Susan points out that corporations do not pay their fair share, while Dad shouts that the government funds too many social programs and allows too large a number of immigrants to enter the country. These discussions are often discursive and unsatisfying because they are not focused on one clear and precise **question at issue.**

For an argument to be successful, one person does not necessarily have to defeat another; one point of view does not have to be proven superior to another. An argument can also be considered successful if it opens a line of communication between people and allows them to consider—with respect—points of view other than their own. But, if an argument is to establish such a worthwhile exchange, it must focus first on a single issue and then on a particular question at issue.

The Issue

An **issue** is any topic of concern and controversy. Not all topics are issues since many topics are not controversial. Pet care, for instance, is a topic but not an issue; laboratory testing of animals, on the other hand, is an issue. In the hypothetical family discussion above, four issues are raised: taxes, the current administration, immigration, and government-funded social programs. No wonder such a discussion is fragmented and deteriorates into people shouting unsupported claims at one another.

Where and how do you find appropriate topics? In your work or personal life you might need to write an argument that has a real-world purpose. Why product X is superior to all other brands and how using it will turn a customer's business around. Why you are the most qualified applicant for the job. For your classes, you are often assigned topics. But sometimes in a writing class you are asked to select a topic of interest to you, and then you are on your own. Newspapers, in your community and on your campus, can suggest issues, as can news broadcasts. The Internet has opened up a vast new world of information from which you might select a topic once you have identified a broad category that interests you. Although it can be useful to choose a subject that you know something about, particularly if you want to take a strong stand right away, don't be afraid of exploring new areas. In a freshman history class some years ago, one of us was handed the unknown name *Leon Trotsky*. That required paper led to a whole new world of knowledge: Russia, the Soviet Union, the Russian Revolution, and communism. Your writing assignments can be a way of opening new worlds.

The Question at Issue

Whether you choose you own issue or are assigned one, the next step is to select one **question at issue**—a particular aspect of the issue under consideration. Affirmative action, for instance, is an issue that contains many distinct questions at issue.

> Should affirmative action play a role in university admissions?
>
> Should affirmative action play a role in the work place?
>
> Should affirmative action play a role in government contracts?
>
> Has affirmative action led to discrimination against white males?
>
> Should affirmative action based on gender be separated from affirmative action based on ethnic origin?

A writer who does not focus on one and only one question at issue risks producing a disorganized essay, one that is difficult to follow because the readers will not be sure they understand the point the writer is arguing. Writing on the issue of how affirmative action has benefitted women, one student kept drifting away from that question at issue to another: Should affirmative action play a role in university admissions? Since both her questions at issue were part of the **same issue,** affirmative action, and hence related, she was unaware that her paper was going in two different directions. The result was a disorganized, disjointed essay.

The following diagram illustrates that a single issue may contain any number of separate and distinct questions as issue. Your task as a writer is to isolate a particular question at issue and stay focused on it.

AFFIRMATIVE ACTION

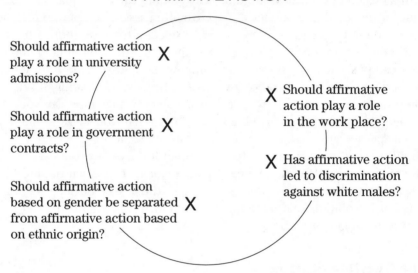

Should affirmative action play a role in university admissions? X

Should affirmative action play a role in government contracts? X

Should affirmative action based on gender be separated from affirmative action based on ethnic origin? X

X Should affirmative action play a role in the work place?

X Has affirmative action led to discrimination against white males?

The Thesis

The final step in establishing the focus of an essay is determining the **thesis.** Although the issue and question at issue state, respectively, the subject and focus of the paper, they are neutral statements; they do not reveal the writer's opinion nor should they. To encourage objective analysis, the question at issue should be expressed in neutral rather than biased or emotionally charged language. The **thesis,** however, states the writer's position, her response to the question at issue, the *conclusion* of her argument, the primary claim she is making. Your thesis takes central stage in both the final paper you write and the thinking you do as you conduct your research and prepare drafts. It controls the evidence you gather and clarifies the stand you want to take.

Suppose you want to write a paper about affirmative action and narrow the issue to a more focused question at issue:

Should affirmative action play a role in university admissions?

You might start with a sentence that states the topic:

> Affirmative action in university admissions has become a controversial subject.

Yes, your reader would say. You're right on target with the topic, but what about the assertive edge? Where is your opinion? What have you to prove in such a statement? Not much. Not many people would argue that affirmative action is a controversial issue. You need to move on to an assertion of something you want to prove in your paper, a statement that lays out the grounds for an argument.

Perhaps you want to convince your university that affirmative action is necessary on your campus.

> Affirmative action has played an important role in bringing minorities into our university and thus into society as a whole. Our country is not ready to abandon the significant gains it has made under affirmative action guidelines for university admissions.

You have set up reasonable expectations for what you need to develop and support your point: convincing evidence of the "important role" affirmative action has played, further evidence of why "our country is not ready to abandon" these gains, and elaboration of the term "significant." (See *Definition* in Chapter 5.)

Or, you may want to join others who have argued that affirmative action in admissions must stop.

> Because affirmative action in university admissions has created more problems than it has solved, the time has come to end special admissions for minorities.

Here you need to provide detailed examples of problems created by affirmative action and show how affirmative action is responsible for such problems. You also need to recognize any advantages that have come from affirmative action and balance them with the problems you identify.

With either of these thesis statements, your reader will know the point you are advocating in your paper and the purpose behind your choice of question at issue. Just as important, you will have pinned down your ideas so that you have a road map to guide you as you search for and sift through the evidence necessary for supporting your position.

Sometimes when we begin exploring a topic for a paper, we may not know our position. We may need to learn more about the question at issue through research before arriving at a conclusion. If, however, our question at issue is clear and precise, we can proceed without a definite thesis or with only a tentative one since the writing process itself will help us to arrive at one. (Refer to Chapter 1.)

We don't necessarily have to arrive at a completely yes or no response to the question at issue. For example, if the question at issue is whether or not school administrators should have the right to censor student newspapers, our response may not be an unequivocal yes or no but a qualified response:

> School administrators should not have the right to censor student newspapers unless an article is libelous.

After completing the necessary research and examining various points of view, we may still be unable to reach a final conclusion. In this case, the thesis of the paper may be an evaluation of these different points of view with a tentative stand based on the unfolding of future events.

Keep in mind that arguments don't always have to be adversarial. Often you will find yourself taking a tentative position, researching the issue, and finally arbitrating a conclusion, settling for a consensus. This option can be more challenging to write on successfully but often reflects reality since careful examination of issues frequently reveals that both sides have reasonable arguments. Your thesis for this kind of paper also requires careful thought and should reflect the compromise position you have chosen. Take, for example, the conflict in Yugoslavia. Your thesis might run something like this:

> When they were able to return to their ravaged country, Kosova Albanians maintained that atrocities committed against them by Serbs required retribution. Although much of the world understood their bitterness, international peacekeepers were morally obligated to protect the Serbs just as they had tried to defend the Kosovas.

Your paper would have to explore the degree of atrocity carried out by both sides and then show why peace would be best served by protecting Serbs as well as Kosovas. You would not be taking an adversarial position on either side yet would be mounting an argument for a complex solution to a perplexing issue. In Writing Assignment 11 on page 115, we ask you to try such an approach.

In essays by professional writers, the thesis is sometimes indirectly stated; it may be implicit rather than explicit. For instance, writer Sheila Koran argues in an essay that gay and lesbian couples should have the same legal spousal rights as married couples. She never directly states this thesis as she describes the life she lives with her mate, a life like any other family's, but the point is clearly made; the reader is never confused about the purpose of the essay. In general, the more experienced the writer, the more she is able to write a focused essay without an explicit thesis. But for the most part, writer and reader are best served by a clearly defined thesis.

In summary, you should take the following steps as you prepare your topic:

Select an **issue** that is debatable, an issue on which you can argue more
than one position.
Narrow that issue to a focused **question at issue.**
Write a "working" **thesis** that makes an assertion about this question at issue; your thesis states your opinion on the question at issue.

Two Kinds of Thesis Statements

Another option we have when writing a thesis is to decide whether or not
it should be "complete" or "open." An open thesis states the writer's opinion but not the reasons for her opinion. A complete thesis includes both
the writer's opinion and all of the reasons or premises that support this
conclusion. For example:

An "open" thesis:
Access to the Internet should be controlled.
A "complete" thesis:
Because children need protection from pornography, our right to pri-
vacy is threatened, and "intellectual property" can be too easily
pirated, access to the Internet should be controlled.
A compromise:
Access to the Internet raises serious moral, legal, and even constitu-
tional questions, the nature of which suggests that such access should
be controlled.

Which thesis statement is preferable? It is a matter of choice, the writer's
choice. Some writers fear that the complete thesis will not capture the
reader's interest, believing that if all the reasons for the conclusion are
given in the thesis, the reader's curiosity will not be aroused. On the other
hand, a writer may prefer the greater clarity of the "complete" thesis, for
herself and her readers. In any case, even if a writer chooses the open thesis approach, at some point in the process she should be just as clear about
the reasons for her position as the writer who chooses the complete thesis.

As a general guideline to assist you in deciding the most suitable thesis
approach to take, consider the complexity of the topic, the length of the
paper, the needs of your audience, and the purpose of your project. In a
long paper on a complex topic, the reader may welcome the clarity of the
complete thesis or at least a modified one, but in a short essay on a simple
topic, the complete thesis is probably not necessary and may sound too
mechanical.

A thesis is not necessarily restricted to one sentence. In fact, it's not
unusual for a complete thesis to require a paragraph. As your work progresses and new ideas change your thinking on your topic, you may need
to revise your thesis. You may also find yourself refining the language of

your thesis during the final editing process. But a well thought out and clearly expressed thesis guides writer and reader, keeping both focused on the question at issue and on the position the writer has taken.

EXERCISE 4A

Identifying the Issue, Question at Issue, and Thesis

Complete the following sets by supplying the missing element.

1. *Issue:*

   Question at Issue: Should universities put a cap on fee increases?
   Thesis: To ensure an economically diverse student population, universities should put a cap on fee increases.

2. *Issue:* First Amendment rights to free speech and the Internet

   Question at Issue:
   Thesis: Because the safety of children using the Internet is a growing concern to parents and educators, some restrictions on free speech are necessary and inevitable.

3. *Issue:* Private militias

   Question at Issue: Should the government have the right to control the public speech of private militias?
   Thesis:

4. For the following example, supply two examples of a thesis: (1) An open thesis and (2) a complete thesis.

   Issue: Gambling on the Internet
   Question at Issue: Should gambling on the Internet be available and unrestricted?

Shaping a Written Argument—Rhetorical Strategies

What do we mean by *rhetorical*? The term **rhetoric** has various shades of meaning, but the following definition adapted from the Greek philosopher Aristotle provides the most useful approach for our purposes: "The art of using language to good effect, to prove, to convince, to persuade."

And thus to argue. The structure of written argument as we know it today dates back to the orations of Greeks and Romans. The following features of classical argument, modified by contemporary rhetoric, can serve us well as long as we recognize that they are options, not requisite components. We write to communicate, not to fit a formula or fulfill a set of narrow expectations.

The Introduction

How you begin your argument depends on the issue, the audience, and your own style. The key question is: How much can you expect your readers to know about your question at issue? If your subject has received a great deal of recent media attention, you probably do not need to supply much background. If, on the other hand, your subject is obscure or technical, then you will probably have to give your readers the necessary background information—the history of the case or the specific circumstances that give rise to the present problem—so that they can understand the argument to follow.

If not much background is required, you may want to begin your essay with a relevant narrative, either actual or fictional, which illustrates your question at issue. For example, if your subject is euthanasia, you may want to describe a day in the life of a terminally ill patient. Such a scene captures the reader's interest—not a necessity but sometimes a valuable rhetorical strategy. A relevant quotation can also provide an interesting way into your argument. Or you may choose to open with an opposing view and build your argument on a refutation of what is often the prevailing wisdom on an issue.

No matter what approach you choose, you have considerable flexibility. Your introduction may be a single paragraph or run to three or four paragraphs depending on the strategies you choose and the amount of background required. Usually, you will state your thesis (your position, your opinion) somewhere in the introductory paragraphs so that your reader is clear about the purpose of the essay.

For a variety of introductory strategies, examine the three sample essays in 4E, page 104. The author of "Alternative Sentencing" starts with the broad issue of crime, moves to problems associated with sentencing, offers a short concession, and states the thesis, all in the first paragraph. The author of "Rap Takes a Bum Rap" includes an analogy and a statement of what Rap is not before stating his thesis. Journalist Cynthia Tucker presents her position on affirmative action in university admissions in the form of two questions, a more indirect approach than the two previous essays but nonetheless clear.

The Development of Your Argument

Once again, the possibilities, although not infinite, are numerous. You need to present as many strong premises in support of your position as necessary. These in turn have to be elaborated, explained, and defended with as much specific detail, example, and illustration as you can provide. You may draw on personal experience, research, and respected authorities to support your position. Called, in classical rhetoric, the *confirmation* of your position, this support should be connected explicitly to your thesis unless the logical ties are self-evident. As the Greek philosopher and rhetorician Plato said in the *Phaedrus*, "What is stated outright will be clearer than what is not."

Sometimes one premise requires a whole paragraph or more. Others may need only a few sentences and can be effectively grouped with additional premises. Audience and purpose as well as your topic play a role in your choices. Here are two examples of paragraphs lifted from the middle of student essays, one that develops a single premise in some detail, another that groups a series of premises together in one paragraph.

A single premise paragraph:

Since the NCAA (National Collegiate Athletic Association) policy of random drug testing was begun some years ago, public debate on this issue has increased, and the idea of drug testing for college athletes has been challenged for a variety of reasons. The strongest argument against drug testing of college athletes is that it is unconstitutional. An athlete should be entitled to the same constitutional rights as other citizens, and drug testing violates both the Fourth Amendment's provisions against unreasonable search and seizure, and the Fifth Amendment's provision of the right to refuse to furnish potentially incriminating evidence about one's self.* As various forms of drug testing were subjected to legal challenges, the courts needed to rule that drug testing is, indeed, unconstitutional. *Time* magazine reported that ". . . a number of judges have already ruled that mass testing violates workers' constitutional rights to privacy and protection from self-incrimination," and quoted Federal Judge Robert Collins, who called a U.S. Customs Service drug testing program "unreasonable and wholly unconstitutional." In the late 1980s, the Appellate Division of the New York State Supreme Court ruled that probationary teachers in a Long Island school district could not be compelled to submit to urinalysis because the tests would be an unconstitutional invasion of privacy (Kaufman 19). In the case of Simone LeVant, the Stanford diver who has so far been the only athlete to challenge the NCAA drug tests in court, *The New York Times* reported that Judge Peter G. Stone of the Santa Clara county Superior Court agreed with the athlete and her attorney that mandatory urine tests were an obtrusive, unreasonable, and unconstitutional invasion of privacy.

---

*Given the length of this paragraph, some writers might choose to divide it in two, starting a new paragraph here where the examples begin. Paragraphing, while certainly not arbitrary, can be flexible and should serve the needs of the reader as well as the logic of the argument.

A Multipremise Paragraph:

Although it is a controversial proposition, legalizing drugs has many advantages. First of all, it will free the now overburdened legal system to do its job dispensing justice. Cases will be processed with greater speed because the system won't be overwhelmed with drug cases. With the legalization of drugs, violent drug-related crimes will decrease. As a result, prisons will be less crowded, which in turn will allow serious offenders to serve longer terms. Legalizing drugs will free law enforcement officials to combat other serious crimes more effectively. With the money saved from law enforcement and legal procedures, a more effective campaign of educating the public on the maladies of drugs can be mounted, and more money will be available for the rehabilitation of drug addicts. Finally, by legalizing drugs, we can slow down the spread of AIDS among IV drug users, who will be able to get clean needles and not have to share with other drug addicts, many of whom are infected with the AIDS virus. The positive results of legalizing drugs definitely outweigh the negative consequences.

In the second paragraph, the writer has only just begun with such a summary approach to a broad subject. Each individual premise will have to be given specific support in subsequent paragraphs.

How Many Premises Should an Argument Have?

It would seem that the greater the number of premises, the stronger the argument, but this quest for quantity should not be at the expense of quality; in other words, weak or questionable premises should not be included just to increase the number of premises. It's possible to have a strong argument with only one or two premises if those premises are extremely convincing and are developed in detail.

The Conclusion

We have no simple rule of thumb here other than to suggest you conclude your essay rather than simply stop. If your paper is long and complex, you need to help your reader by briefly summarizing where you have been and what you propose. If you present only a tentative or partial thesis in the introduction, then you need to be sure that your final position is clear in the conclusion. If you think that further investigation is still needed before you can arrive at a responsible "conclusion" on the issue, then recommend what direction you think such investigation should take. If, as a result of your argument, you have definite recommendations for action, your conclusion can carry such suggestions.

You and your readers should feel satisfied at the close of your paper. This does not mean that every paper needs a long and redundant formulaic conclusion. Once again, we refer you to the sample essays in Exercise 4E for models.

And so your argument assumes its shape. Commenting on effective rhetoric, Plato, quoting Socrates, summed it up in his *Phaedrus:*

> Every discourse, like a living creature, should be so put together that it has its own body and lacks neither head nor feet, middle nor extremities, all composed in such a way that they suit both each other and the whole.

A Dialectical Approach to Argument

Effective argument is more than the straightforward presentation of a thesis, premises, and their support. Most issues worth arguing today are complex, with evidence sometimes contradictory or ambiguous. Arguments on such issues should reflect a flexible mind, one capable of thinking dialectically. From this term's various meanings, we can extract a definition of **dialectic** appropriate for written argument: a process of examining an issue by looking at it from opposing points of view; or, to elaborate a little: a method of argument that systematically weighs contradictory ideas with a view to resolution of their contradictions.

It is this interplay of conflict among seeming opposites that can help us arrive at some form of "truth" or resolution. The German writer Goethe said that what we agree with leaves us inactive, but contradiction makes us productive. The world is full of contradictions. Those trained in dialectical thinking are better equipped to handle such contradictions. Through logical disputation we test and explore our ideas as we search for a viable position. As philosopher Georg Hegel saw it, the dialectic is a *process* of change whereby an idea, a *thesis,* is transformed into its opposite, *antithesis.* The combination of the two is then resolved in a form of truth, *synthesis.* Aristotle described this final common ground as *stasis.*

The English philosopher John Stuart Mill was trained by his father to argue both sides of every question and was taught that you had no right to a belief unless you understood the arguments for its opposite.

Eleanor Roosevelt advised women in politics to "argue the other side with a friend until you have found the answer to every point which might be brought up against you." We would second her advice.

And cognitive psychologist Piaget maintained that one mark of a maturing mind is the ability to take another's point of view and thus be capable of considering two conflicting views on the same issue.

A book reviewer takes Camille Paglia and her book *Sex, Art, and American Culture* to task for not having this capability:

. . . she is constitutionally incapable of splitting a difference. She is one of the least dialectical minds that ever claimed to be critical. Her style is a style of pure assertion. It has no philosophical shading or depth.

Dialectical thinking moves us to a richer form of argument in which the process of interweaving premises and counterarguments leads us to a new, stronger position on the issue.

Addressing Counterarguments

To take this dialectical approach to argument, you as a writer must pay careful attention to opposing views, acknowledging within your paper important **counterarguments** and thus those members of your audience who might hold them.

But, one might ask, why aid and abet the opposition by calling attention to their arguments? For a number of good reasons, such strategies can actually strengthen your own position.

know when writing an argument.

- By *anticipating* your opponent's reasoning, you can often disarm the opposition. The "I recognize that . . ." approach can be very effective, showing the writer's knowledge of the opposition's viewpoint.
- You can make your own position stronger when you state and then *refute* opposing premises by demonstrating their weakness or falseness. You must handle refutation tactfully, however, if you hope to convince those opposed to your position. If you treat them with contempt, as though they are shortsighted and thickheaded for holding the position they do, you only alienate them and defeat your own purpose, which is to have your views heard.
- By addressing counterarguments to your position, you also appear more reasonable, more fair. You are seen not as narrow-minded, dogmatic, or unheedful of others' views, but as broad-minded and aware of complexity and so ultimately as more intelligent, reliable, and thus credible.
- And when you *acknowledge* the possibility of merit in some of your opponents' reasoning, you have taken the ultimate step in establishing yourself as a "generous" thinker. Arguments are rarely truly one-sided, no matter how strong your convictions. When you can *concede* a point, you move closer to a middle ground, opening a line of communication and thus increasing your chances of winning your final point.
- You may even discover weaknesses and contradictions in your own thinking as you sort through the reasoning of your opponents. It is not easy to abandon cherished beliefs, but clear thinkers often must.

How Much Counterargument?

How much counterargument should writers include in their papers? There is no precise answer. If the writer has strong refutations for every one of the opposition's premises, then she may want to address all these counterarguments. If, on the other hand, a writer thinks the premises she has to support her conclusion are stronger than her refutation of the opposition, she may want to include only a minimum of counterargument. In any case, a writer cannot ignore the most compelling opposing premises even if they provide the greatest challenge to the writer's own view.

For a paper on limiting gun ownership, one would have to address the fact that many Americans believe the Second Amendment to the Constitution guarantees the right to own guns, and acknowledge that, in the eyes of some, hunting rifles should form a category separate from assault weapons or small handguns. And in a paper in favor of euthanasia, the writer would have to deal with the widely held belief that euthanasia is a form of murder or suicide. Precisely how the writer would present these counterarguments would depend on the evidence she presents and the precise position on the issue she decides to take. Once again, this is where the wording of the thesis is important.

Refutation and Concession

As you can see from this discussion, there is more than one way to address counterarguments. But address them you must, since to present a contradictory position and then leave it alone would confuse your reader. Here are two possible responses.

1. **Refutation:** Present a counterargument and then explain why this position is false, misleading, irrelevant, or weak; discredit it in some well-reasoned way.

   From a student essay in support of a law sanctioning active euthanasia:

   Some say death and suffering are in keeping with God's universal plan for humanity. Functioning to educate, to prepare people for the painless eternity of heaven, the dying process, no matter how long or how agonizing, has both spiritual and moral purpose. **To believe this argument though, one must believe there is life after death and many do not. So why can't people live and die in accordance with their own value system? Let both the religious and secular have some control of their own destiny; give those who choose to die that alternative, while honoring the belief of those who do not.** [emphasis added]

2. **Concession:** Recognize the merit of a counterargument and so concede that point or (as in our example below) a feature of it. If, for example, you are arguing in favor of euthanasia and want to refute the counterargument that euthanasia is a form of murder, you might begin this way:

> **Although I also believe that life is sacred and murder is wrong, I** don't think that ending the life of a brain-dead patient is equivalent to murder since in the true sense of the word "life," this patient is not living.

Visually, the relationship between counterargument and refutation and concession looks something like this:

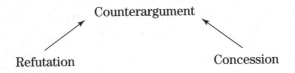

Rogerian Strategy

For a deeper appreciation of concession, we turn to the psychology of communication, particularly the work of Carl R. Rogers, a psychotherapist and communication theorist. Carl Rogers recognized that people tend to establish barriers and to grow more rigid in their beliefs when threatened and are thus less open to alternatives. If we view argument, whether spoken or written, not as a hostile contest between adversaries but as a dialogue, as an open exchange of ideas directed toward mutual understanding, we may find a more responsive audience and thus have greater success with changing people's opinions. If we are genuinely concerned with communicating our ideas to others, we must cultivate the audience to whom we direct these ideas. To achieve this end, we must develop *empathy*—the ability, in Rogers' words, "to see the expressed idea and attitude from the other person's point of view, to sense how it feels to him, to achieve his frame of reference in regard to the thing he is talking about." It is through empathy that we can most successfully understand another's position and so concede appropriate points, often gaining rather than losing ground in the process.

Take, for example, the issue of the death penalty. If a writer can understand why someone believes the death penalty serves as a deterrent and can acknowledge that understanding, a reader who favors the death penalty will be more inclined to consider the writer's arguments opposing the death penalty. The reader will feel less threatened as the writer reduces the gap between them and replaces hostile judgment with "mutual communication," helping a defensive opponent to see alternatives to her beliefs. Such a commitment can, as Rogers points out, carry risks. As a writer begins to "really understand" another person's point of view, she runs "the risk of being changed" herself. This spirit of conciliation and cooperation can sometimes be painful. But the gain in understanding can pay off handsomely as rigidity and defensiveness evolve into problem solving.

A British politician turned to Rogerian strategy when Iran and Britain were in a political crisis over the publication of Salmon Rushdie's *The Satanic Verses*, a novel which offended Moslems to such a degree that the then ruler of Iran, the Ayatollah Khomeini, called on Moslems around the world to kill Rushdie, sending the author into hiding for 10 years. The British government, while providing the author with continuous police protection, tried to temper Iran's fury. Britain's foreign secretary, Sir Geoffrey Howe, in a BBC radio broadcast meant to be heard by Iran, delivered the following message:

> We do understand that the book itself has been found deeply offensive by people of the Moslem faith. We can understand why it has been criticized. It is a book that is offensive in many other ways as well. We are not upholding the right of freedom to speak because we agree with the book. The book is extremely rude about us. It compares Britain with Hitler's Germany. We don't like that any more than people of the Moslem faith like the attacks on their faith.

He concluded with his belief that no matter how offensive its content, "nothing in the book could justify a threat to the life of the author." His comments were meant to forge a bond of empathy between the British and the Iranians—both groups, both governments were criticized by Rushdie—so of course, the British understand the anger of the Iranians. Through this mutual understanding, the foreign secretary hoped to persuade Iran to withdraw its demand that Rushdie be assassinated. We wish we could claim success for Rogerian strategy in this instance, but in fact, it was not until the Ayatollah Khomeini died, that the death sentence was lifted from Rushdie's head.

The Rogerian approach is not entirely new. Well over two thousand years ago, Aristotle spoke of an essential triad in argument, *logos, ethos,* and *pathos:*

logos the argument itself (derived from the Greek, meaning both "word" and "reason")

ethos the disposition of the writer (speaker) to present herself well

pathos empathy with the audience

MACHLIS

In this chapter we have already addressed *logos* when discussing the elements of mounting a successful written argument. In Chapter 1 and in this chapter, we discuss the ways you, the writer, must think about how you present yourself to your audience—the *ethos*. And *pathos* is precisely what Carl Rogers means when he talks of cultivating the audience, making them sympathetic to your point of view.

Aristotle saw the essential bond between writer and reader that leads to meaningful communication. To write convincing argument, you, the writer, must present yourself as a reasonable, sympathetic person at the same time that you convey respect for your readers. Both Carl Rogers and Aristotle suggest that effective argument depends not only on a well-informed writer but also on a writer who is acutely aware of her audience and well disposed toward them. The same holds true for public speaking.

The alternatives for organizing Rogerian concessions within an essay are the same as those discussed above under refutation and concession and as illustrated in the sample essays in Exercise 4E.

Can you identify the Rogerian strategy in this cartoon?

"He says his ballads sing of the brotherhood of man, with due regard for the stabilizing influence of the nobility."

When There Is No Other Side

What makes an issue worth arguing? While there are no fast rules, issues inappropriate for argument fall into three general categories. Some positions are simply too offensive to the majority of writers or readers. Arguments advocating racial bigotry or denial of the Holocaust, for example, fall into this category. Others are so personal or so self-evident that they don't lend themselves to intelligent debate. Take for example the following claims:

Chocolate ice cream is far superior to strawberry.

or

Free, quality education should be provided for all children in America.

Neither proposition lends itself to the kind of exploration we have been discussing in this chapter, in the first instance because it concerns a personal and insignificant preference, and in the second because no one could in all seriousness argue against such a proposition.

FOR AN EFFECTIVE ARGUMENT

express your thesis clearly
support your own position as thoroughly as possible
present relevant opposing views
provide appropriate concessions and refutations
develop empathy with your audience

Application to Writing

Logical Joining of Contrasting and Concessive Ideas

To express contrast and concession, so necessary for effective written argument, you need to manipulate your sentences to create a coherent flow of ideas and to convey logical relationships. We introduced principles of logical joining with the discussion of conjunctions in Chapter 3 and continue that discussion here.

EXERCISE 4B

Expressing Contrast and Concession

Below are three different attitudes on smoking in the workplace. Read the passages carefully, examine the logical relationship between ideas, then state the position of each writer and explain how you reached your decision.

1. The battle rages on. Whereas some contend that smoking, as a direct threat to health, should be banned in the workplace, others maintain that forbidding smoking is too extreme a measure. Medical evidence demonstrates that cigarette smoke is harmful to nonsmoking bystanders as well as to smokers, but smokers argue that

their emotional health is at stake. They point out that such discrimination threatens their constitutional civil rights, whereas executives and nonsmoking employees claim that medical costs from health problems and time lost from work justify such restrictions of personal choice.

2. Although most people recognize that smoking is a direct threat to health, making nonsmoking a condition of employment constitutes a new form of discrimination.

3. While banning smoking on the job can create serious personnel problems for a company, current medical evidence strongly supports those who insist on a completely smoke-free work environment.

As you have no doubt noticed, it is through the different choices of joining words that these writers established their slant on the issue here. Let's review these distinctions:

Coordinating Conjunctions	Subordinating Conjunctions	Major Transitions
contrast:	contrast & concession:	contrast & concession:
but	while	however
yet	whereas	on the other hand
	although	
	though	

The Concessive Sentence

The degree to which subordinating conjunctions express concession can vary according to the content of the sentence. In sentence 3 above, the writer recognizes the merit of a counterargument. But in some cases you may simply acknowledge your opponent's position without really conceding it, as in the following example:

> *Although* smokers defend their constitutional rights, the health of a nonsmoker should come first.

EXERCISE 4C

Making Rhetorical Choices

Try joining the following pair of sentences in three different ways: from the perspective of a film buff, a responsible student, and someone genuinely uncommitted.

1. I desperately want to see the latest Star Wars movie.
2. I know I need to work on my report due next week in my economics class.

More on Coherence

While you can manipulate ideas with grammatical word choice to signal relationships at the sentence level, you also need to develop rhetorical patterns of coherence throughout your paper. The form of your paper can take many shapes, but you want the whole to be held together by an almost invisible glue. Your thesis should guide you as you build paragraphs and create a thread that weaves its way from opening sentence to conclusion, each paragraph relating back to the thesis. The result will be a unified whole. Every sentence should follow from the sentence before it; each paragraph must follow logically from the one preceding it. As a writer, you take your reader's hand, never letting that reader stray from the flow of your argument. If you were to cut your paper into individual paragraphs, shake them up, and throw them in the air, a stranger should have no difficulty putting them together in the original order. The same is true of sentences within a paragraph.

To accomplish this logical flow from sentence to sentence, you will arrange points in a logical sequence, select joining conjunctions and major transitions carefully, and repeat or echo key words to keep your reader focused on your train of thought. Pronouns, those words that refer back to nouns (his, him, hers, her, they, this, that, these), can help relate one sentence to another, as can synonyms for nouns when repetition begins to sound monotonous. For more on keeping ideas connected within a paragraph, see *Sentence Focus—Techniques for Sharpening the Flow of Ideas and Parallel Structure* in Chapter 8.

To develop coherence between paragraphs within the essay, be sure that each paragraph connects to and makes a point about your thesis; follows a logical, clearly organized sequence; and creates a link to the one preceding it. The first sentence of a paragraph can pick up a phrase or idea expressed in the last sentence of the paragraph before it. A transitional word may signal the logical relationship, as discussed previously under joining words. Or the opening sentence might echo the thesis and so keep the main idea moving forward. All writers from time to time are tempted to include a graphic but unrelated example or an irrelevant line of reasoning, especially if time is short and material is thin. To be sure that your paper conveys a unified, coherent argument, one that "sticks" together and keeps your reader's attention, depend on details that clearly support major points and connect ideas logically.

A caution: Coherence devices should not be heavy-handed or too obvious. Remember to go lightly on the major transitions. It is the logical progression of your ideas that is important, not the deployment of conjunctions alone.

EXERCISE 4D

Identifying Coherence Strategies

It is difficult to create artificial coherence strategies without a context. But, as you revise your papers, you can look back at the suggestions given here. To illustrate some of these strategies in action, we ask you to select one of the essays that follows in Exercise 4E and identify the ways in which the writer has achieved coherence, both between sentences and between paragraphs. Explain the precise way in which each example works to create these links.

Sample Essays

To help you see some of the rhetorical features of effective written argument in action, we have selected three examples for you to examine closely. The first two are by students; the third is by a professional journalist. Note that all three address topics that could be relevant to you as a college student. Academic arguments don't always have to consider global topics such as world trade, euthanasia, or the death penalty.

EXERCISE 4E

Identifying Rhetorical Features of Argument

In the first essay, we identify the elements of written argument presented in this chapter. In the second and third essays, we ask you to do the same.

   thesis

   premises

   counterarguments

   concessions and refutations used to address the counterarguments

   Rogerian strategy

This model of a student essay, used in our classes to illustrate effective written argument, shows one way to organize, support, and advocate a position on a pressing problem.

Alternative Sentencing

As the newspapers confirm daily, Americans are worried about crime. Often responding emotionally to the many reports of crime we read and see on TV, people want to throw into prison everyone convicted of a crime. But our prisons are overcrowded and costly to run. In addition they are now producing more repeat offenders than reformed citizens. To begin to deal with this problem, we need to explore new solutions. First we should distinguish between violent and non-violent criminals. Then we could find alternative sentences for the non-violent ones. Instead of automatically choosing a jail sentence, a number of judges have begun to order non-violent offenders to perform a set number of hours of community service tailored to the criminal and the crime committed. While this solution has its critics, I believe the advantages of alternative sentencing outweigh any negative risks. We should support this innovative response to the pressing problem of rising crime.

Prisons are not only dangerously overcrowded, but prison programs are completely insufficient to rehabilitate criminals or to help them re-enter society as productive citizens. The number of repeat offenders tells us this. Most prisons are depressing places of despair, which instill anger and resentment in the prisoner. Taken from family and friends, deprived of normal relationships and privacy, caged under the most humiliating circumstances, often threatened and raped by other inmates, the prisoner is constantly reminded of his misdeed. We shouldn't be surprised that when these prisoners are released, they have become hostile, bitter, depressed people who lack the motivation to become useful citizens.

With the option of alternative sentencing, judges will be able to devise sentences that, while punishing the offender, also benefit the community. For example, instead of sending a drug dealer to prison, where he can continue to sell drugs, a judge might order him to work 200 hours in a drug crisis center, a place where he would be forced to help the very people he had been hurting and where he would have to face the misery of the addict and thus have the chance of becoming less inclined to push drugs. One such sentence, which a judge gave to an offender who had killed a man while driving drunk, illustrates how the community can benefit from an alternative sentence. The driver was allowed to continue working so that his family wouldn't have to go on welfare, thus saving the taxpayers money. Still, the offender had to live at the county jail and pay for his room and board there. And for one year he was ordered to work 200 hours in a hospital trauma center and to spend 200 hours on the lecture circuit describing the catastrophic results of his actions. Sentences like this one benefit everyone involved and help us realize how conventional sentencing can sometimes be worthless.

But what about the drug-dealers, shop-lifters, embezzlers who decide they need not fear prison? With no threat of prison, won't they receive the wrong message and feel that their crimes are insignificant? Surprisingly, alternative sentences can deter crime better than conventional sentences. *The*

Thesis

Premise

Counter-argument

New York Times reported the interesting case of Morris Cage, an apartment building owner in the Bronx, who was fined and ordered to pay $198,000 in civil penalties to correct code violations in one of his buildings. He was also sentenced to serve 22 days in an apartment in that decrepit building, forced to live alongside tenants who daily endured leaking pipes, falling plaster, little heat and less water. Tenants greeted Mr. Cage with a banner: "Welcome, You Rodent." The judge also ordered Cage to develop a housing plan and to spend 20 hours a week for five years carrying it out. That was 5,000 hours of community service. Such sentences will catch the attention of other slum landlords, who will want to avoid similar sentences which deprive them of their freedom and force them to confront the horrible problems they have created.

Statistics also shed light on the advantages of alternative sentencing. According to *The Baltimore Sun,* in 1997 the state of Maryland had, after only three years, reduced the chance of an offender committing a new crime by 50 percent and "saved the state from having to construct a new prison." The report came from Maryland's Correctional Options Program which was seen as "a national model by the U.S. Department of Justice." Programs include "home detention, which requires offenders to wear electronic ankle bracelets, drug abuse treatment, and military-style boot camps to rehabilitate convicts and return them to society." Intensive supervision is included, ensuring "that offenders stay off drugs and go to work instead of being kept in prison."

"'The bottom line behind all these programs is, who do you want in prison?' said Leonard A. Sipes, Jr., a spokesman for the Department of Public Safety and Correctional Services. 'Do you want the rapist? Do you want the armed robber? Or do you want the shoplifter? The program was designed to save prison beds for violent offenders,' Sipes said. 'And the findings have been nothing short of outstanding.'" Although the options program was relatively new at the time of the report, results so far certainly support alternative sentencing.

Further bolstering the arguments for such sentencing, Bob Pendergrass, an alternative sentencing advocate for the 5th Judicial District public defender's office in New Mexico, "estimates that he has saved the state of New Mexico more than $18 million."

"At first, the alternative program met a lot of resistance," he conceded. Ten years earlier, public sentiment was running against alternative programs because people were afraid criminals would be set loose to commit new crimes. But Pendergrass recognized that locking up non-violent offenders was not the answer; it only taught them to be better criminals (*Roswell Daily Record*).

"'It's not about letting them out. It's about providing them what they need so they don't recycle,' Pendergrass said."

Margin annotations (top to bottom): Refutation; Premise; Premise; Refutation Concession; Refutation

Concession (Rogerian)

Counter-argument

Refutation

Some may question Pendergrass's financial claims, thinking that the kinds of specialized intervention required to make alternative programs work would be very costly. While it is true that effective alternatives come at a high price, it is also true that the costs of incarceration are even higher. According to the Maryland report cited above, "the program costs $4,100 for each inmate, compared with $18,000 per inmate in prison." Add to that difference the cost of a new prison with its high operating expenses and we can see that the state would have had to earmark enormous sums for prisons beyond what they already must spend.

Concession (Rogerian)

Counter-argument

Refutation

But even if innovative sentencing works in some cases, how can we be assured that judges aren't being given too much flexibility in devising sentences? This too is a valid concern, but if our judges are well trained in alternative sentencing, if strict guidelines are set up for them, and if they work closely with the criminal reform specialists—criminologists, rehabilitation experts, psychologists, and directors of alternative services programs—most judges will be able to give fair and appropriate sentences. After evaluating each case by interviewing the persons involved, deciding whether the offender is criminally oriented and whether he or she has a good chance of rehabilitation, and then determining which type of program would be the most appropriate, the experts can advise the judge.

Rogerian

While crime remains a terrible problem in our society, we must find ways of dealing more effectively with the less dangerous criminals and, at the same time, better serve those who need to be incarcerated. We can deal effectively with violent criminals only if we have room for them in our prisons. I recognize that no one proposal can solve a problem so complex. But one way to remove the hardened criminal from our streets is to keep non-violent offenders out of the prisons so that we have more space for those who truly belong there. And, with some states forced to transfer money from their education budgets to prison construction, we might wonder why every judge in every state doesn't take a closer look at sentence reform.

Works Cited

"Bronx Apartment Owner Cited." *The New York Times* 17 March. 1994.

Penn, Ivan. "Alternative Sentencing." *The Baltimore Sun* 21 Oct. 1997. 21 Jan. 1999
<http://library.northernlight.com/pn19990630030073894.html?cb=o&dx=10048&sc=odoc>.

Sanner, Tammy. "Alternative Sentencing Advocate Retiring." *Roswell Daily Record* 3 March. 1998. 25 Jan. 1999
<http://www.roswell-record.com/news1326.html>.

In the following essay, student John Herschend defends popular music.

Rap Takes a Bum Rap

Even the president and vice president have gotten into the act, posturing about Ice-T's "Cop Killer" (as if boycotting Time Warner would reduce the national debt).

—SHERLEY ANNE WILLIAMS

Since its birth, Rap music has taken the blame for many of the problems plaguing America's inner cities—violence, drugs, AIDS, you name it. But Rap music cannot take the blame for these problems any more than, say, soap operas can shoulder the blame for infidelity in America. Rap is an art form, a medium which expresses, enrages and educates like most other art forms. As Guru says in the introduction to his album *Jazzmataz,* Rap is "musical, cultural expression based on reality." It does not cause problems but, instead, expresses them just as some movies, television shows and other forms of music do. However, unlike most of the mindless violence depicted in today's popular movies—*True Lies, Killing Zoe, Pulp Fiction*—Rap is a constructive outlet which brings attention to our country's problems in a creative, innovative and sometimes positive fashion.

In fact, the roots of rap are based in creativity and innovation. With its humble beginnings in the black ghettoes as filler between songs at parties, Rap has become a multi-million dollar business and one of the most established forms of new music in the past decade. The original idea was simple: two turntables and a microphone. The DJ, in command of the turntables, manipulates the records in order to form a beat or provide snippets of musical accompaniment. The "MC" then "busts out" in a fit of rhyme based stories, usually about the DJ's ability to "spin" or the MC's ability to "rap." However, as rap became more and more popular, the rappers began focusing their attention on the larger issues of life in the ghetto—violence, drugs, and oppression—forming two separate branches of Rap.

The first, and currently the most popular, is known as "gangsta" rap, a rough mix of extreme violence and heavy rhythms, sounding something like broken glass on an inner city basketball court. The second, which is quickly gaining momentum, is known as hip-hop, a jazz based, dance mix which is much more complex and layered than gangster. The music of hip-hop evokes the feel of a smoky, Soho jazz club in the 1950s while the words relate stories of ghetto life in the 1990s. The message of hip-hop is upbeat, oftentimes offering solutions or alternatives to the problems rather than focusing solely on them. Although gangsta and hip-hop differ in their style and message, both forms are important for their ability to educate and to offer a creative outlet.

Rap's ability to educate its listeners is an often overlooked but crucial element of the music. Several groups envision the music as their way to speak directly to kids. Groups such as the Bay Area's Disposable Heroes of Hiphoprisy believe that they, as Rap artists, are the only role models the children may have and therefore work to fill their music with thoughts on politics, environmentalism and other social issues in hopes of raising the consciousness of their listeners. Many of their songs are like quick morality plays. For instance, on the Disposable Heroes' latest album, *Hypocrisy Is the Greatest Luxury*, they have a song entitled "The Language of Violence" about a boy who goes to jail for killing another boy. In the song, the killer is caught and sent to jail where he is raped by the inmates. Michael Franti, the lyricist of the group, writes, "He had never questioned his own sexuality but this group of men didn't hesitate their reality, with an awful powerful showerful an hour full of violence." In the end, the song takes a more philosophical vein and asks: "is this a tale of rough justice in a land where there's no justice at all. Who is really the victim? Or are we all the cause, and victim of it all." Franti's aim is to get the kids who might commit acts of violence to think not only of the immediate physical consequences of their actions, but of the larger picture of violence and victimization. He says that "death is the silence in this circle of violence." The same is true of other rap artists such as the Digable Planets, The Pharcyde and Guru. These groups fill their albums with a smoky coolness of life on the streets and the choices available to the kids. They tell stories of street life with a more positive and hopeful edge, working to expand the vision of the listener, to help them see beyond the ghetto. Their music doesn't seek to exploit or cause violence but rather paint a picture of reality and offer alternatives.

But not all Rap music offers such positive alternatives. A good portion of Rap, particularly gangsta, offers little or no alternatives. It simply paints a picture of a bleak world where the gun is king. And it is here where Rap foes focus their efforts and here where I would agree with them. They say that Rap glamorizes the violence on the streets. They say that kids look to these groups as heroes and follow their lyrics as a zealot Christian might follow the Bible. In fact, a recent *Newsweek* article entitled *A Gangster Wake-Up Call* questions whether kids will "change their attitudes about money, sex, and violence now that gangster rap appears to be doing a drive-by on itself?" In essence, the article is assuming that Rap is the only place that kids get these ideas. The article is about the death (due to AIDS) of Eazy-E, one of the first major Rap stars, and the jailing of three other Rap superstars because of their violent ways. It seems that the Rap foes are making an important point: Rap stars live the life they sing about. But all this is presupposing the fact that the listeners of Rap are motivated by the lyrics to take action in the streets. In fact, it completely bypasses the notion that violence has existed in our streets before Rap and that the musicians, particularly the ones indicated in the *Newsweek* article, are victims of these streets.

Rather than say that Rap lyrics are a cause of street violence, I would like to offer the idea that violence is the cause of Rap lyrics, and that our society seems to have a double standard when it comes to judging the violence of Rap music versus the violence of popular cinema and television. If we are to isolate Rap for its violence what, then, do we make of movies like

Killing Zoe, Pulp Fiction, Reservoir Dogs or *The Bad Lieutenant.* Or while we're on the subject, how about such popular TV shows as *Cops, Rescue 911* and *Real Stories of the California Highway Patrol?* It seems that violence is an obsession with Americans and still we don't indict these shows as being the cause of it. They are accepted and even called "artistic," and works of genius. For instance, in "Vox Populi," an article which appeared in *The Atlantic* magazine, Francis Davis credits Quentin Tarantino for his subtle handling of an extremely violent scene in *Reservoir Dogs.* In the scene, a captive cop is bound to a chair while Mr. Blonde, played by Michael Madsen, dances around with a razor in his hand, eventually cutting off the cop's ear and dousing him in gasoline. Davis is impressed with the scene because it takes our emotions for a ride. He writes about the scene, saying that Madsen

> *does a series of graceful little dance steps to Stealers Wheel's "Stuck in the Middle with You," and closes in on his defenseless, screaming captive. "Was that as good for you as it was for me?" Madsen asks the cop afterward. . . . Madsen might also be asking those of us who sat through the scene without averting our eyes.*

Davis feels that this form of violence is more acceptable because it is complex and plays with the audience's emotions. Conversely, Rap artist Ice-T was forced, due to heavy protest from police organizations, to remove the song *Cop Killer* from an album with the same name. The police groups, who felt that the album encouraged kids to kill police officers, won their argument and Ice-T had to pull the song and change the name of the album. Interestingly enough, Tarantino did not meet the same criticism and was praised by many for his "genius" in handling the violence of the police scene. A double standard? To say that one form of violence is better or more acceptable than another is ridiculous. The hard edges of gangsta Rap are no different than Tarantino's violence. By stating that the violence of movies and TV shows does not cause acts of aggression while at the same time indicting Rap music as a reason for aggression, we set an absurd double standard.

Rap music is violent because it reflects the real life struggles of life on the inner city streets. And although this is not an appealing vision for many, it is still a telling story, one that deserves attention. Of course many songs are often blown out of proportion, but the kernel of struggle is still discernible. When groups sing about drive-bys, drugs and beer drinking, it's because the singers grew up with these realities. These are not imaginary issues that are drummed up to sell records; they are the incidents of real life for many kids in America. Rap music is a window to real life, an expression of frustration and a way for Americans to understand what is going on in our streets. This is not to validate the violence, but to say that the expression is a positive release for both listener and singer, something that should not be so readily ignored and dismissed.

We look to expression—music, literature, cinema—as a way of release. Indeed, it is powerful; it can change hearts and minds. But expression is ultimately a product of experience. It is an interpretation of life and all the emotions that go along with it—fear, love, anger, happiness—feelings as old as our ability to express them. Rap, as a member of this community, cannot and should not be singled out as the cause of violence. It is an expression of life in our inner cities, a vision that is sometimes hopeful and sometimes violent but always based in reality. And if we listen without prejudice, we might begin to hear the words behind the violence. We might even be able to begin focusing on the real factors of ghetto life rather than constantly blaming the messenger for the delivery of bad news.

Works Cited

Davis, Francis. "Vox Populi." *Constellations: A Contextual Reader for Writers.* 2nd ed. Ed. John Schilb, Elizabeth Flynn & John Clifford. New York: HarperCollins, 1995: 603–610.

Marriott, Michel. "A Ganster Wake-Up Call." *Newsweek* 10 Apr. 1995: 74–76.

Atlanta Constitution editor Cynthia Tucker, in her weekly column "As I See It," addresses the grave concerns many people have about the abandonment of affirmative action in several states and the threat in others. Note how effectively she summons arguments to support her points and how skillfully she keeps her opponents with her by acknowledging their views.

A Case for Affirmative Action

Why are many Americans—white Americans, mostly—so upset about college admissions programs that take race into account for a handful of students whose test scores are slightly below standards? Why are programs that boost the chances of black and brown students so controversial, while similar programs that benefit white students go without notice?

For example, the country's premier colleges and universities have long reserved places for the lesser-achieving children of their well-heeled graduates and donors. At the University of Georgia, family connections are one of the dozen or so factors—along with race—used to assess about 20 percent of its applicants who don't quite meet academic standards. In other words, a kid whose test scores and grades are not quite good enough may get into Georgia anyway if his mom or dad is a graduate.

That practice allows weaker students—most of them white—to be admitted at the expense of better students. Yet no one bemoans it as an assault on the vaunted "meritocracy."

College admissions also grant athletic "preferences," a device that happens to benefit many kids—black, white, and brown—who otherwise could

premise

not get near their chosen college. For some reason, a black kid with low SATs who can score touchdowns and generate a lot of money for the university is not nearly as offensive as a black kid with low scores who just wants an education.

concession

To be fair, some criticism of college admissions efforts is legitimate. Awarding scholarships based on race makes no sense, since they would often end up giving financial aid to the black upper-middle-class but not to the white poor. Besides that, poorly run affirmative-action programs, such as the contracting set-aside program run by the city of Atlanta, tend to generate resentments that splash over onto better-run and more necessary programs.

refutation

But much criticism of affirmative action in college admissions is based on myth, misunderstanding and—how shall I say this?—simple bigotry. Affirmative-action programs exist only in 25 percent to 40 percent of the nation's institutions of higher learning; the other 60 percent to 75 percent accept all applicants. So the controversy centers around the nation's most prestigious institutions.

premise

Admission to those elite colleges is highly competitive, because a diploma from Harvard or Emory nearly guarantees a financially rewarding career. Rejected white applicants, looking for an explanation for their failure, often believe they were unfairly supplanted by an unqualified minority student.

Consider, however, an analogy used by Thomas Kane of the Brookings Institution, likening affirmative action in colleges to the handicapped parking space:

support

"Eliminating the reserved space would have only a minuscule effect on parking options for non-disabled drivers. But the sight of the open space will frustrate many passing motorists who are looking for a space. Many are likely to believe that they would now be parked if the space were not reserved."

Scaling back affirmative action would cripple the prospects for black participation in this nation's economic, political and social elite. William Bowen, former president of Princeton University, and Derek Bok, former president of Harvard University, recently conducted a landmark study of affirmative action at 28 elite institutions, including Atlanta's Emory University. They found that black graduates of those colleges go on to earn advanced degrees—medicine, law, MBAs—at slightly higher rates than their white counterparts, and also become more active in civic affairs.

Because America proffers advancement through education, programs to enhance educational opportunities for students of color remain critical—perhaps more important than any other form of affirmative action. Since my grandfathers would not have been admitted to white universities, it does not seem unreasonable to create a form of "legacy" for their descendants.

Four Approaches to Writing Arguments

The next four writing assignments all focus on argument. Writing Assignment 9 serves as preparation for Writing Assignment 10. Writing Assignment 11 presents a more complex and thus more challenging approach to an issue. Assignment 12 focuses on working collaboratively with classmates on complex issues chosen by the class.

WRITING ASSIGNMENT 9

Arguing Both Sides of an Issue

The Topic

Below is a list of proposals advocating a position on a social issue. Choose *one* and write two arguments, one defending and one refuting the proposal. For each argument, convey clearly the position you are taking by writing a short thesis (the conclusion of your argument) at the top of the page. For each position, provide relevant reasons (premises) that are, to the best of your knowledge, accurate. You will have two separate papers with a paragraph for each reason. Although each paragraph should be written coherently with fluent sentences, you don't, at this stage, need to provide logical transitions between paragraphs for a coherent whole. And you need not provide an introduction or conclusion. All this will come later in Writing Assignment 10.

Make your selection with care, for you will be spending considerable time on this one issue.

1. Free speech may have to be limited in order to protect children from pornography on the Internet.

2. If economics is not a factor, the mother of a young child or children is still justified in choosing to work outside the home.

3. School administrators should be permitted to censor student Web sites.

4. Online gambling should be prohibited by federal law.

5. Nationwide standardized tests throughout elementary and secondary school have a negative effect on education.

6. The genetic engineering of plants used for food poses a danger to consumers.

7. Basic Education requirements at my college place an unnecessary burden on students.

8. The use of car phones while a driver is in motion should be prohibited.

9. All medical research on animals should be forbidden by law.

If another issue interests you more—for instance, a campus topic or a controversy in your neighborhood—you may write on it. Be sure the issue is one worth arguing from both sides and can be expressed as a proposal similar to those above. You may, of course, change any of the given topics to suit your own purpose.

Audience

A wide range of your peers: those who would agree with you, those who would disagree, and those who have not, as yet, formed any opinion

Purpose

To present both sides of a controversial issue so you and your readers are forced to consider alternatives to one position

WRITING ASSIGNMENT 10

Taking a Stand

The Topic

In this essay, take a stand on the issue you debated in Writing Assignment 9, constructing as persuasive an argument as possible.

Your thesis may express a strong position either for or against the proposition you addressed in the previous assignment or may be qualified as appropriate to reflect your view of the issue. (See the discussion of the thesis earlier in this chapter.)

To support your position fully, draw on the premises you presented in Writing Assignment 9, discarding reasoning that seems weak or irrelevant, adding reasons where you find gaps in your earlier paper. Strengthen your argument with as much available data as you think necessary to make your case. As you expand your argument, you will probably need to consult outside sources—newspapers, magazines, books, and individual authorities—for supporting information. Be sure to cite all references. For guidelines, consult Chapter 9, Research and Documentation.

To address opposing views, select the most important premises from your list of arguments on the other side of your position and briefly address them, acknowledging, conceding, and refuting in the manner best suited to your stand on the issue. Do not elaborate the opposing views in the same way you have your own premises.

For help in organizing your paper, refer once again to the sample essays in Exercise 4E.

Important: To complete the assignment, include the following attachments written out on a separate page:

Your issue, question at issue, and thesis

Your principal argument set out in standard form (see Chapter 3)

Peer Editing

If your instructor can find the time, you will find it useful to edit a first complete draft with classmates. Bring photocopies of your paper to class and exchange papers with one or more students, asking questions and noting strengths and weaknesses on each others' drafts.

Audience

The same as for Writing Assignment 9

Purpose

To present a convincing, balanced, fair argument for your position on a controversial argument in order to persuade your readers to adopt your point of view

---

A CHECKLIST OF ESSENTIAL COMPONENTS FOR ASSIGNMENT 10:

A clear thesis to guide you as a writer and prepare your reader

Support for this thesis—plenty of well-reasoned premises supported with examples, explanation, and analysis

Counterarguments with appropriate concessions and refutations

Sentences logically joined for contrast and concession, cause and effect, and coherence

WRITING ASSIGNMENT 11

Exploring an Argument in Depth

Not all issues lend themselves to a pro or con, yes or no argument. In Writing Assignment 9, you argued two opposing positions on the same question at issue, and then in Writing Assignment 10, took a position on that issue. For this paper, address an issue in more of its complexity, considering arguments from as many sides as possible and coming to a conclusion that seems reasonable in light of your in-depth exploration. Such topics often present paradoxes in which two contradictory claims may both merit approval. In such a conclusion, you may incline to one position or another or may settle for explaining and clarifying the issues without going so far as to make a definitive decision.

The Topic

Choose a current controversial issue of interest to you, one that suggests more than a simple pro and con approach. Because you will present a number of viewpoints, you must make sure your readers know which point of view you are expressing at any given point in the paper. Clear and logical transitions between points will help you accomplish this (note discussion of joining words in Chapter 3 and contrast and concession earlier in this chapter), as will smooth attributions of quotations and references to the ideas of others (see Chapter 9).

Be prepared to face a degree of chaos as you sort out the different perspectives. Don't be afraid of the inevitable confusion that a more complex issue often produces. It is through such a thinking and writing process that critical thinking takes place.

Once again, you may want to edit a draft with classmates.

Audience

The same as for Assignments 9 and 10

Purpose

To clarify your audience's understanding of a complex controversial issue

---

A CHECKLIST FOR WRITING ASSIGNMENT 11

An introduction that presents the question at issue with appropriate background, acknowledges its complexity, and suggests your thesis even though you may not be taking a clear stand either pro or con

A detailed discussion of arguments for as many positions as possible

Refutations and concessions as appropriate for a thoughtful examination of alternatives

Your personal recommendation on the issue, based on an evaluation in which you weigh the strengths and weaknesses of the positions you have presented, a synthesis of them, a call for further investigation, or a summary of possible alternatives.

WRITING ASSIGNMENT 12

Collaborating on a Complex Issue

Here we offer an alternative approach to writing the kind of argument presented in Assignment 11. Rather than preparing your paper on your own, you will be working with a group of classmates. Once out in the world, writing for business, politics, for many jobs, you will find that much of the writing you do is collaborative.

The Topic

Each member of the class will submit two or three controversial issues. From this list, the class will select four or five topics around which research groups will form on the basis of preference. You should end up with groups of five or six students.

Here are the guidelines for working with classmates to construct a written argument:

1. The topic research groups will meet in class to narrow the issue to a specific question at issue.

2. Students will conduct research to find at least one relevant article each that addresses the question at issue. They will make copies for

members of the group. Because these articles are to represent the various positions on the question at issue, members of the group must confer to ensure that the articles together reflect the diverse points of view.

3. Students will reduce the central argument of their own articles to standard form (see Chapter 3).

4. Each group will meet as often as necessary, in class and out as time permits, to share and discuss these materials. Members of each group will also have an opportunity to discuss the organization and development of their papers.

5. The class will choose whether students complete these papers on their own or whether they work together as a group to compose one final product as a fully collaborative effort.

6. Each group may want to select the best paper to read to the class, or in the case of collaborative papers, there may be time to hear them all.

Audience

The same as for Writing Assignments 9, 10, and 11

Purpose

To present different perspectives on an issue and to engage or persuade an audience through collaborative effort

SUMMARY

Convincing arguments usually contain an introduction to the topic, a thesis stated or clearly implied, well-supported premises, acknowledgment of opposing views, and a conclusion. Successful written argument depends on a dialectical approach in which writers address both their own position and opposing views.

A well-written argument requires joining sentences for logic and fluency and developing coherent links to express relationships.

Collaboration on the production of a written argument can be helpful and reflects the process often used in the working world.

KEY TERMS

Concession   a statement that grants the opposing view.

Counterargument   an opposing view in an argument.

Dialectic   a method of argument that systematically weighs contradictory ideas with a view to resolution of their contradictions.

Issue   any topic of concern and controversy.

Question at issue   a particular aspect of the issue under consideration.

Refutation   an explanation of why a position is false or weak.

Rhetoric   the art of using language to good effect, to prove, to convince, to persuade.

Rogerian strategy   an explicit effort to see ideas from an opponent's point of view; the cultivation of empathy with the opposition; a concept derived from the research of psychologist Carl Rogers.

Thesis   a statement of a writer's position; in argument, a response to the question at issue, the conclusion of the central argument in an essay.

CHAPTER 5

The Language of Argument—Definition

"When I use a word," Humpty Dumpty said in rather a scornful tone, "it means just what I choose it to mean—neither more nor less."
— LEWIS CARROLL, *ALICE THROUGH THE LOOKING GLASS*

In Chapter 4, we discuss how to construct written arguments that explore an issue in depth, weigh evidence, and address opposing views. Now we'd like to concentrate on the precise use of language, on paying close attention to how we choose our words, and thus on how we make our meaning precise and clear to others. As Francis Bacon put it four hundred years ago, "Men imagine that their minds have the command of language, but it often happens that language bears rule over their minds." Language itself, he suggests, can shape—even control—our thoughts. Poet W. H. Auden agrees: "Language is the mother, not the handmaiden, of thought; words will tell you things you never thought or felt before." While scholars today disagree about the possibility of thought without language, it remains enormously important that we know the meaning of the words we use and that when we write, our readers, to the degree possible, share our understanding of words. To achieve this clarity in our writing, we must, when necessary, define our terms.

Logical Definition

Cicero, the Roman orator, claimed that every discourse should begin with a definition in order to make clear what the subject under consideration is. French philosopher Voltaire wrote, "If you would argue with me, first define your terms."

Ellen Willis, writing in *Rolling Stone*, admonishes us, "Find out who controls the definitions, and you have a pretty good clue who controls everything else." Toni Morrison, in her novel, *Beloved*, illustrates the brutal oppression of slavery with the story of the slave Sixo. When the school teacher accused him of stealing the shoat (a piece of pork), Sixo claimed he wasn't *stealing* but *improving his property*. The teacher beat Sixo "to show him that definitions belonged to the definers—not the defined."

For a close look at the importance of definition in today's world, let's examine the following sentences:

1. Was Bill Clinton an effective president?
2. Does money mean success?
3. Is the violence portrayed in today's movies obscene?
4. Is television addictive?
5. Is alcoholism an illness?
6. Should we encourage entrepreneurs?

Remembering our discussion in Chapter 4, you will note that each sentence is a question at issue. Examine these questions more closely and you will notice that each contains at least one key term that is open to interpretation. For example, what does it mean to be an "effective" president? If you were to write a paper based on this question at issue, you would first have to define "effective," to list the criteria for such a presidency before applying them to Bill Clinton.

You need to define, to stipulate, to pin down precise meaning for terms such as these. To supply useful definitions, where do you begin? A good dictionary is the best *initial* source. Following the tradition of classical rhetoric laid down by Plato and Aristotle, first place the term in its general *class* and then narrow the definition by determining the **distinguishing characteristics,** the ways in which it differs from other terms in the same class.

Such a rigorous process is hardly necessary for a concrete term such as "fork," which belongs to the class of eating utensils and is distinguished from other members of its class, other eating utensils, by its shape, a handle at one end with two or more pointed prongs at the other. But abstract terms such as "success" and "obscene" must be carefully defined.

A definition of key terms in questions two and three above would look like this:

Term	Class	Distinguishing Characteristics
Success	(is) a favorable result	(which) implies economic and social achievement in one's chosen professional field.
Obscene	(is) a negative quality	(which) offends prevailing notions of modesty or decency.

Note that the distinguishing characteristics are still subject to interpretation, to individual assessment. Another writer could define success in terms of personal relationships or contributions to the community rather than professional achievement. And, of course, stipulating the precise meaning of "obscene" is a task that has long bedeviled our courts and has continued to do so with cases such as the violence in rap lyrics and the on-going controversy over censorship of the Internet.

GUINDON

5-7

John White is my idea of an intellectual. He buys Playboy magazine, cuts out the interviews and hangs them all over his bedroom.

EXERCISE 5A

Defining Key Terms

For the remaining three questions at issue above (4–6), identify terms that require clarification and stipulate a definition. Place each term first in its general class and then narrow your definition with distinguishing characteristics as we have done. You may find it interesting to compare your definitions with those of classmates.

Definition and The Social Sciences

In a study on child abuse and health, which we cite in Chapter 7, the researchers first had to define child abuse before they could determine its effect on women's health. They separated child abuse into three categories—emotional, physical, and sexual. Then they defined each category.

> *emotional abuse:* repeated rejection or serious physical threats from parents, tension in the home more than 25 percent of the time, and frequent violent fighting among parents.
>
> *physical abuse:* strong blows from an adult or forced eating of caustic substances; firm slaps were excluded.
>
> *sexual abuse:* any nonvoluntary sexual activity with a person at least five years older.

Researchers interviewed 700 women from a private gynecological practice and tabulated their responses according to these categories. Without clearcut definitions to guide them, social scientists would be left with subjective impressions rather than quantifiable results.

Definition and Perception

Our definitions can reveal how we see people—as individuals and collectively. In his book *Days of Obligation,* writer Richard Rodriguez points out that American feminists have appropriated the word *macho* "to name their American antithesis," a man who is "boorish" and "counterdomestic." But in Mexican Spanish, he tells us that "*Machismo* is more akin to the Latin *gravitas.* The male is serious. The male provides. The Mexican male never abandons those who depend upon him." As this example illustrates, when different cultures share languages, shifts in meaning often occur, reflecting cultural bias.

Feminist Gloria Steinem points out our culture's sexual bias in its traditional definitions of the following terms, definitions that have played crucial roles in determining how women and men view themselves and others.

> *work:* something men do, go to; as distinguished from housework and childcare, which is what women do
>
> *art:* what white men produce
>
> *crafts:* what women and ethnic minorities do

We can hope that these definitions are changing. And indeed, we have historical precedent for scientific definitions shifting to conform to new ways of thinking. In the 19th century, alcoholism was defined as criminal behavior. When the term was redefined as an illness after World War I, considerable progress in treatment became possible.

Conversely, when the American Psychological Association recently stopped classifying homosexuality as an illness, the homosexual community was understandably gratified by the revision of a definition it found unjust and damaging to its members.

Writer Katie Roiphe, author of *The Morning After: Sex, Fear, and Feminism on Campus,* inspired angry responses when she claimed that the definition of date rape had gone too far. "It's creating stereotypes of men as predatory beasts and women as delicate vessels. It's destructive. When you use rape to mean so many things, the word itself loses its meaning."

Language evolves over time. It's a natural process. But when expanded meaning results in loss of precision, we do well to examine the causes and effects of the revised meaning.

Language: An Abstract System of Symbols

As you have noticed from the preceding discussion, abstract words can present particular difficulties when it comes to stipulating precise meaning. But language itself, whether it refers to an abstract concept or a concrete object, is an abstract system of symbols. The word is not the thing itself, but a *symbol* or *signifier* used to represent the thing we refer to, which is the *signified.* For example, the word "cat" is a symbol or signifier for the animal itself, the signified.

"Cat"

THE SYMBOL or SIGNIFIER
(the word)

THE SIGNIFIED
(the thing being referred to)

But meaning is made only when the signified is processed through the mind of someone using or receiving the words. This process serves as an endlessly destabilizing force. Whenever a speaker, writer, listener, or reader encounters a word, a lifetime of associations renders the word, and thus the image it conjures up, distinct for each individual.

As literary theorist Stanley Fish points out, meaning is dependent not only on the individual but also on the context, situation, and interpretive community. To illustrate this point, let's look at the word "host." It means one thing if we are at a party, something different if we're discussing parasites with a biologist, and something else entirely if we are at church. Hence, the context or situation determines our understanding of "host."

If, however, you are not a member of a religion that practices the ritual of communion or are not conversant with parasitology, then you may understand the meaning of "host" *only* as the giver of a party. You are not part of the interpretive community, in this case a religious community or a scientific discipline, which understands "host" as a consecrated wafer, a religious symbol, or as an organism on which another lives.

As you can see, language remains perpetually contingent and thus, as a means of communication, slippery. Even when the signified is *concrete*, individual experience and perception will always deny the word complete stability; the range of possible images will still be vast. Take the word "table." Nothing of the essence of table is part of the word "table." Although most words in English (or any modern language) have roots and a history in older languages, the assignation of a particular meaning to a given term remains essentially arbitrary. While all English speakers share a *general* understanding of the word "table," each user or receiver of this word, without having considerably more detail, will create a different picture.

If the symbolic representation of a *concrete*, visible object such as a table is as unstable as our discussion suggests, think how much more problematic *abstract* terms must be. Were we to substitute the abstraction "freedom" for the concrete "table," the range of interpretations would be considerably more diverse and much more challenging to convey to others. Visual pictures, which arise when concrete objects are signaled, don't

concrete: real, tangible-
abstract; apart from · ?

come to mind as readily when we refer to abstractions, a distinction that required us to define the abstract terms in the questions at issue above and led Shakespeare to explain why poets give "to airy nothing a local habitation and a name."

Semanticist S. I. Hayakawa discusses the idea of an abstraction ladder in which language starts on the ground, so to speak, with an object available to our sense of perception, and moves up to concepts abstracted from, derived from, the concrete source—for example, from a specific cow to livestock to farm assets to assets. He stresses that our powers of abstraction are indispensable. "The ability to climb to higher and higher levels of abstraction is a distinctively human trait without which none of our philosophical or scientific insights would be possible." But he cautions against staying at too high a level of abstraction.

(handwritten margin note: Study history of language)

> The kind of "thinking" we must be extremely wary of is that which *never* leaves the higher verbal levels of abstraction, the kind that never points *down* the abstraction ladder to lower levels of abstraction and from there to the extensional world:
> "What do you mean by *democracy*?"
> "Democracy means the preservation of human *rights*."
> "What do you mean by *rights*?"
> "By rights I mean those privileges God grants to all of us—I mean man's inherent privileges."
> "Such as?"
> "Liberty, for example."
> "What do you mean by *liberty*?"
> "Religious and political freedom."
> "And what does that mean?"
> "Religious and political freedom is what we enjoy under a democracy."

The writer never moves down to the essential lower levels on the abstraction ladder, and a discourse consisting only of abstractions, devoid of concrete details and examples, is necessarily vague, often difficult for the reader to understand and, in this definition of democracy, circular.

The Importance of Specificity

To avoid the confusion that unclarified abstractions can generate, Hayakawa suggests pointing down "to extensional levels wherever necessary; in writing and speaking, this means giving *specific examples* of what we are talking about," grounding our arguments in experience.

Compare the empty, circular definition of democracy Hayakawa quotes above with the concrete illustrations that illuminate E. B. White's celebrated World War II definition of the same term.

BIZARRO *Piraro*

www.uexpress.com

July 3, 1943

We received a letter from the Writers' War Board the other day asking for a statement on "The Meaning of Democracy." It presumably is our duty to comply with such a request, and it is certainly our pleasure. Surely the Board knows what democracy is. It is the line that forms on the right. It is the don't in don't shove. It is the hole in the stuffed shirt through which the sawdust slowly trickles; it is the dent in the high hat. Democracy is the recurrent suspicion that more than half of the people are right more than half of the time. It is the feeling of privacy in the voting booths, the feeling of communion in the libraries, the feeling of vitality everywhere. Democracy is a letter to the Editor. Democracy is the score at the beginning of the ninth. It is an idea that hasn't been disproved yet, a song the words of which have not gone bad. It's the mustard on the hot dog and the cream in the rationed coffee. Democracy is a request from a War Board, in the middle of a morning in the middle of a war, wanting to know what democracy is.

Such specificity is what writer Annie Dillard values when she says, "This is what life is all about: salamanders, fiddle tunes, you and me and things . . . the fizz into particulars" (*Teaching a Stone to Talk*). And what novelist Vladimir Nabokov prizes when he asks us to "Caress the details, the divine details" (*Lectures on Literature*).

The Manipulation of Language

Sometimes abstractions are used, consciously or unconsciously, to confuse, distort, conceal, or evade, in short, to manipulate others—a practice Hemingway comments on in *A Farewell to Arms,* his World War I novel.

I was always embarrassed by the words sacred, glorious, and sacrifice and the expression in vain. We had heard them, sometimes standing in the rain almost out of earshot, so that only the shouted words came through, and had read them, on proclamations that were slapped up by billposters or other proclamations, now for a long time, and I had seen nothing sacred, and the things that were glorious had no glory and the sacrifices were like the stockyards at Chicago if nothing was done with the meat except to bury it. There were many words that you could not stand to hear and finally only the names of places had dignity. Certain numbers were the same way and certain dates and these with the names of the places were all you could say and have them mean anything. Abstract words such as glory, honor, courage, or hallow were obscene beside the concrete names of villages, the numbers of roads, the names of rivers, the numbers of regiments and the dates.

Hemingway eloquently indicates the power of concrete nouns to generate precise meaning readily visualized.

Closer to home, during debates on the complex environmental issue of preserving wetlands, then-President George Bush declared that "All existing wetlands, no matter how small, should be preserved." But when pressured by real estate, oil, and mining interests to open protected wetlands to development and exploration, Bush expediently redefined the word, a definition that left at least 10 million acres of wet lands unprotected. Such examples lend fresh meaning to our opening claims of power for those who control the definitions.

In the 1940s, British writer George Orwell addressed the political significance of language in his celebrated essay, "Politics and the English Language," claiming that "political speech and writing are largely the defense of the indefensible. . . . Defenceless villages are bombarded from the air, the inhabitants driven out into the countryside, the cattle machinegunned, the huts set on fire with incendiary bullets: this is called pacification." In his novel *1984,* he satirizes the official use of deceptive language, coining, among other terms, the words "doublethink" and "newspeak."

We continue to have had our own share of befuddling language, dubbed psychobabble, spacespeak, doublespeak, gobbledygook. Euphemisms, indirect, less expressive words or phrases for sensitive ideas, are sometimes justified as a means of sparing feelings: Someone passed away rather than died, or a large woman is referred to as mature in size. And the specialized lingo of a particular discipline may be necessary even though it appears as needless jargon to a lay person.

We must be particularly wary of language that deliberately camouflages precise meaning. When opposition to building the controversial MX missiles grew heated, the proponents began to call the missiles "peacemakers." Such an example reminds us of our claim, earlier in this chapter, that those who hold the power want to control the definitions.

EXERCISE 5B *dysphemism — opposite of.*

Beware the Euphemism — *expression making terms sound nicer.*

1. Below is a list of paired terms or phrases. For each, briefly explain how the language of the second phrase dulls the meaning, and thus the reality, of the initial term, and discuss why you think such euphemistic language crept in. For some of these terms, you may need to do a little research in order to fully understand the meaning.

    foreign   /   offshore
    taxes   /   revenue enhancement
    civilian losses   /   collateral damage
    cloning   /   "somatic cell nuclear transfer"

THE FAR SIDE   By GARY LARSON

"Well, actually, Doreen, I rather resent being
called a 'swamp thing.' ... I prefer the term
'wetlands-challenged mutant.'"

2. From newspapers, magazines, television, or the Internet find a current example of usage that you think represents a manipulative euphemism. Advertising is often a good source of deceptive language.

WRITING ASSIGNMENT 13

Composing an Extended Definition of an Abstract Term

Step 1

Choose a word from the list of abstract terms below, think about its implications for a few minutes, and then start writing a definition that captures its meaning and significance for you. (If an abstract term other than one of those on the list comes to mind and interests you, substitute it, but clear it with your instructor first.) Using a freewriting approach (see Chapter 1), keep going for about 20 minutes. If time and your instructor permit, do this in class; you will find the combination of spontaneity and structure imposed by writing during class to be an aid to composing. You can't get up to make a phone call or clean the refrigerator.

education	addiction
originality	defeat
machismo	courage
maturity	leisure
creativity	progress
cult	trend
gossip	art
pornography	political correctness
imagination	character
sexual harassment	marriage
soul	generosity
intelligence	heroism

Volunteers can enlighten (and entertain) the class by reading these drafts aloud.

Step 2

With more time for reflection and revision, take the spontaneous draft you have written and, in a page or two, expand and edit your definition. In the process of defining your term, analyze and clarify what it means to you, arriving at, or at least implying, a significant point.

THE LOCKHORNS

"IT'S NOT GOSSIP....IT'S ORAL HISTORY!"

You may want to argue a point, to use the term you are defining as a springboard for a complete written argument. With this option, your paper would grow into one of persuasion. As the discussion in this chapter has emphasized, you must include specific detail to animate your abstraction. If, for example, you have selected the phrase *burn out*, then, after clarifying what you mean by the term, you might decide to argue that the pressure and stress of life in today's society leads to *burn out* with serious consequences for both the individual and society as a whole, and then possibly suggest solutions.

If time permits, multiple definitions of the same term can be read to the class for comparison and discussion.

Here are some possible strategies for writing an extended definition; do not feel compelled to use them all.

- stipulate your precise meaning (see logical definition above), but don't include a dictionary definition unless you plan to use it or disagree with it
- provide examples of the term
- explain the function or purpose of the term
- explore etymology (origin and history of a word). The most fruitful source for such explorations is *The Oxford English Dictionary*, a multivolume work available in most college libraries, and a dictionary well worth your acquaintance. Use the history of a term to help make a point.

- examine the connotations of the term
- discuss what it is not (Use this sparingly.)
- draw analogies (Here you will want to be precise; be sure the analogy really fits.)

A few cautions

- define or illustrate more complex words with more familiar ones
- stick to one sense of the word unless you clarify an intended distinction
- avoid circularity

Look ahead to Chapter 8, The Language of Argument: Style, for helpful sentence hints:

> *appositives* for inserting short definitions, identifications, and concrete examples into your sentences
>
> clear *"focus"*—appropriate sentence subjects and active verbs
>
> *parallel structure* to organize and balance points and give emphasis

Audience

The instructor and other members of the class

Purpose

To make an abstraction concrete or to establish the focal point of an argument

---

Extended definitions: Student examples Several of our students have contributed their efforts on this topic. Here is a sampling.

Two different approaches to the same term

Radical

The word "radical" has been defined in *The Oxford-English Dictionary* as "going to the root or origin, touching or acting upon what is essential and fundamental." Thus, a radical reform is said to be a fundamental, "thorough reform." In a political sense, an advocate of "radical reform" was described as "one who holds the most advanced views of political reform on democratic lines, and thus belongs to the extreme section of the Liberal party." While this may have been a commonly accepted usage of the term in England at the time, the word "radical" has drifted away from its original specific meaning to a rather vague term for anyone who appears to be trying to disrupt the status quo.

In the late 1800s and early 1900s, socialists, Communists, and anarchists alike were popularly categorized by the general American public with the term "radical." With the controversy surrounding the political goals of these different activists, "a radical" was at the very least a controversial figure. More often than not, the word "radical" brought to mind some sort of disruptive character, a nonspecific image of an extremist, most probably from the far left. On the political spectrum the "radical" is still viewed as an individual on the extreme left, opposite the "right" or "conservative" parties. "Conservatives" holding radically different views and goals are not normally termed "radicals"; they are merely part of the "ultraright."

The term "radical" today is used less as a description of political intent and more as a critique of overall manner and appearance. While many of the"radicals" in the 1960s did indeed advocate numerous political reforms, the general public was more impressed by their personal character and style of advocacy. It is not surprising that when asked to define "a radical," most individuals conjure up a vague image of some young person wearing ragged clothes and long hair. It is a pity that in this society, where progressive change is so essential, the term "radical" has been imbued with so much negativity, so many connotations which really have nothing to do with political reform.

Radical

A radical is an algebraic symbol which tells a person to carry out a certain mathematical operation. The end result of this operation will tell a person the root or origin of a number or problem.

Recently, while in Los Angeles, I overheard someone describe a car as radical. I immediately thought to myself, something is wrong here. Radicals do not have engines. They may contain a number, like 32, underneath their top line, but never a stock Chevy 302 engine. It simply would not fit. When I asked this person why he called the car a radical, he replied, "Because the car is different and unusual." Once again, I thought to myself, he has made a mistake. Radicals are quite common. In fact, they are an essential part of most algebraic theories. I had to infer that this man knew nothing about algebra. If he did, he would have realized that radicals are not different or unusual at all, and would not have called the car one.

While I was in New York this past summer, I happened to see a group of people carrying signs of protest in front of the United Nations Building. As I watched them, a man came over to me, pointed at the group and muttered, "Radicals." I thought to myself, man are you ever wrong. Radicals do not carry signs saying, "Feed the Poor." They may carry a number, like 2, in their top right hand corner, but this number only means to find the root of a problem. It does not mean, "Feed the Poor."

These two events show that there is a great deal of misunderstanding throughout the country in regards to what a radical is. At their simplest level, radicals tell us to find the root of a problem. At their most complex level, they tell us the same thing.

A student's definition in which the approach reflects the word itself:

Fun

What's fun? In the black community fun means trippin'.[1] For example, the fellas pitchin' pennies, shootin' dice, playin' three-card molly[2] on the back of the bus, or playin' stick ball in the streets from the time they are five until they are 25. Little girls and big girls playin' Double Dutch,[3] jumpin' ropes and singin' to the rhythm of their feet. Blastin' the ghetto box to the latest beat and watching the brothuhs break. Bustin' open the fire hydrants on a hot day in order to cool off by runnin' through the water. Listenin' to the dudes standing on the street corner rappin' to a sistuh as she strolls down the street. "Hey, Mamma, what it is! You sho' is lookin' mighty fine today! How 'bout slidin' by my pad for a bit?" Gettin' happy in church and callin' out, "Lordy, Lordy! Lordy have mercy! Yes, Lord! Help me Lord!" Helpin' Mamma wash the collard greens and sweet potatoes, stirrin' the corn bread and slicin' the fatback[4] for Sunday supper after church. The whole family sittin' on the stoop in the evening listenin' to grandmamma tell stories 'bout the ol' days while fussin' about the young folk. All of this comes down to trippin', enjoying one's self, and havin' fun in the hood.[5]

Stipulating Personal Meaning

Through the centuries, people have been defining what they consider themselves to be, using the term "man" in a number of inventive ways.

---

[1]trippin'—enjoying yourself

[2]three-card molly—a card game involving three different-colored cards

[3]Double Dutch—a jump rope game involving two ropes swung in opposite directions. The jumping technique involves intricate rhythm and style and is often accompanied by a song or a chant recited by a child.

[4]fatback—discarded meat in the back of a butcher shop

[5]hood—the African-American community or neighborhood

Plato

First, he put man in the class "biped" and differentiated him from others in the class by describing him as "a featherless biped." When his rival, Diogenes, produced a plucked chicken, Plato had to add "having broad nails" as a further distinguishing characteristic.

Shakespeare

"What a piece of work is a man! How noble in reason! how infinite in faculty! in form, in moving, how express and admirable! in action how like an angel! in apprehension how like a god! the beauty of the world! the paragon of animals! And yet, to me what is this quintessence of dust? Man delights not me; no, nor woman neither." (*Hamlet*, II.ii. 316)

Ambrose Bierce

"An animal so lost in rapturous contemplation of what he thinks he is as to overlook what he indubitably ought to be. His chief occupation is extermination of other animals and his own species, which, however, multiplies with such insistent rapidity as to infest the whole habitable earth and Canada." (*Devil's Dictionary*)

Inventing New Words to Fill a Need

Contemporary American writer Alice Walker sought to rectify some of the linguistic imbalance in gender representation when she coined the term *womanist* for her collection of nonfiction, *In Search of Our Mothers' Gardens: Womanist Prose.* Why, we might ask, did she need to invent such a word? We can assume that she experienced a condition for which there was no term, so she created one. To stipulate the meaning of her neologism (a newly coined word or phrase), she opens the book with a series of definitions. What inference can you make from her decision to coin such a word and define it as she does?

Womanist:
   1. From womanish. (Opp. of "girlish," i.e., frivolous, irresponsible not serious.) A black feminist or feminist of color. From the black folk expression of mothers to female children, "You acting womanish," i.e., like a woman. Usually referring to outrageous, audacious, courageous or *willful* behavior. Wanting to know more and in greater depth than is considered "good" for one. Interested in grown-up doings. Acting grown up. Being grown up. Interchangeable with another black folk

expression: "You trying to be grown." Responsible. In charge. *Serious.*

2. Also: A woman who loves other women, sexually and/or nonsexually. Appreciates and prefers women's culture, women's emotional flexibility (values tears as natural counter-balance of laughter), and women's strength. Sometimes loves individual men, sexually and/or nonsexually. Committed to survival and wholeness of entire people, male *and* female. Not a separatist, except periodically, for health. Traditionally universalist, as in: "Mama, why are we brown, pink, and yellow, and our cousins are white, beige, and black?" Ans.: Well, you know the colored race is just like a flower garden, with every color flower represented." Traditionally capable, as in: "Mama, I'm walking to Canada and I'm taking you and a bunch of other slaves with me." Reply: "It wouldn't be the first time."

3. Loves music. Loves dance. Loves the moon. *Loves* the Spirit. Loves love and food and roundness. Loves struggle. *Loves* the Folk. Loves herself. *Regardless.*

4. Womanist is to feminist as purple to lavender.

Writer and performer Rich Hall created the word *sniglet* for "any word that doesn't appear in the dictionary, but should." Two examples from his collection:

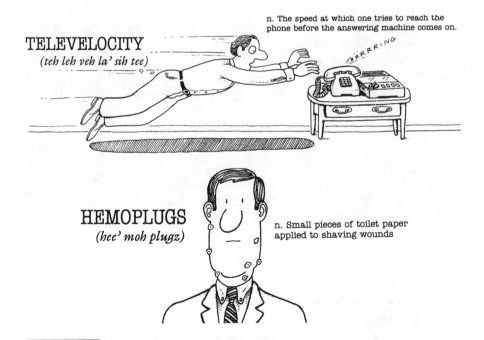

TELEVELOCITY
(teh leh veh la' sih tee)

n. The speed at which one tries to reach the phone before the answering machine comes on.

HEMOPLUGS
(hee' moh plugz)

n. Small pieces of toilet paper applied to shaving wounds

WRITING ASSIGNMENT 14

Creating a New Word

Now it's your turn to create a new word. Give the word an extended definition so that those in your class can see how to use it and why our culture
needs such an addition to the language. Here, again, you have an opportunity to develop an argument, using your new word as a springboard.

Audience

The instructor and other members of the class

Purpose

To identify a meaning in need of a name

SUMMARY

Words at a high level of abstraction such as "success" and "obscene"
must be defined.

Definitions can affect how people view themselves and others,
"addiction" being one example of many such terms.

Language is an abstract system of symbols.

The assignation of a particular meaning to a given term remains
essentially arbitrary.

Meaning is dependent to a large degree on the individual, the
context, and the interpretative community.

Political systems and advertising often manipulate abstract language for their own purposes.

The power to abstract is what makes us human. Specific, concrete details are what flesh out our ideas so our readers can grasp, visualize, and retain meaning.

Rather than contradictory, these two imperatives—the abstract
and the concrete—are best seen as complementary in both our writing and our thinking.

KEY TERM

Distinguishing characteristics   in logical definition, the ways in which
a term differs from other terms in the same class.

CHAPTER 6

Fallacious Arguments

So convenient a thing it is to be a reasonable creature, since it enables one to find or make a reason for everything one has a mind to do.
—BENJAMIN FRANKLIN

What is a Fallacious Argument?

To answer this question, we ask you to look carefully at two short arguments.

Short people do not make good presidents.

The democratic candidate is short.

Therefore, the democratic candidate will not be a good president.

Senator Smith was expelled from college for cheating on an exam.

His wife divorced him because of his numerous affairs.

Therefore, he is a man without honor, a politician who cannot be trusted, and we should not support his National Health Bill.

Which of these two arguments is more persuasive? Technically, the line of reasoning in the first argument is logical because the two premises lead inescapably to the conclusion. There is nothing fallacious in the *form* of this argument. The difficulty lies in the first premise; it is an absurd claim and an unacceptable premise. This argument is not persuasive and would convince no one. (Look ahead to Chapter 7, Deductive and Inductive Arguments, for a detailed explanation of form and acceptability of premises.)

But what about the second argument? Would you be in favor of a National Health Bill created by such a man? Some might find it persuasive, believing that such a man could not propose worthwhile legislation. But because nothing in the premises indicates flaws in the bill—only flaws in the man—the conclusion is not logically supported. The bill may be worthwhile despite the nature of the man who proposes it. This then is a fallacious argument, an argument that is persuasive but does not logically support its conclusion.

Because fallacious arguments are both appealing and abundant, we as critical readers and writers must guard against them. The first step in this defense is to familiarize ourselves with the most common fallacies. Fallacious reasoning may be intentional, as is sometimes the case with unscrupulous merchandisers and politicians, or it may be an innocent mistake resulting from fuzzy thinking or unexamined bias. In any case, if we are familiar with fallacies we can avoid them in our own thinking and writing. We can also spot them in the arguments of others, a skill that makes us wiser consumers and citizens.

There are many fallacies, a number of which tend to overlap. Our intention here is not to overwhelm you with an exhaustive list of fallacies and a complex classification scheme. Instead, we offer a list of the more common fallacies, presented in alphabetical order for easy reference.

Appeal to Authority

The opinion of an authority can support an argument only when it reflects his special area of expertise; the authority must be an expert on the subject being argued, as is the case in the following examples:

> The Surgeon General warns that smoking is injurious to health.
>
> Vladimir Horowitz, the internationally acclaimed pianist, preferred the Steinway piano.
>
> Studies conducted by *The New York Times*, the *Los Angeles Times*, and the ABC Network suggest that increasing numbers of viewers object to TV violence.

But, if the appeal is to an authority who is not appropriate, the appeal is fallacious, as is the case in the following example:

> Abortion to save the life of a mother is an irrelevant issue because a former surgeon general, a well-known pediatric surgeon, claimed that in all his years of surgical practice he had never seen a case in which such a dilemma had arisen.

The problem here is that a pediatric surgeon is not an appropriate authority on an issue involving obstetrics, a different medical specialty.

Fallacious appeals to authority are bountiful in advertising, which employs well-known actors and athletes to sell us everything from banking services to automobiles to coffee. Since many of these celebrities have no specialized knowledge—no authority—on the particular service or product they are promoting, they are not credible sources. Some may remember an actor known for his role as a TV doctor who endorsed a painkiller on television commercials.

Appeals to authority also appear in the form of snob appeal or appeal to the authority of the select few. The following advertisement for a resort hotel illustrates this fallacy, which appeals to people's desire for prestige and exclusivity:

> Palmilla's not for everyone. The best never is.

Keep in mind that fallacious appeals to authority should not cause us to doubt all authorities but rather should encourage us to distinguish between reliable and unreliable sources. In constructing your own arguments, be prepared to cite, explain, and, if necessary, defend your sources when relying on authority.

THE FAR SIDE   By GARY LARSON

"Why, yes . . . we do have two children who won't eat their vegetables."

Parents often rely on appeals to fear to persuade their children.

Appeal to Fear

An appeal to fear attempts to convince by implicitly threatening the audience. Its efforts to persuade are based on emotion rather than reason. An ad for a business college uses this approach.

> Will there be a *job* waiting when *you* leave college?

This ad attempts to frighten students by implying that unless they attend this business college, they will be unable to get a job after attending a four-year traditional college.

Senator Jesse Helms of North Carolina raised millions in campaign funds by sending voters a letter that contained the following warning:

> Your tax dollars are being used to pay for grade school classes that teach our children that **CANNIBALISM, WIFE-SWAPPING** and the **MURDER** of infants and the elderly are acceptable behavior.

Appeal to Pity

An appeal to pity attempts to win our sympathy in order to convince us of the conclusion. Like an appeal to fear, it appeals to our emotions rather than our intellect. Some students use this approach when arguing for a particular grade.

> Professor Hall, I must get an A in your course. If you don't give me an A, I won't be able to go to law school.

As we know, a student's work in a course—papers, exams, participation—determines the final grade. The consequences of a grade, no matter how dire they may be, should have no effect in determining that grade.

Emotion may play a part in argument, but its role must be secondary, a backdrop to logical reasoning. In fact, effective arguments often begin with frightening statistics—"If nothing is done about the Greenhouse Effect, the earth's temperature will increase 10 degrees by the year 2010 with disastrous consequences for our environment." Or they may begin with an emotional illustration. For example, an argument for mandatory fencing around all private swimming pools may open with a description of a mother caring for a child who is brain damaged as a result of almost drowning in a private pool. Either of these introductions will capture the emotions and interest of the audience, but they should be followed by facts, appropriate appeals to authority, and logical reasoning.

Begging the Question

When a person begs the question, he offers no actual support for his conclusion while appearing to do so. Instead, he may argue in a circle, just restating, as a premise, his conclusion in different words.

Students like rock music because it is the most enjoyable music around.

The writer is simply stating that students find rock music enjoyable because it is enjoyable. He begs the question. "They like it" means the same as "They find it enjoyable."

Or, take a couple of classics:

Parallel lines will never meet because they are parallel.

. . . your noble son is mad.
Mad call I it, for to define true madness,
What is't but to be nothing else but mad?

—POLONIUS TO QUEEN GERTRUDE IN *HAMLET,* II.ii

[We can discern something of Polonius' character from the manner of his argument.]

"You know what I like about power? It's so damn empowering."

Some such fallacious arguments beg the question not by restating the conclusion but by supporting the conclusion with assumptions (stated or hidden) that are as much in need of proof as the conclusion. A familiar example is frequently offered by those opposed to rent control who argue that rent controls should be removed because such decontrol could result in a significant rise in housing construction and thus relieve the shortage of affordable rental units. A letter to the editor points out the weakness.

> Editor: In your editorial concerning the housing crisis, you rely on one of the oldest rhetorical tricks of accepting as a given that which you could not possibly prove, that is, "There can be little question that removal of rent controls would result in a boom in apartment house construction. . . ." If rent control is such an important factor, construction should have been booming in the '70s before rent control laws existed in our state. It wasn't. . . .

Before we can accept the conclusion, the "truth" of the premise—that construction of new housing will increase if rent control laws are abolished—must be established.

We can also encounter question begging (avoiding the issue) in the form of an actual question, **a loaded question.**

> An example: Have you started paying your fair share of taxes yet?

First, the questioner would have to establish what he means by "fair share" and then establish that the person to whom he addressed the question had not been paying it.

In some arguments, just a single word—reactionary, negligent, warmonger, deadbeat—can beg the question. Be on the alert for such prejudicial language.

Equivocation

Equivocation is the shifting of the meaning of a given term within a single argument. This fallacy stems from the often ambiguous nature of language. A term may be ambiguous because it has more than one meaning; for instance, the word "affair" may mean a party, a controversial incident, or an extramarital relationship. Look at this example:

> We are told by the government that to discriminate against a person in employment or housing is wrong and punishable by law. But we must discriminate when we hire an individual (Does he have the necessary experience?) or rent an apartment (Does he have sufficient income?). Discrimination is a necessary part of making such decisions.

The word "discriminate" is the culprit. In the first sentence, "discriminate" refers to prejudice, to denying an individual employment or housing because of his or her race, sex, or religion. In the second sentence, "discriminate" refers to making careful distinctions between applicants on the basis of relevant issues.

Often equivocation is used to manipulate the language for rhetorical effect and positive associations, especially in advertising. A color film company refers to its product as "The Color of America," a slogan that is superimposed over images of African-American and Asian-American families. Hence, color refers to color film and to race, a clear case of equivocation.

"Tonto, when I said put silver on the table, I meant knives, forks, spoons."

Tonto annoys the Lone Ranger when he equivocates, mistaking the horse Silver for tableware.

In writing our own arguments, we can avoid equivocation by defining all ambiguous terms and being consistent in our use of them. (See Chapter 5 for definition strategies.)

False Analogy

One creative way to mount an argument can be through analogy. An argument by analogy compares two or more things, alike in certain respects, and suggests that since they share certain characteristics, they probably share other characteristics as well. A doctor argues effectively for drug therapy over psychotherapy as the best treatment for schizophrenia or severe depression by comparing the brain to the heart. "The brain is an organ, like the heart, and like that organ, can malfunction as a result of biochemical imbalances."

But in a **false analogy,** one compares two things in which the key features are different. A mountain climber offers this analogy to minimize the danger of his sport:

> I don't want to die falling off a rock. . . . But you can kill yourself
> falling in the bathtub, too.
>
> —JOHN BACHAR

He is comparing two extremely dissimilar acts: climbing a mountain and taking a bath, one a sport, the other a daily routine. And while it is possible to kill oneself slipping in the bathtub, if we were to compare the number of deaths in proportion to the number of bathers and the number of mountain climbers, we would surely find a higher incidence of deaths in mountain climbing than in bathing. To construct a more convincing analogy, the mountain climber should compare the risk in mountain climbing with that in another high-risk sport such as race-car driving.

A "Dear Abby" reader writes in response to Abby's recommendation that young people use contraceptives for premarital sex, "We know that premarital sex is wrong, just as we know shoplifting is wrong." Dear Abby's reply points out the fallaciousness of this comparison.

> One of the most powerful urges inborn in the human animal is the sex drive.
> Nature intended it to ensure perpetuation of our species. It is not comparable
> with the temptation to swipe a candy bar or a T-shirt.

In debating whether or not it is appropriate for Miss America beauty contestants to have plastic surgery, those in favor of allowing such surgery compare it with other practices women use to improve their appearance such as makeup and hair color. *The Boston Globe* columnist Ellen Goodman points out that this analogy is false since cosmetics are superficial while cosmetic surgery, such as breast implants, is physically invasive. She then offers a more accurate analogy—cosmetic surgery for beauty contestants is like steroids for athletes—each gives an unfair advantage to contestants involved in a competition.

The following letter to "Miss Manners" argues on the basis of analogy, an analogy that in her reply Miss Manners shows to be false:

> Dear Miss Manners:
>   If I were to entertain someone at dinner whom I knew to be a vegetarian, I
> would make certain there would be plenty of things on the menu that a vege-
> tarian could eat. Besides my lamb chop, there would be plenty of vegetables,

breads, salads, etc. I would not feel compelled to become a vegetarian myself for the occasion.

Were I to dine at the home of vegetarians, I would expect of them a similar accommodation, so that in addition to their usual fare, they might serve me a small steak, perhaps, though of course they wouldn't need to partake of it themselves.

Miss Manners replies:

Gentle Reader:

You lose the argument. Here is the problem: Serving vegetables to guests does not violate your principles, nor does it make you a vegetarian. However, expecting your vegetarian friends to serve you something that they exclude from their households would require their violating their principles.

"For all his brilliance, we're going to have to replace Trewell. He never quite seems able to reduce his ideas to football analogies."

Reasoning by analogy is appealing because it is vivid and accessible. But we must not accept analogies without careful examination. We must ask if the two things being compared are similar in ways that are significant to the point being made. Pay particular attention to advertising that relies on analogies to sell its products, sometimes effectively, sometimes approaching the absurd.

False Cause

The fallacy of **false cause** is also called post hoc reasoning, from the Latin *post hoc, ergo propter hoc*, which means "after this, therefore because of this." As this translation indicates, the fallacy of false cause assumes a cause–effect relationship between two events because one precedes another. It claims a causal relationship solely on the basis of a chronological relationship. Mark Twain uses this relationship for humorous effect.

> I joined the Confederacy for two weeks. Then I deserted. The Confederacy fell.

We know, as Twain did, that his desertion did nothing to end the Civil War, but this fallacy is not always so obvious. Look at the following example:

Governor Robinson took office in 1998.

In 1999, the state suffered a severe recession.

Therefore, Governor Robinson should not be re-elected.

(Hidden assumption: The governor caused the recession.)

Elected officials are often credited with the success or blamed for the failure of the economy. But in fact, anything as complex as the economy is affected by numerous factors such as inflation, environmental changes, the laws of supply and demand, just to name a few. Elected officials may indeed affect the economy but are unlikely to be the sole cause of its success or failure.

In a letter to *The New York Times Book Review*, a doctor takes exception with a book in which the author claims that his nephew's autism resulted from brain damage due to a vaccination.

> To the Editor:
> There will always be people who are convinced that because the signs of mental retardation or a seizure disorder or autism first became evident after an immunization, then certainly the immunization caused their problems; millions of dollars have been awarded in damages because some such people served on juries.
> For those people of reason who remember that **post hoc, ergo propter hoc** is a logical fallacy and not a standard of proof, let me state categorically that careful review of the literature confirms that a DPT shot might result in a fever or a sore leg or an irritable child. But it will not cause retardation, it will not precipitate epilepsy, and it never has and never will lead to autism.
> DIANE LIND FENSTER, M.D.
> GREEN BAY, WIS.

Some have argued that the atomic bombs we dropped in Hiroshima and Nagasaki caused Japan to surrender at the end of World War II. Others argue that this is a case of post hoc reasoning, that other factors such as Russia's threat to enter the war against Japan caused Japan to surrender, so that the killing of 110,000 Japanese, many of them women and children, was unnecessary.

Determining the cause of all but the simplest events is extremely difficult. Post hoc reasoning is appealing because it offers simple explanations for complex events.

False Dilemma

A **false dilemma** presents two and only two alternatives for consideration when other possibilities exist. For this reason, a false dilemma is often referred to as either/or reasoning.

> Either you are in favor of recalling the mayor, or you are a supporter of his political platform.

We are presented with only two positions when in fact we may hold neither. We may want the mayor to continue in office because we believe him to be a strong administrator, but we may object to his proposal to encourage big business by lowering the business tax.

In his essay, "Love One, Hate the Other," movie critic Mick LaSalle rails against what he calls "false polarities." He offers the following examples: Lennon or McCartney, Monroe or Bardot, Hemingway or Fitzgerald, Freud or Jung. He calls them false "because, in each case, two elements are arbitrarily set apart as opposites when they are not opposite at all, and the idea is that we must choose between the two when there's no legitimate need to do that."

Narrowing to two choices is a strategy designed to forestall clear thinking and force a quick decision. This kind of reasoning can be seductive because it reduces the often difficult decisions and judgments we must make by narrowing complex problems and issues to two simple options.

Columnist Anna Quindlen comments on how this either/or reasoning shaped the public's opinion and the trial of Erik and Lyle Menendez, two brothers accused of murdering their parents for financial gain.

> . . . the question has become: venal rich kids or tormented victims? Which are the Menendez brothers? Few seem to consider a third possibility: maybe both. . . . Lyle and Erik [are] either tormented, abused child-men or cold-blooded climbers in Porsches. Not both. Never both.
>
> The ultimate either-or decision belongs to the jurors in the Menendez case. But perhaps they will consider things that we overlook when we are turning public tragedy into social mythology: sometimes bad things happen to bad people, that it is possible to be both victim and victimizer. Life is so messy that the temptation to straighten it up is very strong. And the result's always illusory.

Columnist Ellen Goodman offers an example of one young critical thinker who refused to accept the limits of either–or thinking.

Remember the story of Heinz, the man whose wife was dying for lack of medicine or the funds to buy it? Children are asked to decide whether it's OK for
Heinz to steal the drugs. On the one hand it's wrong to break the law, on the
other, it's wrong to let the woman die.

What I remember most about the Heinz dilemma is the response of an 11-
year-old little girl named Amy, as described in Carol Gilligan's book, *In a Different Voice*. Amy didn't think that Heinz should steal the drugs because if he did
he might end up in jail—and what would happen next time his wife needed
the pills? Nor did Amy think she should die.

This 11-year-old refused to choose from column A or column B. She thought
they should "talk it out," get a loan, or find another way out of the dilemma.
Traditional moralists thought Amy was "illogical." But the truth was that she
took the long, wide moral view—six steps down the road, up a side road and
back to the main road. Amy stepped outside the multiple-choice questionnaire.

*"Damn it, Eddie! If you don't believe in nuclear war
and you don't believe in conventional war, what the
hell kind of war <u>do</u> you believe in?"*

What alternative has the speaker completely overlooked?

Hasty Generalization

A **hasty generalization** is a conclusion based on a sample that is too small
or in some other way unrepresentative of the larger population.

> Students in Professor Hall's eight o'clock freshman composition class are often
> late. There's no doubt that people are right when they claim today's college
> students are irresponsible and unreliable.

In this case the sample is both unrepresentative and too small; unrepresentative because we would expect an eight o'clock class to have more

late students than classes offered later in the day, and too small because one section can't represent an entire freshman class.

It is impossible to avoid making generalizations, nor should we try to. But we must examine the basis for our generalizations to determine their reliability (see Chapter 7).

One way to avoid this fallacy is to qualify your generalizations with words such as "many" or "some." Most of us would accept the claim that "some women are bad drivers" but would reject and even be offended by the claim that "women are bad drivers."

Personal Attack

Often called by its Latin name, *ad hominem* ("against the man"), the fallacy of **personal attack** substitutes for a reasoned evaluation of an argument an attack against the person presenting the argument. By discrediting the source, often in an abusive or irrelevant way, a person can disguise the absence of a substantive position.

> Because she is extremely wealthy and owns two luxurious homes, our mayor, Carolyn Quinn, cannot properly represent the people of this city.

But does a person's economic status necessarily rule out understanding of those in different circumstances?

A few years ago, conservative John H. Bunzel wrote a controversial book, *Challenge to American Schools*. In it he attacked the National Education Association for criticizing some reform ideas he admired—merit pay and standardized tests. He focused on their "leftist" politics rather than examining the reasons for their opposition.

When Rachel Carson's *Silent Spring*, a seminal work on the health hazards of insecticides and pesticides, was published in 1962, a leading scientist (male), questioned her concern for future generations because she was a spinster who had no children. He attacked her personally, not her argument that certain commonly used chemicals caused cancer.

Those given to Latin names like to label a particular kind of personal attack as ***tu quoque***—"you also." In this instance, a person and thus his arguments are discredited because his own behavior does not strictly conform to the position he holds. We've all heard about the parent who drinks too much but admonishes his child about the dangers of drinking.

Antigun-control groups were delighted when Carl Rowan, a prominent Washington columnist and a staunch advocate of gun control, used an unregistered pistol to wound a young man who broke into his backyard. But Rowan's failure to follow his own beliefs does not necessarily make his argument for gun control a weak one.

BIZARRO *Piraro*

Poisoning the Well

A person **poisons the well** when he makes an assertion that precludes or discourages an open discussion of the issue. This assertion will intimidate the listener, who fears that any resistance on his part will lead to a personal disagreement rather than a critical discussion.

> Every patriotic American supports legislation condemning the desecration of the flag.

The listener must now prove his patriotism rather than express his doubts about the legislation, and the speaker avoids having to defend his conclusion with relevant premises.

Slippery Slope

We know the **slippery slope** fallacy by other names too: the domino theory, the ripple effect. One thing leads to another. People often claim that an action should be avoided because it will inevitably lead to a series of extremely undesirable consequences. Sometimes such a chain reaction is probable, but often it can be exaggerated for effect.

Writer Wendy Kaminer, reviewing *Under Fire: The NRA and the Battle for Gun Control,* presents one group's position on gun control:

> What seems like reasonable restrictions on guns with no legitimate civilian purpose (assault rifles, for example) will lead inevitably to total prohibition of gun ownership that ends in virtual slavery at the hands of a totalitarian regime.

The argument here is that if we allow the government to take one step—the banning of assault weapons—the next step will be the banning of all guns—and the final step, loss of all freedom for all citizens.

In this argument, the downward slope is more precipitous than the evidence warrants, leading to an erroneous conclusion and, tragically, to private militias and the Oklahoma City bombing.

Look, if you give them a nuclear freeze, the next thing you know they'll want to outlaw war altogether.

If only all slippery slopes led to such a desirable outcome.

Special Pleading

When an argument contains the fallacy of **special pleading,** it judges and labels the same act differently depending on the person or group who performs the act. It is the application of a double standard.

When Shannon Faulkner, the first woman ever admitted, dropped out of The Citadel, a military college in South Carolina, the other cadets cheered as she departed the campus and the media covered her departure in great detail. What neither the jeering male cadets nor the media paid any attention to were the 34 other first-year students, all men, who also dropped out. Shannon Faulkner and her classmates made the same decision, but she was subjected to ridicule and close media scrutiny while her 34 male classmates were not; a double standard was applied.

Sometimes a double standard can be applied subtly though the manipulative use of language. A well-known defense lawyer, while discussing legal strategies on television, stated that he "prepares" his witnesses while the prosecution "coaches" theirs. "Prepares" suggests professional legal preparation for the courtroom whereas "coaches" suggests that a witness is encouraged to say what the lawyer tells her to whether it is true or not. Both lawyers are working with their clients before trial, but the lawyer's subtle use of language casts a negative slant on opposing counsel.

Straw Man

In a **straw man** argument, a person creates and then attacks a distorted version of the opposition's argument.

> The democratic candidate wants the federal government to house everyone, feed everyone, care for everyone's children, and provide medical care for everyone. And he's going to take 50 percent of every dime you make to do it.

This argument overlooks the candidate's proposal to reduce defense spending to meet his goals. Hence, this is an unfair presentation of the opposing view, but one that could be extremely effective in discouraging votes for the democratic candidate. And this is the purpose of a straw man argument: to frighten supporters away from the opponent's camp and into one's own.

Columnist Ellen Goodman comments on this strategy in an essay titled "The Straw Feminist."

> The straw man has been a useful creature throughout history. Whenever people argued, he could be pulled together quickly out of the nearest available haystack, and set up as an opponent. The beauty of the straw man was that he was easily defeated. The straw man was also useful as a scarecrow. The arguments attributed to him were not only flimsy, they were frightening.
>
> So I wasn't surprised when the straw feminist was sighted burning her bra at a "Miss America" pageant. The fact that there never was a bra-burning was irrelevant. Feminists became bra-burners. Not to mention man-haters.

The straw feminist wanted to drive all women out of their happy homes and into the workforce. The straw feminist had an abortion as casually as she had a tooth pulled. The straw feminist was hostile to family life and wanted children warehoused in government-run day and night care. At times, the straw feminist was painted slightly pinko by the anti-Communists or rather lavender by the anti-lesbians. But it was generally agreed upon that she was a castrating—well, you fill in the blank.

This creature was most helpful for discrediting real feminists but also handy for scaring supporters away.

A caution: German philosopher Arthur Schopenhauer [1788–1860] pointed out that "It would be a very good thing if every trick could receive some short and obviously appropriate name, so that when a man used this or that particular trick, he could at once be reproved for it." Fallacies provide us with those short and appropriate names for tricks or errors in reasoning, but we must not assume that all such errors can be labeled. Whenever we find fault with a particular line of reasoning, we should not hesitate to articulate that fault, whether or not we have a label for it. On the other hand, we must be careful not to see fallacies everywhere, perhaps even where they don't exist. We must *read critically*, informed by our knowledge of fallacies; at the same time we should avoid tedious witch hunts on the charitable assumption that most arguments are offered in good faith.

EXERCISE 6A

Identifying Fallacies

Identify by name the fallacies in each of the following arguments and justify your responses. You may want to turn to the end of the chapter for a chart of the fallacies.

Competition and collaboration: An interesting approach to this exercise combines competition and cooperation. The class is divided into two teams who compete in identifying the fallacies, with team members cooperating on responses.

---

1. "You say 'Why do I think [America is] in danger?' and I say look at the record. Seven years of the Truman–Acheson Administration and what's happened? Six hundred million people lost to the Communists, and a war in Korea in which we have lost 117,000 American casualties." (From Richard Nixon's Checkers Speech, September 23, 1952)

2. "Students should not be allowed any grace whatsoever on late assignments. Before you know it, they will no longer complete their work at all. If they don't do their assignments, they will be ignorant. If the students who are being educated are ignorant, then all of America will become more ignorant." (Thanks to a former student)

3. America: Love it or leave it.

4. You can't expect insight and credibility from the recent book *The Feminist Challenge* because its author David Bouchier is, obviously, a man.

5. Politicians can't be trusted because they lack integrity.

6. Closing the gay baths to prevent the spread of AIDS is like closing bars to prevent the spread of alcoholism.

7. How long must we allow our courts to go on coddling criminals?

8. "I'm firm. You are stubborn. He's pig-headed." (philosopher Bertrand Russell)

9. Anyone who truly cares about preserving the American way of life will vote Republican this fall.

10. "Why is it okay for people to choose the best house, the best schools, the best surgeon, the best car, but not try to have the best baby possible?" (A father's defense of the Nobel Prize winners' sperm bank)

11. Socrates, during his trial in 399 B.C.: "My friend, I am a man, and like other men, a creature of flesh and blood, and not of wood or stone, as Homer says; and I have a family, yes, and sons, O Athenians, three in number, one almost a man, and two others who are still young; and yet I will not bring any of them hither in order to petition you for an acquittal." (Plato, the "Apology")

12. "All Latins are volatile people." (Senator Jesse Helms, on Mexican protests against Senate Foreign Affairs subcommittee hearings on corruption south of the border)

13. Mark R. Hughes, owner of Herbalife International, was questioned by a Senate subcommittee about the safety of the controversial diet products marketed by his company. Referring to a panel of three nutrition and weight-control authorities, Hughes asked: "If they're such experts, then why are they fat?"

14. During these same hearings, Senator William Roth, R-Delaware, the Senate subcommittee chairman, reminded Hughes of criticism by some physicians that Herbalife fails to recommend that consumers seek guidance from doctors about their diets. "Do you be-

lieve it's safe to use your products without consulting a doctor?" Roth asked. "Sure," replied Hughes, 29. "Everybody needs good, sound, basic nutrition. We all know that."

15. When the Supreme Court ruled that school officials need not obtain search warrants or find "probable cause" while conducting reasonable searches of students, they violated freedoms guaranteed under the Bill of Rights. If you allow a teacher to look for a knife or drugs, you'll soon have strip searches and next, torture.

16. Since I walked under that ladder yesterday, I've lost my wallet and received a speeding ticket.

17. Sometimes, the *best* is not for everyone. (an ad for a "Parisian boutique")

18. "I'm being denied the right to own a semiautomatic firearm simply because someone doesn't like the way it looks. If you look at all the different automobiles out there, the majority of them travel on regular roads. So how do you explain the dune buggies or off-road vehicles? They're different, but you don't hear anybody saying, 'Why does anyone need to have a dune buggy or an off-road vehicle? What's wrong with your regular run-of-the-mill traditional automobile?' It's all a matter of personal preference." (Marion Hammer, president of the National Rifle Association, in *George* magazine)

19. We are going to have to ease up on environmental protection legislation or see the costs overwhelm us.

20. Any rational person will accept that a fetus is a human being.

21. "Editor—Is anyone really surprised that students' grades haven't improved when all they do is listen to rock 'n' roll? Rock lyrics don't ever develop into anything cohesive and the music never expands itself like real music does. All it does is just sit there and make a lot of very loud noise that goes boom, boom, boom, boom, boom that blots off the mind completely. How can a mind ever expand when that's all it ever takes in? It all started about 35 years ago with bubble-gum rock and then went into heavy metal and grades have been going down steadily ever since." (Bob Grimes in a Letter to the Editor, *San Francisco Chronicle*)

22. Heat Wave Blamed For Record Temperatures Across U.S. (a Grass Valley *Union* headline)

23. The erosion of traditional male leadership has led to an increase in divorce because men no longer possess leadership roles.

24. "**Dear Ann Landers**: I have been a nudist for 36 years and am firmly convinced that if everyone would accept the concept of nudism, there would be no more wars, no crime and no greed, and we would live together in perfect harmony as God intended us to. Anyone who reads the Bible knows that all the trouble started when Eve ate that apple and put on the fig leaf." (*San Francisco Examiner*)

25. Now, all young men, a warning take,
    And shun the poisoned bowl; (alcohol)
    'Twill lead you down to hell's dark gate,
    And ruin your own soul.
    (ANONYMOUS, FROM CARL SANDBURG, ED., *THE AMERICAN SONGBAG*)

26. While our diplomats in France were gathering intelligence, their diplomats in Washington were practicing espionage.

27. I recently read about a homeless man with a burst appendix who was turned away from a hospital emergency room to die in the street. It's obvious that hospitals don't care about people, only money.

28. Do the vastly inflated salaries paid to professional athletes lead them into drug abuse?

29. The Nuclear Freeze movement was misguided and dangerous from the beginning, dependent as it was on "unilateral" disarmament. (A common argument of the movement's opponents. Those supporting the Nuclear Freeze movement actually proposed "bilateral" disarmament.)

30. Haemon: So, father, pause, and put aside your anger.
    I think, for what my young opinion's worth,
    That, good as it is to have infallible wisdom,
    Since this is rarely found, the next best thing
    Is to be willing to listen to wise advice.
    Creon: Indeed! Am I to take lessons at my time of life
    From a fellow of his age?
    (SOPHOCLES, *ANTIGONE*)

31. S & W vegetables are the best because they use only premium quality.

32. "We would not tolerate a proposal that states that because teenage drug use is a given we should make drugs more easily available." (Archbishop John R. Quinn in response to a National Research Council's recommendation that contraceptives and abortion be made readily available to teenagers.)

33. Reading test scores in public schools have declined dramatically. This decline was caused by the radical changes in teaching strategies introduced in the 1960s.

34. The rates of teen pregnancy, youth violence, and drug use have increased rapidly in the years since school prayer was banned. The evidence is clear: We must bring prayer back to the classroom.

35. "Just as instructors could prune sentences for poor grammar, so the principal was entitled to find certain articles inappropriate for publication—in this situation because they might reveal the identity of pregnant students and because references to sexual activity were deemed improper for young students to see."

36. "Editor: Now that it has been definitely established that nonsmokers have the right to tell smokers not to pollute their air, it follows that people who don't own cars have the right to tell car owners not to drive. Right?" (Jim Hodge, *San Francisco Chronicle*)

37. The Black Panthers—Were they criminals or freedom fighters? (From a televison ad promoting a documentary on the radical group from the 1970's)

38. We must either give up some of our constitutional liberties to ensure that the government can protect us against terrorism or we will again fall prey to terrorists.

39. "I give so much pleasure to so many people. Why can't I get some pleasure for myself?" Comedian John Belushi to his doctor in justification of his drug use.

EXERCISE 6B

Analyzing a Short Argument

The following letter is not a genuine letter to the editor but a critical thinking test devised by educators. Test yourself by writing a critique of this deliberately flawed argument. It contains at least seven errors in reasoning, some of them fallacies that you have studied in this chapter, some of them weaknesses that can be identified and described but not labeled.

230 Sycamore Street
Moorburg
April 10

Dear Editor:
    Overnight parking on all streets in Moorburg should be eliminated. To achieve this goal, parking should be prohibited from 2 a.m. to 6 a.m. There are a number of reasons why an intelligent citizen should agree.
    For one thing, to park overnight is to have a garage in the streets. Now it is illegal for anyone to have a garage in the city streets. Clearly then it should be against the law to park overnight in the streets.

Three important streets, Lincoln Avenue, Marquand Avenue, and West Main Street are very narrow. With cars parked on the streets, there really isn't room for the heavy traffic that passes over them in the afternoon rush hour. When driving home in the afternoon after work, it takes me thirty-five minutes to make a trip that takes ten minutes during the uncrowded time. If there were no cars parked on the side of these streets, they could handle considerably more traffic.

Traffic on some streets is also bad in the morning when factory workers are on their way to the 6 a.m. shift. If there were no cars parked on these streets between 2 a.m. and 6 a.m., then there would be more room for this traffic.

Furthermore there can be no doubt that, in general, overnight parking on the streets is undesirable. It is definitely bad and should be opposed.

If parking is prohibited from 2 a.m. to 6 a.m., then accidents between parked and moving vehicles will be nearly eliminated during this period. All intelligent citizens would regard the near elimination of accidents in any period as highly desirable. So we should be in favor of prohibiting parking from 2 a.m. to 6 a.m.

Last month the Chief of Police, Burgess Jones, ran an experiment which proves that parking should be prohibited from 2 a.m. to 6 a.m. On one of our busiest streets, Marquand Avenue, he placed experimental signs for one day. The signs prohibited parking from 2 a.m. to 6 a.m. During the four-hour period there was *not one accident* on Marquand. Everyone knows, of course, that there have been over four hundred accidents on Marquand during the past year.

The opponents of my suggestions have said that conditions are safe enough now. These people don't know what "safe" really means. *Conditions are not safe if there's even the slightest possible chance for an accident.* That's what "safe" means. So conditions are not safe the way they are now.

Finally let me point out that the director of the National Traffic Safety Council, Kenneth O. Taylor, has strongly recommended that overnight street parking be prevented on busy streets in cities the size of Moorburg. The National Association of Police Chiefs has made the same recommendation. Both suggest that prohibiting parking from 2 a.m. to 6 a.m. is the best way to prevent overnight parking.

I invite those who disagree as well as those who agree with me to react to my letter through the editor of this paper. Let's get this issue out in the open.

Sincerely,

Robert R. Raywift

WRITING ASSIGNMENT 15

Analyzing an Extended Argument

From the following collection of editorials, choose one (or find one in a newspaper or periodical) on which to write an essay evaluating the argument. We suggest the following process for approaching this paper:

Analyze each paragraph of your chosen editorial in order. Compose a list of the fallacies you find in each paragraph—give names of fallacies or identify weaknesses in reasoning (not all weaknesses can be precisely named) and illustrate with specific examples from the editorial. Avoid the trap of being too picky; you won't necessarily find significant fallacies in every paragraph.

During this paragraph-by-paragraph analysis, keep the argument's conclusion in mind and ask yourself if the author provides adequate support for it.

Next, review your paragraph-by-paragraph analysis to determine the two or three major problems in the argument. Then group and condense your list of faults or fallacies and, in a coherently written essay organized around these two or three principal categories of weaknesses, present your evaluation of the argument. For example, if you find more than one instance of personal attack, devote one of your paragraphs to this fallacy and cite all the examples you find to support your claim. Follow the same procedure for other weaknesses. Identify each specific example you cite either by paraphrase or direct quotation, imagining as you write that the reader is not familiar with the editorial you are critiquing.

Audience

College-age readers who have not read the editorial and who are not familiar with all of the fallacies listed in the text

Purpose

To illustrate to a less critical reader that published arguments written by established professionals are not necessarily free of fallacious reasoning

On Date Rape

Dating is a very recent phenomenon in world history. Throughout history, women have been chaperoned. As late as 1964, when I arrived in college, we had strict rules. We had to be in the dorm under lock and key by 11 o'clock. My generation was the one that broke these rules. We said, "We want freedom—no more double standard!" When I went to stay at a male friend's apartment in New York, my aunts flew into a frenzy: "You can't do that, it's dangerous!" But I said, "No, we're not going to be like that anymore." Still, we understood in the '60s that we were taking a risk.

Today these young women want the freedoms that we won, but they don't want to acknowledge the risk. That's the problem. The minute you go out with a man, the minute you go to a bar to have a drink, there is a risk. You have to accept the fact that part of the sizzle of sex comes from the danger of sex. You can be overpowered.

So it is women's personal responsibility to be aware of the dangers of the world. But these young feminists today are deluded. They come from a protected, white, middle-class world, and they expect everything to be safe. Notice it's not black or Hispanic women who are making a fuss about this—they come from cultures that are fully sexual and they are fully realistic about sex. But these other women are sexually repressed girls, coming out of pampered homes, and when they arrive at these colleges and suddenly hit male lust, they go, "Oh, no!"

These girls say, "Well, I should be able to get drunk at a fraternity party and go upstairs to a guy's room without anything happening." And I say, "Oh, really? And when you drive your car to New York City, do you leave your keys on the hood?" My point is that if your car is stolen after you do something like that, yes, the police should pursue the thief and he should be punished. But at the same time, the police—and I—have the right to say to you, "You stupid idiot, what the hell were you thinking?"

I mean, wake up to reality. This is male sex. Guess what, it's hot. Male sex is hot. There's an attraction between the sexes that we're not totally in control of. The idea that we can regulate it by passing campus grievance committee rules is madness. My kind of feminism stresses personal responsibility. I've never been raped, but I've been very vigilant—I'm constantly reading the signals. If I ever got into a dating situation where I was overpowered and raped, I would say, "Oh well, I misread the signals." But I don't think I would ever press charges.

The girl in the Kennedy rape case is an idiot. You go back to the Kennedy compound late at night and you're surprised at what happens? She's the one who should be charged—with ignorance. Because everyone knows that Kennedy is spelled S-E-X. Give me a break, this is not rape. And it's going to erode the real outrage that we should feel about actual rape. This is just over-privileged people saying they want the world to be a bowl of cherries. Guess what? It's not and it never will be.

—CAMILLE PAGLIA, HUMANITIES PROFESSOR AND CULTURAL CRITIC,
SAN FRANCISCO EXAMINER

Boxing, Doctors—Round Two

Before I went on vacation a few weeks ago, I wrote a column criticizing the American Medical Association for its call to abolish boxing. As you might have expected, I have received letters from doctors telling me I'm misinformed and scientifically naive. One doctor even said I must have had terrible experiences with doctors to have written what I wrote.

That just shows how arrogant doctors are. It never would occur to them that I might have a defensible position. If I disagree with them, it's because I'm ignorant.

Doctors are used to being right. We come into their offices sick and generally not knowing what's wrong with us. We are in awe of their expertise and afraid for our well-being. We have a tendency to act like children in front of them. "If you can only make me well, Doc, I will love you for life." Doctors, who start out as regular human beings, come to expect us to worship them. They thrive on the power that comes from having knowledge about life and death.

Which brings us to their misguided stand against boxing. Doctors are offended by injuries in boxing, although they don't seem as mortified by the people who die skiing or bike riding or swimming every year. You rarely hear a peep out of them about the many injuries football players sustain—that includes kids in the peewee leagues and high school. Why the outrage over boxing?

Because many doctors are social snobs. They see people from ethnic minorities punching each other in a ring and they reach the conclusion that these poor, dumb blacks and Latinos must be protected from themselves because they don't know any better. The AMA is acting like a glorified SPCA, arrogantly trying to prevent cruelty to animals. They would never dare preach this way to football players, because most of them went to college. Nor would they come out against skiing, because many doctors love to ski.

Boxers know the risks of taking a right cross to the jaw better than doctors, and they take up the sport with a full understanding of its risks. A man should have the right to take a risk. Doctors may want to save us from adventure, but there still is honor in freely choosing to put yourself on the line. Risk is why race-car drivers speed around treacherous tracks. Danger is why mountain climbers continue to explore the mystery of Mount Everest. Yet doctors do not come out against auto racing or mountain climbing.

One physician wrote a letter to the Sporting Green saying the AMA's position against boxing is based on medical evidence. As I read the letter's twisted logic, I wondered if the AMA causes brain damage in doctors. "Skiing, bicycle riding and swimming kill more people each year (than boxing)," he writes. "Obviously, far more people engage in those activities than enter a boxing ring."

Does his position make sense to you? We should eliminate boxing, the sport with fewer negative consequences, but allow the real killer sports to survive. Amazing. If this doctor were really concerned with medical evidence, as he claims, he would attack all dangerous sports, not just boxing.

But he doesn't. The truth is, boxing offends the delicate sensibilities of doctors. They don't like the idea that two men *intentionally* try to hurt each other. They feel more comfortable when injuries are a byproduct of a sport—although ask any batter who has been beaned by a fastball if his broken skull was an innocent byproduct.

In other words, doctors are making a moral judgment, not a medical judgment, about which sports are acceptable. Every joker is entitled to ethical opinions, but doctors have no more expertise than you or I when it comes to right and wrong. If preaching excites them, let them become priests.

What if the AMA is successful in getting boxing banned? Will the sport disappear? No way. As long as man is man, he will want to see two guys of equal weight and ability solve their elemental little problem in a ring. If the sport becomes illegal, it will drift off to barges and back alleys, where men will fight in secret without proper supervision. And then you will see deaths and maiming like you never saw before.

Whom will the AMA blame then?

—LOWELL COHN, A SPORTSWRITER
SAN FRANCISCO CHRONICLE

Guns Save Lives

The data from the 1990 Harvard Medical Practice Study suggest that 150,000 Americans die every year from doctors' negligence—compared with 38,000 gun deaths annually. Why are doctors not declared a public health menace? Because they save many more lives than they take. And so it is with guns.

Every year, good Americans use guns about 2.5 million times to protect themselves and their families, which means 65 lives are protected by guns for every life lost to a gun. For every 101 California tragedy, many others are averted.

An unsurprising 1 percent of America's 240 million guns are used for protection annually. The U.S. Bureau of Justice Statistics has repeatedly shown that guns are the most effective means of self-protection. If guns are as dangerous for self-defense as the alarmists claim, why does their leading researcher, Dr. Arthur Kellermann, want his wife to have a gun for defense?

Physicians who advocate gun prohibition have promoted confiscatory taxation and fees on guns, ammunition, and gun owners, in hopes that those taxes will be funneled into their research and their emergency rooms. To strengthen their case, they ignore the lives protected by guns and exaggerate the medical costs, claiming $20 billion per year in costs from gun violence.

In fact, the cost of medical care for gun violence is about $1.5 billion per year, less than 0.2 percent of our $800 billion annual health care costs. So advocates of gun prohibition routinely include estimates of "lost lifetime earnings," assuming gang bangers, drug dealers and rapists to be as productive as teachers and factory workers.

Even the virulently anti-self defense New England Journal of Medicine and Journal of Trauma have published studies showing that three-fourths of gun homicide "victims" are drug dealers or their customers. On the street, they cost society an average of $400,000 per criminal per year. In prison, they cost an average of $30,000 per criminal per year and, some cold-hearted analysts have noted, in the ground, they hurt no one and cost us nothing.

Cost-benefit analysis is necessarily hardhearted and, though it may be repugnant to consider, the gun deaths of those predators may be a savings to society on the order of $5.5 billion annually, more than three times the medical "costs" of guns.

—EDGAR A. SUTTER, NATIONAL CHAIRMAN OF DOCTORS FOR INTEGRITY IN
RESEARCH AND PUBLIC POLICY

KEY TERMS

Term	Description	Example
Fallacious argument	Persuasive but does not logically support its conclusion.	Senator Smith was expelled from college for cheating on an exam. His wife divorced him because of his numerous affairs. Therefore, he is a man without honor, a politician who cannot be trusted, and we should not support his National Health Bill.
Appeal to authority (2 forms)	**1.** Appeals to an authority who is not an expert on the issue under discussion.	Abortion to save the mother is irrelevant because a pediatric surgeon has never seen a case in which such a dilemma has risen.
Snob appeal	**2.** Appeals to people's desire for prestige and exclusivity.	Pamilla's not for everyone. The best never is.
Appeal to fear	Implicitly threatens the audience.	Will there be a *job* waiting when *you* leave college?
Appeal to pity	Attempts to win sympathy.	Professor Hall, I must get an A in your course. If you don't give me an A, I won't be able to go to law school.
Begging the question	**1.** Offers no actual support; may restate as a premise the conclusion in different words.	Students like rock music because it is the most enjoyable music around.
Loaded question	**2.** Asks a question that contains an assumption that must be proven.	Have you started to pay your fair share of taxes yet?
Question-begging epithet	**3.** Uses a single word to assert a claim that must be proven.	Reactionary, negligent, warmonger, deadbeat.

Equivocation	Shifts the meaning of a term within a single argument.	We are told that to discriminate in employment or housing is punishable by law. But we must discriminate when we hire an individual or rent an apartment.
False analogy	Compares two or more things that are not in essence similar and suggests that since they share certain characteristics, they share others as well.	I don't want to die falling off a rock. But you can kill yourself falling in the bathtub too.
False cause [Latin name: *post hoc, ergo propter hoc*]	Claims a causal relationship between events solely on the basis of a chronological relationship.	I joined the Confederacy for two weeks. Then I deserted. The Confederacy fell.
False dilemma	Presents two and only two alternatives for consideration when other possibilities exist.	Either you are in favor of recalling the mayor, or you are a supporter of her political platform.
Hasty generalization	Generalizes from a sample that is too small or in some other way unrepresentative of the target population.	Students in Professor Hall's eight o'clock freshman composition class are often late. Today's college students are irresponsible and unreliable.
Personal attack [Latin name: *ad hominem*]	1. Attacks the person representing the argument rather than the argument itself.	Because she is extremely wealthy, our mayor cannot properly represent this city.
Tu quoque ("you also")	2. Discredits an argument because the behavior of the person proposing it does not conform to the position he's supporting.	A teenager to his father: Don't tell me not to drink. You drink all the time.
Poisoning the well	Makes an assertion which will intimidate the audience and therefore discourage an open discussion.	Every patriotic American supports legislation condemning the desecration of the flag.

Slippery slope	Claims that an action should be avoided because it will lead to a series of extremely undesirable consequences.	What seems like reasonable restrictions on guns with no legitimate civilian purpose will lead inevitably to total prohibition of gun ownership that ends in virtual slavery at the hands of a totalitarian regime.
Special pleading	Judges and labels the same act differently depending on the person or group who performs the act.	The supplying of weapons to Central America by the Russians was an act of aggression. Our military aid to the region, however, helped the Freedom Fighters in their quest for peace.
Straw man	Creates and then attacks a distorted version of the opposition's argument.	The democratic candidate wants the federal government to house everyone, feed everyone, care for everyone's children, and provide medical care for everyone. And he's going to take 50 percent of every dime you make to do it.

CHAPTER 7

Deductive and Inductive Argument

There is a tradition of opposition between adherents of induction and deduction. In my view, it would be just as sensible for the two ends of a worm to quarrel.

—ALFRED NORTH WHITEHEAD

Sometimes arguments are classified as inductive or deductive. Induction and deduction are modes of reasoning, particular ways of arriving at an inference. Different logicians tend to make different distinctions between deductive and inductive reasoning, with some going so far as to declare, as Whitehead did, that such a distinction is spurious. But classifications, if carefully made, help us to understand abstract concepts, and scientists and humanists alike often refer to patterns of reasoning as deductive or inductive. This classification also helps us to distinguish between conclusions we must accept and those we should question, a valuable skill for both reading critically and writing logically.

Key Distinctions

The key distinctions between deduction and induction are generally seen as falling into two categories.

Necessity Versus Probability

In a **deductive argument**, the conclusion will follow by *necessity* from the premises if the method of reasoning is valid, as in this familiar bit of classical wisdom:

1. All men (updated—people) are mortal.
2. Socrates is a man (person).
   ∴ Socrates is mortal.

In an **inductive argument,** the conclusion can only follow with some degree of *probability* (from the unlikely to the highly probable). British philosopher Bertrand Russell made the point implicitly but emphatically in *The Problems of Philosophy:* "The man who has fed the chicken every day throughout its life at last wrings its neck instead." The chicken reasons thus—

1. He has fed me today.
2. He has fed me this next day.
3. He has fed me this day too.
4. He has fed me yet another day, etc.
   ∴ He will feed me tomorrow.

The poor chicken has made a prediction, and a reasonable one, based on its past experience.

A related distinction here becomes clear. The premises of a deductive argument contain all the information needed for the conclusion, whereas the conclusion of an inductive argument goes beyond the premises. For this reason, some prefer the certainty of deduction to the probability of induction. Italian writer Italo Calvino describes such a person in his novel, *Mr. Palomar:*

> To construct a model—as Mr. Palomar was aware—you have to start with something; that is, you have to have principles, from which, by deduction, you develop your own line of reasoning. The principles—also known as axioms or postulates—are not something you select; you have them already, because if you did not have them, you could not even begin thinking. So Mr. Palomar also had some, but since he was neither a mathematician nor a logician, he did not bother to define them. Deduction, in any case, was one of his favorite activities, because he could devote himself to it in silence and alone, without special equipment, at any place and moment, seated in his armchair or strolling. Induction, on the contrary, was something he did not really trust, perhaps because he thought his experiences vague and incomplete. The construction of a model, therefore, was for him a miracle of equilibrium between principles (left in shadow) and experience (elusive), but the result should be more substantial than either.

Ambrose Peré, an Italian Renaissance physician, revealed his distrust of induction when he defined inductive diagnosis as "the rapid means to the wrong conclusion." One assumes that he would have argued for the value of a few well-learned principles behind one's observations.

From General to Specific, Specific to General

In a *deductive* argument, the inference usually moves from a generalization to a particular, specific instance or example that fits that generalization. Two examples:

1. All students who complete this course successfully will fulfill the critical thinking requirement.
2. Jane has completed this course successfully.
   ∴ Jane has fulfilled the critical thinking requirement.

1. Children born on a Saturday will "work hard for a living."
2. Nick was born on a Saturday.
   ∴ Nick will work hard for his living.

You may not believe this folk wisdom, especially if you were born on a Saturday, but the line of reasoning is still deductive.

In an ***inductive*** argument, the inference usually moves from a series of specific instances to a generalization.

1. Droughts have been more frequent in some areas.
2. Skin cancers related to ultraviolet rays have been increasing.
3. The tree line is moving north about 40 meters a year.
4. Polar ice has been melting more rapidly than in the past.
5. Oceans have been rising at measurable annual rates around the globe.
   ∴ The early stages of the dreaded "Greenhouse Effect" are upon us.

"Gentlemen, it's time we gave some serious thought to the effects of global warming."

Sometimes in inductive reasoning, we begin with a hypothesis, an unproved theory or proposition, and gather the data to support it. For instance, when Jonas Salk thought his vaccine would cure polio, he first had to test it inductively by administering it to a broad sample before concluding that the vaccine prevented polio.

The Relationship Between Induction and Deduction

In Exercise 7B we ask you to distinguish between inductive and deductive reasoning, but in reality the two are inextricable. Consider the source for the generalizations upon which deductions are based. In some cases they seem to be the laws of nature (or of God if one is religiously inclined), but more often than not we arrive at these generalizations by means of repeated observations. Throughout history, people have observed their own mortality, so we can now take that generalization—all people are mortal— as a given from which we can deduce conclusions about individual people. Induction has, in this case, led to a trusted generalization that in turn allows us a "necessary," or deductive, inference.

Humorists have sometimes turned these concepts on their heads. Here's Woody Allen reflecting on deduction: "All men are Socrates." And Lewis Carroll, in "The Hunting of the Snark," on induction: "What I tell you three times is true."

In a more serious approach, Robert Pirsig, in his philosophical novel, *Zen and the Art of Motorcycle Maintenance*, attempts to explain deduction, induction, and the relationships between them in language we can all understand. These terms were never intended to be the exclusive domain of academics but, rather, descriptive of the ways in which we all think every day.

Note how the following excerpt from Pirsig's novel explains both the differences between induction and deduction and their dependence on one another.

Mechanics' Logic

Two kinds of logic are used (in motorcycle maintenance), inductive and deductive. Inductive inferences start with observations of the machine and arrive at general conclusions. For example, if the cycle goes over a bump and the engine misfires, and then goes over another bump and the engine misfires, and then goes over another bump and the engine misfires, and then goes over a long smooth stretch of road and there is no misfiring, and then goes over a fourth bump and the engine misfires again, one can logically conclude that the misfiring is caused by the bumps. That is induction: reasoning from particular experiences to general truths.

Deductive inferences do the reverse. They start with general knowledge and predict a specific observation. For example, if, from reading the hierarchy of facts about the machine, the mechanic knows the horn of the cycle is powered exclusively by electricity from the battery, then he can logically infer that if the battery is dead the horn will not work. That is deduction.

Solution of problems too complicated for common sense to solve is achieved by long strings of mixed inductive and deductive inferences that weave back and forth between the observed machine and the mental hierarchy of the machine found in the manuals. The correct program for this interweaving is formalized as scientific method.

Actually I've never seen a cycle-maintenance problem complex enough really to require full-scale formal scientific method. Repair problems are not that hard. When I think of formal scientific method an image sometimes comes to mind of an enormous juggernaut, a huge bulldozer—slow, tedious, lumbering, laborious, but invincible. It takes twice as long, five times as long, maybe a dozen times as long as informal mechanic's techniques, but you know in the end you're going to *get* it. There's no fault isolation problem in motorcycle maintenance that can stand up to it. When you've hit a really tough one, tried everything, racked your brain and nothing works, and you know that this time Nature has really decided to be difficult, you say, "Okay, Nature, that's the end of the *nice* guy," and you crank up the formal scientific method.

For this you keep a lab notebook. Everything gets written down, formally, so that you know at all times where you are, where you've been, where you're going and where you want to get. In scientific work and electronics technology this is necessary because otherwise the problems get so complex you get lost in them and confused and forget what you know and what you don't know and have to give up. In cycle maintenance things are not that involved, but when confusion starts it's a good idea to hold it down by making everything formal and exact. Sometimes just the act of writing down the problems straightens out your head as to what they really are.

The logical statements entered into the notebook are broken down into six categories: (1) statement of the problem, (2) hypotheses as to the cause of the problem, (3) experiments designed to test each hypothesis, (4) predicted results of the experiments, (5) observed results of the experiments and (6) conclusions from the results of the experiments. This is not different from the formal arrangement of many college and high-school lab notebooks but the purpose here is no longer just busy-work. The purpose now is precise guidance of thoughts that will fail if they are not accurate.

The real purpose of scientific method is to make sure Nature hasn't misled you into thinking you know something you don't actually know. There's not a mechanic or scientist or technician alive who hasn't suffered from that one so much that he's not instinctively on guard. That's the main reason why so much scientific and mechanical information sounds so dull and so cautious. If you get careless or go romanticizing scientific information, giving it a flourish here and there, Nature will soon make a complete fool out of you. It does it often enougli anyway even when you don't give it opportunities. One must be extremely careful and rigidly logical when dealing with Nature: one logical slip and an entire scientific edifice comes tumbling down. One false deduction about the machine and you can get hung up indefinitely.

In Part One of formal scientific method, which is the statement of the problem, the main skill is in stating absolutely no more than you are positive you know. It is much better to enter a statement "Solve Problem: Why doesn't cycle work?" which sounds dumb but is correct, than it is to enter a statement "Solve Problem: What is wrong with the electrical system?" when you don't absolutely *know* the trouble is *in* the electrical system. What you should state is "Solve Problem: What is wrong with cycle?" and *then* state as the first entry of Part Two: "Hypothesis Number One: The trouble is in the electrical system." You think of as many hypotheses as you can, then you design experiments to test them to see which are true and which are false.

This careful approach to the beginning questions keeps you from taking a major wrong turn which might cause you weeks of extra work or can even hang you up completely. Scientific questions often have a surface appearance of dumbness for this reason. They are asked in order to prevent dumb mistakes later on.

Part Three, that part of formal scientific method called experimentation, is sometimes thought of by romantics as all of science itself because that's the only part with much visual surface. They see lots of test tubes and bizarre equipment and people running around making discoveries. They do not see the experiment as part of a larger intellectual process and so they often confuse experiments with demonstrations, which look the same. A man conducting a gee-whiz science show with fifty thousand dollars' worth of Frankenstein equipment is not doing anything scientific if he knows beforehand what the results of his efforts are going to be. A motorcycle mechanic, on the other hand, who honks the horn to see if the battery works is informally conducting a true scientific experiment. He is testing a hypothesis by putting the question to Nature. The TV scientist who mutters sadly, "The experiment is a failure; we have failed to achieve what we had hoped for," is suffering mainly from a bad scriptwriter. An experiment is never a failure solely because it fails to achieve predicted results. An experiment is a failure only when it also fails adequately to test the hypothesis in question, when the data it produces don't prove anything one way or another.

Skill at this point consists of using experiments that test only the hypothesis in question, nothing less, nothing more. If the horn honks, and the mechanic concludes that the whole electrical system is working, he is in deep trouble. He has reached an illogical conclusion. The honking horn only tells him that the battery and horn are working. To design an experiment properly he has to think very rigidly in terms of what directly causes what. This you know from the hierarchy. The horn doesn't make the cycle go. Neither does the battery, except in a very indirect way. The point at which the electrical system *directly* causes the engine to fire is at the spark plugs, and if you don't test here, at the output of the electrical system, you will never really know whether the failure is electrical or not.

To test properly the mechanic removes the plug and lays it against the engine so that the base around the plug is electrically grounded, kicks the starter lever and watches the spark-plug gap for a blue spark. If there isn't any he can conclude one of two things: (a) there is an electrical failure or (b) his experiment is sloppy. If he is experienced he will try it a few more times, checking connections, trying every way he can think of to get that plug to fire. Then, if he can't get it to fire, he finally concludes that *a* is correct, there's an electrical failure, and the experiment is over. He has proved that his hypothesis is correct.

In the final category, conclusions, skill comes in stating no more than the experiment has proved. It hasn't proved that when he fixes the electrical system the motorcycle will start. There may be other things wrong. But he does know that the motorcycle isn't going to run until the electrical system is working and he sets up the next formal question: "Solve problem: what is wrong with the electrical system?"

He then sets up hypotheses for these and tests them. By asking the right questions and choosing the right tests and drawing the right conclusions the mechanic works his way down the echelons of the motorcycle hierarchy until he has found the exact specific cause or causes of the engine failure, and then he changes them so that they no longer cause the failure.

An untrained observer will see only physical labor and often get the idea that physical labor is mainly what the mechanic does. Actually the physical labor is the smallest and easiest part of what the mechanic does. By far the greatest part of his work is careful observation and precise thinking. That is why mechanics sometimes seem so taciturn and withdrawn when performing tests. They don't like it when you talk to them because they are concentrating on mental images, hierarchies, and not really looking at you or the physical motorcycle at all. They are using the experiment as part of the program to expand their hierarchy of knowledge of the faulty motorcycle and compare it to the correct hierarchy in their mind. They are looking at underlying form.

EXERCISE 7A

......

Analyzing Pirsig

1. According to Pirsig, what is the most important part of the mechanic's work?

2. How does Pirsig define induction and deduction?

3. Which method of reasoning—induction or deduction—does the scientific method rely on?

4. Return to the statement by mathematician and philosopher Alfred North Whitehead (1861–1947), which begins this chapter, and explain its meaning.

EXERCISE 7B

Distinguishing Inductive from Deductive Reasoning

A. Read the following passages carefully and determine which are based on deductive reasoning and which on inductive. Briefly explain your answers.

1. Marie must be out of town. She hasn't answered her phone in a week, nor has she returned the messages that I have left on her answering machine. When I drove by her house last night, I noted that the lights inside and out were off.

2. Cat lovers do not care for dogs, and since Colette had numerous cats all of her life, I assume she did not care for dogs.

3. According to polls taken prior to the national convention, the candidate I support held a substantial lead in the presidential race. I am now confident that he will win in November.

4. Every Frenchman is devoted to his glass of *vin rouge*. Philippe is a Frenchman so he too must be devoted to that glass of red wine.

5. Bill Clinton lied to the American people about his relationship with a White House intern. Richard Nixon lied about Watergate. Lyndon Johnson lied about the Gulf of Tonkin and the Viet Nam War. I'll let you draw your own conclusions.

6. As an expert testified on the MacNeil/Lehrer News Hour following the *Challenger* space shuttle disaster, the solid rocket booster had proved safe in over 200 successful launchings of both space shuttles and Titan missiles. It was reasonable to conclude that the same rocket booster would function properly on the *Challenger* mission.

7. Students educated in the past three decades are not as well informed as were students attending universities prior to the mid 1960s. And since our rising generation of leaders has been educated in the past three decades, they must not be as well informed as those leaders who preceded them.

8. When people are confident and cheerful, they are generally inclined to spend more freely. With this in mind, we have designed these ads to project a feeling of cheerful confidence that should encourage viewers to spend more freely on your product. [Ad agency pitch to a potential client.]

B. Read the following passage taken from Arthur Conan Doyle's story, "A Study in Scarlet." Some critical thinkers have presented this passage as an example of deduction, others as induction. What do you think? Explain your decision.

A Study in Scarlet

"I wonder what that fellow is looking for?" I asked, pointing to a stalwart, plainly dressed individual who was walking slowly down the other side of the street, looking anxiously at the numbers. He had a large blue envelope in his hand, and was evidently the bearer of a message. "You mean the retired sergeant of Marines," said Sherlock Holmes.

"Brag and bounce!" thought I to myself. "He knows that I cannot verify his guess."

The thought had hardly passed through my mind when the man whom we were watching caught sight of the number on our door, and ran rapidly across the roadway. We heard a loud knock, a deep voice below, and heavy steps ascending the stair.

"For Mr. Sherlock Holmes," he said, stepping into the room and handing my friend the letter.

Here was an opportunity of taking the conceit out of him. He little thought of this when he made that random shot. "May I ask, my lad," I said, in the blandest voice, "what your trade may be?"

"Commissionaire, sir," he said, gruffly. "Uniform away for repairs."

"And you were?" I asked, with a slightly malicious glance at my companion.

"A sergeant, sir, Royal Marine Light Infantry, sir. No answer? Right, sir."

He clicked his heels together , raised his hand in salute, and was gone.

I confess that I was considerably startled by this fresh proof of the practical nature of my companion's theories. My respect for his powers of analysis increased wondrously. There still remained some lurking suspicion in my mind, however, that the whole thing was a prearranged episode, intended to dazzle me, though what earthly object he could have in taking me in was past my comprehension. When I look at him, he had finished reading the note, and his eyes had assumed the vacant, lack-lustre expression which showed mental abstraction.

"How in the world did you deduce that?" I asked.

"Deduce what?" said he, petulantly.

"Why, that he was a retired sergeant of Marines."

"I have no time for trifles," he answered, brusquely; then with a smile, "Excuse my rudeness. You broke the thread of my thoughts; but perhaps it is as well. So you actually were not able to see that that man was a sergeant of Marines?"

"No, indeed."

"It was easier to know it than to explain why I know it. If you were asked to prove that two and two made four, you might find some difficulty, and yet you are quite sure of the fact. Even across the street I could see a great blue anchor tattooed on the back of the fellow's hand. That smacked of the sea. He had a military carriage, however, and regulation side whiskers. There we have the marine. He was a man with some amount of self-importance and a certain air of command. You must have observed the way in which he held his head and swung his cane. A steady, respectable, middle-aged man, too, on the face of him—all facts which led me to believe that he had been a sergeant."

"Wonderful!" I ejaculated.

"Commonplace," said Holmes, though I thought from his expression that he was pleased at my evident surprise and admiration.

C. Arthur Conan Doyle would often tell this story about his first American lecture tour in 1894. A cabby, dropping him off, asked for a ticket to that night's lecture instead of a fare.

"How on earth did you recognize me?" Doyle asked.

The cabman replied: "If you will excuse me, your coat lapels are badly twisted downward, where they have been grasped by the pertinacious New York reporters. Your hair has the Quakerish cut of a Philadelphia barber, and your hat, battered at the brim in front, shows where you have tightly grasped it, in the struggle to stand your ground at a Chicago literary luncheon. Your right shoe has a large block of Buffalo mud just under the instep; the odor of a Utica cigar hangs about your clothing. . . . And, of course, the labels on your case give a full account of your recent travels—just below the brass plaque reading 'Conan Doyle.'"

We can safely infer that the creator of Sherlock Holmes had a sense of humor. Is our inference arrived at inductively or deductively?

Deductive Reasoning

Class Logic

Having established the differences between deductive and inductive reasoning, we can now examine each in greater detail. Underlying both forms of reasoning is an understanding of class logic. In fact, good reasoning in general often depends on seeing relationships between classes.

A **class** in logic is all of the individual things—persons, objects, events, ideas—that share a determinate property, a common feature. What is that determinate property? Anything under the sun. A class may consist of any quality or combination of qualities that the classifier assigns to it. A class may be vast, such as a class containing everything in the universe, or it may be small, containing only one member, such as Uncle Fred's last girlfriend. Making classes and assigning members to those classes is an essential part of everyday reasoning—it's how we order our experience. Indeed, each word in the language serves as a class by which we categorize and communicate experience. We can then take these words in any combination to create the categories or classes that serve our purpose.

A recent article in *The Journal of the American Medical Association,* for example, features a piece titled "Risk of Sexually Transmitted Diseases Among Adolescent Crack Users in Oakland and San Francisco." This title, which identifies one class (and the subject of the article), was created by combining seven classes: the class of things involving risk, the class of things that are sexually transmitted, the class of disease, the class of adolescents, the class of crack users, the class of persons living in Oakland, and the class of persons living in San Francisco.

Relationships Between Classes

There are three possible relationships between classes: **inclusion, exclusion,** and **overlap.**

Inclusion: One class is included in another if every member of one class is a member of the other class. Using letters, we can symbolize this relationship as all As are Bs. Using circle diagrams, also called Euler diagrams after Leonhard Euler, an 18th-century mathematician, we can illustrate a relationship of inclusion this way:

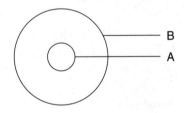

For example, the class of professional basketball players is included in the class of professional athletes because all professional basketball players are also professional athletes. The following diagram illustrates this relationship.

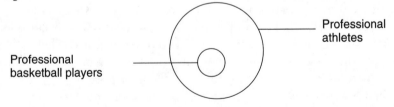

Exclusion: One class excludes another if they share no members, that is, if no As are Bs. Such a relationship exists between handguns and rifles.

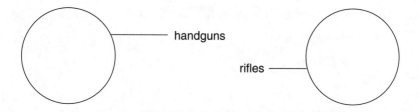

Overlap: One class overlaps with another if both have at least one member in common—if at least one A is also a B—for example, students at this university and students who like classical music.

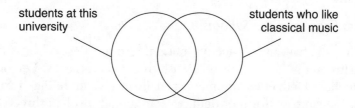

The way our public institutions classify relationships between groups of people can have a significant impact on their lives. The federal department of Housing and Urban Development (HUD) is authorized to allocate housing funds to individuals with disabilities. People with AIDS argued that they were entitled to such funds, but HUD, until recently, had denied them any such subsidy. Clearly, HUD saw the relationship between disabilities and AIDS as one of exclusion, whereas those with AIDS saw their relationship to those with disabilities as one of inclusion, a relationship they were, over time, able to convince HUD of.

EXERCISE 7C

Identifying Relationships Between Classes

Using circle diagrams, illustrate the relationships between the following pairs of classes.

1. cantaloupes and watermelons
2. judges and lawyers
3. Saabs and convertibles
4. mollusks and amphibians
5. cosmetics and hairspray

6. the homeless and the mentally ill

7. euthanasia and suicide

Now create your own classes.

1. Identify two classes, one of which is inclusive of the other.

2. Identify two classes that are exclusive of one another.

3. Identify two classes that overlap one another.

Class Logic and the Syllogism

Both inductive and deductive reasoning often depend on supporting a conclusion on the basis of relationships between classes. Let's look first at deduction. Deductive arguments usually involve more than two classes; in fact, the simplest form of deductive argument involves three classes. Remember this famous argument?

All people are mortal.

Socrates is a person.

∴ Socrates is mortal.

The three classes are "people," "mortality," and "Socrates." We can use circle diagrams to illustrate the relationship between these three classes. The first premise asserts that the class of people is included in the class of mortality. The second premise asserts that the class of Socrates is included in the class of people; and thus the conclusion can claim that Socrates is included in the class of mortality.

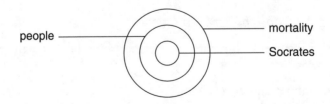

This type of argument is called a **categorical syllogism**—a deductive argument composed of three classes; such an argument has two premises and one conclusion derived from the two premises.

THE SUBJECT AND THE PREDICATE   To help identify the three classes of a categorical syllogism, you may want to identify the subject and predicate of each premise. Categorical propositions, and indeed all English sentences, can be broken down into two parts—the **subject** and **predicate.** These terms are shared by both grammar and logic and mean the same thing in both disciplines. The subject is that part of the sentence about which something is being asserted, and the predicate includes everything being asserted about the subject. In the first premise above, "all people" is the subject and "are mortal" is the predicate; in the second premise, "Socrates" is the subject and "is a person" is the predicate. The subject identifies one class; the predicate, the other.

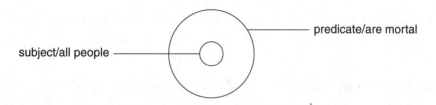

predicate/are mortal

subject/all people

Note: If the premise stated "people are mortal" rather than "all people are mortal," the meaning would be the same because, if a class is not quantified in some way—some, many, few, one—it is assumed that the assertion refers to the entire class.

TRUTH, VALIDITY, AND SOUNDNESS   If the conclusion follows of necessity, inescapably, from the premises, as it does in the syllogism about Socrates, then it is a **valid** argument.

We frequently use the term "valid" in everyday language. For example, we say, "That's a valid point." But in logic **validity** has this very precise meaning: The conclusion follows of necessity from the premises, the form of the argument is correct, the line of reasoning conforms to the rules of logic. When we learn to evaluate the validity of a deductive argument, we can see what it means for a conclusion to follow inescapably from the premises.

Validity, however, is not the only requirement for a successful deductive argument; the premises must also be **"true"** or **"acceptable".** Logicians use the term true, appropriate when a proposition can be evaluated by absolute or mathematical standards. But proof must often fall short of what can be claimed as true, an absolute term too imposing, even intimidating, for many assertions that we would nonetheless be inclined to accept. In most of our arguments, we must settle for what is reasonable to believe, what has been adequately supported and explained. Oliver Wendell Holmes, Supreme

Court Justice 1902–1932, skirted the issue when he said, "What is true is what I can't help believing." We prefer the term "acceptable" to "true." As Tom Bridges of Montclair State University puts it, "The goal of inquiry is not objective truth, but reasonable belief, *pistis*—the state of being persuaded." Here lies the goal of written argument, not to assert a universal, irrevocable truth, but to establish a reasonable, acceptable position.

An important point here is that to evaluate an argument successfully, we must begin by evaluating the premises, one by one, rather than moving in on the conclusion first. The conclusion will only be as acceptable as the sum of its premises.

To summarize, two requirements must be met for us to accept the conclusion of a deductive argument:

1. The structure of the argument must be *valid*—that is, the conclusion must follow of necessity from the premises.

2. The premises must be *acceptable* (true).

A deductive argument whose premises are acceptable and whose structure is valid is a **sound** argument—a successful deductive argument. Put another way, if the argument is valid and the premises are acceptable, then the conclusion cannot be false. Keep in mind that the terms validity and soundness can refer only to the argument as a whole. In contrast, individual statements can only be described as acceptable or unacceptable (true or false). In logic, we don't describe an argument as being true or a premise as valid.

Some examples of sound and unsound arguments:

1. A sound argument—the premises are acceptable and the structure valid.

   Drift-net fishing kills dolphins.
   Mermaid Tuna uses drift nets.
   ∴ Mermaid Tuna kills dolphins.

2. An unsound argument—one of the premises (in this example the first one) is false or not acceptable, even though the structure is valid.

   All Latins are volatile.
   Jesse is a Latin.
   ∴ Jesse is volatile.

3. An unsound argument—the premises are acceptable but the structure is invalid.

   All athletes are people.
   All football players are people.
   ∴ All football players are athletes.

Note that in example 3, all the statements are acceptable, both the premises and the conclusion, but because the structure of the argument is invalid—the premises do not lead inescapably to the conclusion—the argument is unsound. Sketch this argument with circle diagrams to illustrate the principle.

Unreliable syllogisms turn up as accident and as humorous intent in a variety of places. Writer and critic Donald Newlove once claimed that, because he fell asleep while reading Harold Brodkey's *Runaway Soul,* which he also did his first time through literary classics *Moby Dick* and *Ulysses, Runaway Soul* must also be a great work of literature. Writer Ian Frazier found the following graffiti on a library table at Columbia University:

David Bowie is supreme.

God is supreme.

∴ David Bowie is God.

GUILT BY ASSOCIATION   Let's look at another example of an invalid argument with acceptable premises.

Drug dealers wear electronic pagers.

Doctors wear electronic pagers.

∴ Doctors are drug dealers.

All of us would reject this ridiculous argument, but this pattern of reasoning, erroneous as it is, is fairly common. One famous example took place in 1950 when communism was referred to as the "red menace," and Senator Joseph McCarthy and the House Un-American Activities Committee were beginning their witch hunt against anyone who had ever had an association, no matter how slight or distant, with communism. It was in this climate of national paranoia that Republican Richard Nixon, running against Democrat Helen Gahagen Douglas for a California senate seat, presented the following argument, allowing the voters to draw their own conclusions:

Communists favor measures x, y, and z.

My opponent, Helen Gahagen Douglas, favors these same measures.

∴ [Helen Gahagen Douglas is a Communist.]

This kind of reasoning, based on guilt by association, is faulty (but often effective—Douglas lost the election) because it assumes that if two classes share one quality, they share all qualities. Such reasoning is a source of much racism and sexism; it assumes that if two people are of the same sex or race, they share not only that characteristic but an entire set of characteristics as well. But a simple diagram can illustrate where the logic fails.

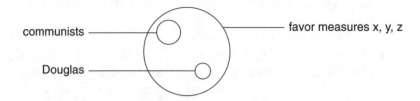

MORE ON SYLLOGISMS   Before you examine some syllogisms on your own, we need to look once again at exclusion, overlap, and inclusion. Examine the following example and use circle diagrams to illustrate the relationship between each of the classes to determine the validity of the reasoning.

> All Alice's friends are Libertarians.
>
> Deborah is not a Libertarian.
>
> ∴ Deborah is not a friend of Alice.

Were you able to illustrate by exclusion that this is a valid argument? Can you do the same for this one?

> None of Alice's friends are Libertarians.
>
> Deborah is not a friend of Alice.
>
> ∴ Deborah is not a Libertarian.

Can you illustrate why this reasoning is not reliable, why the argument is invalid?

So far we have been dealing with what we call a **universal proposition,** an assertion that refers to all members of a designated class. What happens when we qualify a premise with "some" and then have what logicians call a **particular proposition?** Let's look at an example.

> All gamblers are optimists.
>
> Some of my friends are gamblers.
>
> ∴ Some of my friends are optimists.

A diagram illustrates that because the conclusion is qualified, it can follow from one qualified, or "particular," premise. Although it's possible for some friends to fall outside the class of gamblers and thus, perhaps, outside the class of optimists, the second premise guarantees that some (at least two) of my friends are included in the class of gamblers.

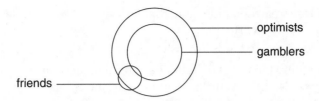

This argument is valid. But if the first premise also says "*Some* gamblers are optimists," you can't necessarily claim that even one friend has to be an optimist. Use a diagram to show the possibility that even the qualified conclusion could be false. When making claims in your written arguments, examine carefully how you use qualifiers and how you state conclusions based on qualified premises. Just because *some* politicians are dishonest, it doesn't necessarily follow that the mayor is dishonest.

EXERCISE 7D

Determining the Validity of Categorical Syllogisms

Use Euler diagrams to determine the validity of the following categorical syllogisms.

Example

1. Stealing is a criminal act.
2. Shoplifting is stealing.
   ∴ Shoplifting is a criminal act.

VALID Inclusion

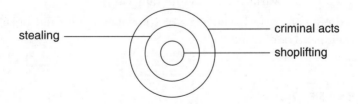

1. Liberals want to ban offshore drilling.
   Conservationists want to ban offshore drilling.
   ∴ Conservationists are liberals.
2. A cautious pilot wouldn't drink before a flight.
   Maxine is a cautious pilot.
   ∴ Maxine wouldn't drink before a flight.

3. All Jose's parrots understand Spanish.
   Pepe is his favorite parrot.
   ∴ Pepe understands Spanish.

4. Gauguin's paintings of Tahiti have brilliant and unrealistic colors.
   "Starry Night" has brilliant and unrealistic colors.
   ∴ "Starry Night" is a Gauguin painting of Tahiti.

5. Young men with shaven heads and swastikas tattooed on their arms
   are racists.
   John is a young man who doesn't shave his head or have a swastika
   tattooed on his arm.
   ∴ John is not a racist.

6. Nations that do not respect human rights shouldn't receive favored
   nation status.
   Tiananmen Square demonstrated China's complete lack of respect
   for the rights of its citizens.
   ∴ China doesn't deserve its favored nation status.

7. Every pediatrician knows that each child develops at his own rate.
   Dr. Haskell knows that each child develops at his own rate.
   ∴ Dr. Haskell is a pediatrician.

8. Some artists are completely self-absorbed.
   Frida Kahlo was an artist.
   ∴ Frida Kahlo was completely self-absorbed.

9. Members of the Christian Coalition believe in family values.
   Carlos and Maria believe in family values.
   ∴ Carlos and Maria are members of the Christian coalition.

10. Killing the innocent is morally wrong.
    Modern warfare always involves killing the innocent.
    ∴ Modern warfare is always morally wrong.

Create three categorical syllogisms of your own—one valid but unsound,
one invalid, and one sound.

EXERCISE 7E

Evaluating Deductive Arguments in Everyday Language

Determine whether the following arguments are sound or unsound. For
each argument follow these steps: First, reduce each one to a categorical
syllogism (supplying any unstated premises or conclusions—see hidden assumptions in Chapter 3); then use circle diagrams to determine validity;
and finally, discuss the truth or acceptability of each premise.

1. Plagiarism is wrong, and paraphrasing the words of others without proper acknowledgment is the same as plagiarism, so paraphrasing the words of others without proper acknowledgment is wrong.

2. Mafia member Joe Bonano was guilty of criminal activities because he claimed the Fifth Amendment in the course of his trial. The Fifth Amendment, you will recall, is the privilege of a witness not to testify on the grounds that the evidence called for might be incriminating. One may choose not to testify against oneself, but there is a risk attached to this privilege. For we cannot avoid the fact that people who take the Fifth Amendment have something to hide—their guilt. In the case of Joe Bonano, that something to hide was his criminal activities.

A Note on Deduction and Written Argument

While understanding the logic of valid syllogisms represents a valuable component of critical thinking, arguments as they appear in written discourse seldom take such a restricted shape. A clear grasp of deductive reasoning, however, is important for ensuring that the conclusions you reach from a given set of premises follow logically. Skeptical opponents of your position may be on the lookout for flawed deductions. Remember, for example, that just because two people, or two circumstances, share one set of common properties, it does not necessarily follow that they share other ideas or qualities. Attempts to smear political candidates often rely on this kind of fallacious reasoning. The case of Richard Nixon and Helen Gahagen Douglas cited above illustrates this point. Advertising, too, may lead us to draw a conclusion based on similar tricks of false association. Why else are beautiful models on hand when the product is an automobile, a vacuum cleaner, a carpet?

Inductive Reasoning

The fundamental distinction between deductive and inductive reasoning lies in the relative certainty with which we can accept a conclusion. The certainty guaranteed when a deductive argument is validly reasoned from acceptable premises cannot be assumed in an inductive argument, no matter how carefully one supports the inference. The terms most appropriate for inductive arguments then are strong and weak, reliable or unreliable rather than valid and invalid.

Some logicians prefer the categories deductive and nondeductive to deductive and inductive, given the varied forms arguments can take when they don't conform to the rigorous rules of inference required for deduction.

Generalization

Determining cause and effect, formulating hypotheses, drawing analogies, and arriving at statistical generalizations are examples of nondeductive reasoning, or as we have chosen to call it, inductive reasoning. In this section, we concentrate on the statistical generalization. **Statistical generalizations** are best characterized as predictions, as claims about the distribution of a **projected property** in a given group or population, the **target population**. From the distribution of such a property in *part* of the target population, the **sample**, we infer a proposition, a conclusion that is either strong or weak depending on how carefully we conduct our survey. We make a prediction, an inference, about the unknown on the basis of the known; on the basis of our observations of the sample, we make a generalization about all of the population, including that part we have not observed closely.

> Suppose we want to determine whether New York taxpayers will support a tax designated specifically for building shelters for the homeless. Here the **projected property** would be the willingness to support this particular tax (what we want to find out). The **target population** would be New York taxpayers. The **sample** would be that portion of New York taxpayers polled. From their answers, we would draw a conclusion, make a generalization about New York taxpayers in general: unanimous support, strong support, marginal support, little support, no support—whatever their answers warrant. But no matter how precise the numbers from the sample, we cannot predict with absolute certainty what the entire population of New York taxpayers will actually do. When we make an inference from some to all, the conclusion always remains logically doubtful to some degree.

Let's look at another example.

> For several years now, scientists and health officials have alerted the public to the increased risk of skin cancer as the thinning of the ozone layer allows more of the harmful ultraviolet rays to penetrate the atmosphere. Imagine that the student health center at your school wanted to find out if students were aware of this danger and were protecting themselves from it. In this case, the **projected property** would be taking preventive measures to protect oneself from the sun. The **target population** would be all the students attending your school, and the **sample** would be the number of students polled. Once again, any conclusions reached by the health center on the basis of its survey would be tentative rather than certain, with the certainty increasing in proportion to the size of the sample—the greater the number of students polled, the more reliable is the conclusion, assuming the sample is representative as well.

The Direction of Inductive Reasoning

The direction of inductive reasoning can vary. We may start by noting specific instances and from them make general inferences, or we may begin with a general idea and seek specific examples or data to support it. The following example moves from specific cases to a generalization.

THAT'S LIFE *Mike Twohy*

© 1999 Mike Twohy. Dist. by Washington Post Writers Group.

"Spin through and see if anything's targeted at us tonight."

Observing a sudden increase in the number of measles cases in several communities, public health officials in the 1990s inferred that too many infants were going unvaccinated.

Even here you may notice that our ability to think both deductively and inductively has a way of intertwining the two modes of thought, but the structure of this argument is still inductive, the conclusion being probable rather than guaranteed.

Often we start with a tentative generalization, a possible conclusion called a **hypothesis,** an assertion we are interested in proving.

Rousel Uclaf, the French manufacturers of a revolutionary new pill to prevent pregnancy and avoid abortion, hoped to prove that it was both effective and safe. To do so, they had to conduct elaborate studies with varied groups of women over time. Until they had gathered such statistical support in a sample population, their claim that it was effective and safe was only a hypothesis, not a reliable conclusion. But once they had tested their product, RU 486, on 40,000 women in several European countries and found only two "incidents" of pregnancies and no apparent harm, they were ready to claim that RU 486 is reasonably safe and statistically effective.

Even here, the conclusion remains inductive—it is a highly probable conclusion but not a necessary one as it would be in deduction. Unfortunately, there are examples of such inductive reasoning leading to false (and

disastrous) conclusions. Approved for use in Europe, the drug thalido-
mide, given to pregnant women for nausea in the 1960s, caused many children to be born with grave deformities. And the Dalkon Shield, an in-
trauterine birth control device of the 1970s, although tested before being
made available, caused sterility in many of its users.

Testing Inductive Generalizations

With inductive arguments, we accept a conclusion with varying degrees of
probability and must be willing to live with at least a fraction of uncertainty.
But the question always remains, how much uncertainty is acceptable?

CRITERIA FOR EVALUATING STATISTICAL GENERALIZATIONS   *How* we infer
our conclusions, the way in which we conduct our surveys, is crucial to determining the strength of an inductive argument. Whether we are constructing our own arguments or evaluating those of others, we need to be
discriminating. Many of our decisions on political, economic, sociological,
even personal issues depend on inductive reasoning. Scarcely a day goes
by without an inductive study or poll reaching the news sections of daily
papers or the evening news on TV: surveys show the president's popularity
is rising or falling, Americans favor socialized medicine, one in five non-
government workers is employed at firms with drug testing programs. A
few principles for evaluating such generalizations can help us all examine
the conclusions with the critical perspective necessary for our self-defense.

In order to accept a conclusion as warranted or reliable, we need to
control or interpret the conditions of the supporting survey.

Two features of the sample are essential:

1. The **size** must be adequate. The proportion of those in the sample
   must be sufficient to reflect the total size of the target population.
   Statisticians have developed complex formulas for determining adequate size proportionate to a given population, but for our general
   purposes common sense and a little well-reasoned practice will
   serve. The Gallup Organization polls 2,500 to 3,000 to determine
   how 80 million will vote in a presidential election and allows for
   only a 3 percent margin of error. This suggests that the size of a survey can often be smaller than we might initially assume.
2. The sample must be **representative**. It must represent the target
   population in at least two different ways.
   a. The sample must be selected *randomly* from the target popula-
      tion.
   b. It must also be *spread* across the population so that all significant
      differences within the population are represented. Such a con-

trived approach might seem contradictory to a random sample, but some conscious manipulation is often necessary to assure a sample that is genuinely typical of the target population.

Examine the following diagram to see these principles illustrated.

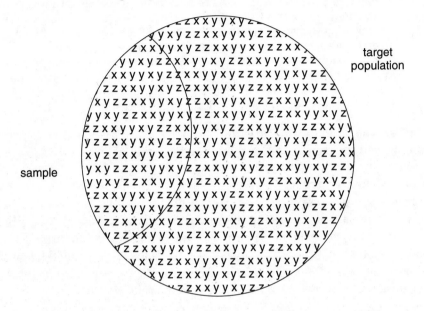

As you can see, we are back to classes (see Class Logic above). The sample is a subclass included in the larger class of the target population. As we make inferences, we move from a conclusion about the smaller class, the sample, to a conclusion about the larger class, the target population.

> *If they remove all the fools from Congress, it wouldn't be a representative Congress.*
>
> —Political commentator Molly Ivins

Let's evaluate the reasoning in the following argument:

A visitor of modest means from a midwestern city comes to San Francisco for five days and is instructed by her friends to assess the prices of San Francisco's restaurants; some of them are considering a trip there in the near future. Our tourist, let's call her Martha, picks up a guidebook and takes the first five restaurants listed in the book: Masas, Campton Place, Postrio, the Ritz Carlton, and Aqua, all of which are located downtown. Verging on bankruptcy, poor Martha returns home with the report that restaurants in San Francisco are staggeringly expensive. For a resident of San Francisco, the error in her conclusion and the flaw in the reasoning that led to her false conclusion are easy to spot—she has inadvertently chosen five of the most expensive restaurants in the city. Before selecting her restaurants, she should have examined her guidebook carefully to be sure that her survey of restaurants was, to some degree, representative. The book clearly began with a list of the major splurges and that was as far as Martha went.

With only five days, she was necessarily limited when it came to the *size* of her sample, and thus she would have to place a strong qualifier on any conclusions she drew. But, with a little care, she could have aimed for a more *random* sample by investigating different sections of her guidebook, referring to more than one guide, and visiting various geographical areas of San Francisco. Such a sampling would also have helped her arrive at examples spread more effectively over different types of cuisines. A visitor intent on savoring the best fare regardless of cost would have done well following Martha's approach, but one interested in the prices was doomed to a distorted picture.

Can you identify the projected property, the target population, the sample, and the conclusion for this inductive argument?

HASTY GENERALIZATIONS   When, like Martha, we leap to an unwarranted conclusion, we commit the common logical fallacy of hasty generalization. If, for example, after one semester at a university as a student having had two professors who failed to return work, often missed class, or arrived late, you concluded that the university had a rotten faculty, you would be guilty of hasty generalization. The sample is clearly too small to warrant such a conclusion. For further discussion of this familiar fallacy, see Chapter 6.

COUNTEREXAMPLES

With any generalization supported by specific examples, one counterexample can discredit, or "embarrass," the conclusion. Warranted conclusions must be consistent with the data used in their support, and where necessary, qualified appropriately—"most," "some," "usually," "occasionally," "in most cases."

Garfield ®   **by Jim Davis**

Garfield doubts his conclusion when he discovers three counterexamples.

Thinking Critically About Surveys and Statistics

Because surveys and statistics suggest an authority they may not warrant, we must read them critically rather than accept them without question. Statistics should contribute to reasoning, not serve as a substitute for it.

Time magazine ran a recent cover story on the high cost of a college degree entitled "How Colleges Are Gouging You," by Erik Larson. In his article Larson accused colleges of protecting their endowment funds while charging whatever the traffic will bear for tuition. The piece elicited this angry response.

> To generalize the situation at the University of Pennsylvania and other Ivy League schools and apply it to major universities across the board is like using the cost of a Lexus to discuss the price of an average family van. In the real world of most institutions, faculty members do not average earnings of $121,000 a year; they are lucky to make $40,000. And they are teaching larger classes with fewer resources and support staff and reduced budgets for essential expenses. Unfortunately, Larson's diatribe will probably be used by state legislatures as justification to cut budgets of many public institutions.
>
> —JOHN BRUNCH, ASSISTANT PROFESSOR
> DEPARTMENT OF MANAGEMENT
> KANSAS STATE UNIVERSITY, MANHATTAN, KANSAS

This professor from a public university is rightfully concerned that a generalization based on a study of private universities will be applied to public universities (which often do not have endowment funds), with the consequence of fewer resources for him and his students.

In 1948 Alfred C. Kinsey published *The Kinsey Report*, one of the first surveys on the sexual mores of Americans. Kinsey concluded among other things that 10% of the population was homosexual. James H. Jones, who wrote a recent biography of Kinsey, points out that the sample on which this conclusion was based was not representative of all Americans.

> Kinsey did a great deal of interviewing in prisons, where the incidence of homosexuality was higher than in the general population. More damaging still to the reliability of his sample was his practice of seeking out individuals on the basis of their sexual tastes and behavior. In compiling his sample of the American population, Kinsey targeted gay people, becoming the first scientist to study in depth the nascent gay communities in large urban areas and elsewhere. In city after city he tapped into gay networks, using the contacts he made with gay subjects to generate introductions to their partners, lovers and friends. This practice enabled Kinsey to collect a large number of gay histories, but, in conjunction with his prison interviews, it also skewed his data in the direction of overestimating the percentage of gay people in the American population.

Bad science is made worse by the media's reporting of all surveys in abbreviated and often sensational ways. Even when a study is carefully done by a reputable institution, the press will often reduces the results to the most attention-getting headline. The media reported that heavy coffee drinkers had two to three times the risk of heart disease on the basis of a study done at Johns Hopkins University that used many subjects over several years. But a careful reading of the study from beginning to end revealed that its authors didn't ask participants about their diet, smoking habits, and exercise levels, mitigating factors in any study of heart disease. The report concluded that there was "a need for further investigation" into the dangers of caffeine, a conclusion the media failed to report. All that one could safely conclude from the Johns Hopkins study is a **correlation** between heavy caffeine use and heart disease, not **causation**. The distinction between correlation and causation is an important one. There is a correlation between home ownership and car accidents. If you are a home owner, you're more likely to own a car, so you're more likely to be in a car accident, but that doesn't mean that home ownership causes car accidents.

Note also subtle slants in the emphasis the media give to statistics. In the same issue of a major daily newspaper, the summary caption on page one stated that, "A new poll finds that 1 in 5 Californians still resent Japan for the attack on Pearl Harbor," while the inside story was headed, "50 years after attack on Pearl Harbor, only 1 in 5 is still resentful, poll shows." What are the different implications of these two captions?

Consider the Source

When evaluating a survey and its conclusions, we must consider the source of the survey—who conducted the survey and who paid for it—to determine if there is a conflict of interest or a hidden agenda. A recent study of silicone breast implants concluded that there was no link between ruptured implants and connective tissue disease. Lawyer and consumer advocate Mary Alexander criticizes this study not only for the limited size of its sample and its failure to allow for the 8.5 years of latency between implantation and silicone disease, but also for two of its authors who "admitted on the threat of perjury that they were paid consultants of breast implant manufacturers." Furthermore, Dow Corning, the world's largest silicone breast implant manufacturer, had donated $5 million to one of the hospitals involved in the study. Such a study is riddled with conflict of interest. It is not in the best interest of those who benefit directly from Dow Corning to find fault with the company's product.

One of the most respected medical publications, *The New England Journal of Medicine*, has been found guilty of violating its conflict-of-interest policy. In 1989, the journal included an article that played down the risks from exposure to asbestos but failed to inform its readers that the

authors had past ties to producers of asbestos. In 1996, the journal ran an editorial claiming that the benefits of diet drugs outweighed the risks but failed to note that the two authors had been paid consultants for firms that made or marketed one of the diet drugs under discussion. In 1997, the journal featured a negative review of a book connecting environmental chemicals and various cancers, a review written by the medical director of a large chemical company.

CRITICAL READING OF SURVEYS

1. Is the sample representative of the target population? Is it large enough?

2. Does the media's report on the survey seem fair and reasonable?

3. Does the survey establish causation or correlation?

4. Who wrote or published or called your attention to the survey? Are they impartial or do they have a hidden agenda or conflict of interest? Is the survey cited in advertising or in another context in which the motive is to sell you something?

EXERCISE 7F

Evaluating Inductive Reasoning

In the following studies, identify the conclusion, the projected property, the target population, and the sample. Then, drawing on the principles of reliable inductive generalizations, evaluate their reliability.

1. The quality control inspector at Sweet and Sour Yogurt removes and tests one container out of approximately every thousand (about one every 15 minutes) and finds it safe for consumption. She then guarantees as safe all the containers filled that day.

2. In her book *Women and Love,* Shere Hite claims that a large percentage of American women are unhappy in their marriages and feel that men don't listen to them. She felt confident in her conclusions after mailing out 100,000 questionnaires to women's political, professional, and religious organizations and having 4 percent of the questionnaires returned.

3. Setting out to document her theory on the prevalence of racism on television, a sociologist examines 40 episodes from the new fall prime-time situation comedies and finds that 36 of them contain racist stereotypes. She concludes that 90 percent of television drama is racist.

4. On November 1, to consolidate his frequent flier miles, businessman Eric Nichols decided to select one domestic airline from his two favorites. He planned to base his decision on each airline's reliability. From November through April he made 20 evenly spaced trips on United, experiencing two cancellations, nine delayed departures, and eight late arrivals. From May through October, he

flew American Airlines 22 times, but improved his record with only one cancellation, seven delays, and five late arrivals. Without further consideration, he chose American as the more reliable of the two.

5. The French Ministry of Social Affairs reported that three well-known research physicians at the Laennec Hospital in Paris had observed "dramatic biological improvements" in a group of patients with AIDS. The physicians reported a "dramatic" slowing of acquired immune deficiency syndrome in one of the six patients and a complete halt in the disease's progress in another after only five days of treatment with a compound called cyclosporine. (Hint: The conclusion is implicit.)

6. A recent study by the University of Medicine and Dentistry of New Jersey concluded that "women who were abused [physically, emotionally, or sexually] as children have more health problems and require more hospital care than women who were not abused." Seven hundred women from a private gynecological practice were interviewed. Mostly white, middle class with college degrees, they ranged in age from 16 to 76.

EXERCISE 7G

Finding Weaknesses in Inductive Arguments

In the following article, a critic points out weaknesses in an inductive argument. Analyze the original inductive study, then the critic's response, and summarize your findings according to these steps:

1. Identify the projected property, the target population, the sample, and the conclusion.

2. Explain the weaknesses as discussed by the critic and conclude with discussion of your own opinion. Do you support the critic or the researchers who first presented the conclusions?

Dispute Over Claims of Ibuprofen Dangers
—UNITED PRESS INTERNATIONAL

Washington
    Federal officials and makers of ibuprofen medicines yesterday disputed the conclusions of medical researchers who claim that a 12-patient study in-

dicates that over-the-counter doses of the pain killer may cause kidney failure in high-risk people.

In a study published in the Annals of Internal Medicine, doctors from Johns Hopkins University medical school in Baltimore looked at the effects of ibuprofen and two other types of nonsteroidal, anti-inflammatory drugs in 12 women with chronic kidney problems but no obvious symptoms. Three of the patients developed complications.

But Food and Drug Administration spokeswoman Bonnie Aikman said yesterday that consumers have no cause for alarm about taking over-the-counter ibuprofen, as long as they read the label telling them to contact a doctor if they experience any unusual symptoms. That advice will be highlighted on ibuprofen labels starting in June, Aikman added.

The patients in the study were given the prescription-level dose of ibuprofen—2,400 milligrams a day—two times the maximum daily dose recommended for over-the-counter versions of the drug. Eight days into an 11-day course of treatment, three of the patients were judged to have severe enough kidney impairment that researchers stopped giving them the drug. When researchers later tried giving them lower doses of ibuprofen, 1,200 milligrams per day—or the top over-the-counter dose, two of the three patients again developed evidence of acute kidney failure.

Ibuprofen was recommended to patients by doctors nearly 50 million times in 1987, according to the National Disease and Therapeutic Index. An estimated 100 million people have used the nonprescription drug since it was introduced in 1984.

T. R. Reid, a spokesman for the Upjohn Co. of Kalamazoo, Mich., maker of Motrin, a prescription ibuprofen medication, and Motrin IB, the over-the-counter version, called the conclusions of the Johns Hopkins study "warped."

Reid noted the study only looked at 12 patients, and all patients were predisposed to kidney failure. But his major objection was that its authors extended the findings about prescription ibuprofen to over-the-counter ibuprofen.

Other common over-the-counter products containing ibuprofen are Nuprin, made by Bristol-Myers Squibb Co. of New York, and Advil, made by Whitehall Laboratories Inc. of New York.

"We do not believe the findings of this study apply to the safety of nonprescription ibuprofen in the general population," Whitehall said in a statement.

Reid said labels on prescription Motrin already inform doctors there is a slim risk—1 percent or less—of kidney complications from prolonged use of the drug.

In addition, the Upjohn Company said labels on nonprescription ibuprofen tell people with serious medical conditions, such as poor kidney function, to consult with their doctors before starting any new over-the-counter medication.

EXERCISE 7H

Collecting Generalizations

Humorist James Thurber, celebrated for his long association with *The New Yorker* magazine, had fun exploiting our tendency to overgeneralize in his essay, "What a Lovely Generalization." Many of his examples are absurd, but some suggest the dangers that can spring from such patterns of thought. For those interested in collecting generalizations, he suggests listening "in particular to women, whose average generalization is from three to five times as broad as a man's." Was he sexist or making a not-so-funny joke? He listed many others from his collection, labelling some "true," some "untrue," others "debatable," "libellous," "ridiculous," and so on. Some examples from his collection: "Women don't sleep very well," "There are no pianos in Japan," "Doctors don't know what they're doing," "Gamblers hate women," "Cops off duty always shoot somebody," "Intellectual women dress funny." And so his collection ran, brimming with hasty generalizations.

Your task is to collect two "lovely generalizations" from the world around you, comment on the accuracy, absurdity, and dangers of each and discuss the implications of your generalizations for those who seem to be the target.

WRITING ASSIGNMENT 16

Questioning Generalizations

Add the two generalizations you chose for Exercise 7H "Collecting Generalizations" to the following list of generalizations and choose one to write a paper in support of, or in opposition to. This list could be even longer and more diverse if your instructor collects the entire classes' generalizations and makes them available to you.

1. Women are better dancers than men.
2. Men are better athletes than women.
3. Everyone is capable of being creative.
4. Nice guys finish last.
5. Appearances can be deceiving.
6. The purpose of a college degree is to prepare an individual for a career.
7. A college graduate will get a higher paying job than a high school graduate.

8. A woman will never be elected president of the United States.

9. All people are created equal.

10. War is a necessary evil.

Audience

A reader who is not strongly invested in the proposition one way or another but who is interested in hearing your point of view

Purpose

To cast a critical eye on a generalization that people tend to accept without question

---

WRITING ASSIGNMENT 17

Conducting a Survey: A Collaborative Project

Conduct a survey at your school to determine something of significance about the student body and then write a report in which you state either a question or a hypothesis, describe the survey, and speculate on the results. (Apologies to statisticians for the oversimplification of a very complex task.)

The class as a whole can brainstorm possible questions to ask the student body, the target population. What do students think about the current administration on campus or in Washington? Our nation's involvement in foreign wars? Or a host of other political issues. How many students take a full academic load and work part-time as well? There are many possibilities.

Choose five or six topics from these many possibilities and divide into groups around them. These groups will then create a survey—a questionnaire appropriate to the topic they are researching—and a strategy for distributing it to a representative sample.

The next step is to collect, tabulate, and discuss the data. Either each student can then write her own report or the group can write a single report, assigning a section to each member of the group.

The report will contain the following:

1. A description of the survey
   What questions did you ask?
   When and where did you ask them?

2. A description of the sample
   Whom did you ask?

How many did you ask?

3. Evaluation of the survey

Was the sample large enough?
Was it representative?
Were your questions unbiased?
What could you do to make it better?

4. Analysis of the results

How does it compare with what you expected the results to be before you began gathering the data?
What do you imagine are the causes that led to these results?
What are the implications of the results?

Audience

Your campus community—students, faculty, and staff

Purpose

To inform your campus community about its student members

Application to Writing

Deduction, Induction, and Organizational Patterns

Textbooks about writing frequently describe organizational patterns for essays as being strictly deductive or inductive. It is true that a written argument may start with a broad generalization offered as a given upon which applications to more specific circumstances may be built. Such a shape does resemble one definition of deduction—a generalization applied to a particular instance or example. A paper that assumes the majority of mothers are working outside the home today could then go on to argue for a particular course of action to address problems surrounding the trend of both parents working outside the home. A deductive paper tends to greater formality, a construction based on defined principles that sets out to prove a stated conclusion.

Often a collection of specific data—empirical observations including personal experience, examples from research, and statistics—can add up to a generalization in the conclusion and thus appear to reflect the inductive process. A survey of urban households, for example, could, with careful analysis, lead to a conclusion about trends in family eating habits. Inductive writing, reflecting its open-ended character, is often looser than its more rigid counterpart.

Legal scholar Patricia J. Williams expresses it this way in describing her personal approach to writing about legal issues:

> Legal writing presumes a methodology that is highly stylized, precedential, and based on deductive reasoning. Most scholarship in law is rather like the "old math": static, stable, formal—rationalism walled against chaos. My writing is an intentional departure from that. I use a model of inductive empiricism, borrowed from—and parodying—systems analysis, in order to enliven thought about complex social problems.

She goes on to explain that she is "trying to create a genre of legal writing to fill the gaps of traditional legal scholarship" by writing "in a way that . . . forces the reader to participate in the construction of meaning."

Ultimately, as Pirsig emphasizes in "Mechanics' Logic," it takes an interplay of the two thinking methods to reflect accurately how we arrive at our conclusions. The writer of the paper on family eating habits would be likely to start speculating on why trends in family meals have changed and possibly on what impact such changes would have on society. Such an approach would not be described as inductive, but, in fact, represents a combination of inductive and deductive reasoning

Our ability to distinguish between inductive and deductive reasoning enables us to see if a conclusion absolutely follows from the evidence or if it is one possibility among others. Understanding our reasoning and the reasoning of others in these terms increases our ability to both think critically and write logically.

SUMMARY

Inductive and deductive reasoning are distinct from one another in two ways.

1. In a deductive argument, the conclusion follows by necessity from the premises if the method of reasoning is valid. In an inductive argument, the conclusion can only follow with some degree of probability.

2. In a deductive argument, the inference moves from a generalization to a particular instance or example that fits that generalization. In an inductive argument, the inference usually moves from a series of specific instances to a generalization.

Induction and deduction are interdependent; it takes an interplay of the two thinking methods to arrive at our conclusions.

There are three possible relationships between classes: inclusion, exclusion, and overlap.

Both inductive and deductive reasoning often depend (
porting a conclusion on the basis of relationships between cla:

For a categorical argument to be sound, the structure of
gument must be valid and the premises acceptable.

The statistical generalization, based as it is on an inducti
from some to all, is never as certain as a conclusion draw
sound deductive reasoning.

The direction of inductive reasoning can vary. We may n(
cific instances and from them make general inferences, or
begin with a general idea and seek specific examples or data
port it.

For a statistical generalization to be reliable, the sample must be
adequate in size and representative of the target population.

With any generalization supported by specific examples, one
counterexample can discredit the conclusion.

KEY TERMS

Categorical syllogism   a deductive argument composed of three
classes; the argument has two premises and one conclusion derived from
the two premises.

Class   in logic all of the individual things—persons, objects, events,
ideas—that share a determinate property.

Deduction   a pattern of reasoning in which the conclusion follows of
necessity from the premises if the reasoning is valid.

Exclusion   a relationship between classes in which classes share no
members.

Hypothesis   a tentative generalization, a possible conclusion, an assertion we are interested in proving.

Inclusion   a relationship between classes in which every member of one
class is a member of another class.

Induction   a pattern of reasoning in which the conclusion follows only
with some degree of probability.

Overlap   a relationship between classes in which classes share at least
one member.

Particular proposition   refers to some members of a designated class.

Predicate   includes everything being asserted about the subject.

Projected property   what is to be determined about the target population.

Sample   the surveyed members of the target population.

Soundness   describes a deductive argument whose premises are acceptable and whose structure is valid.

Statistical generalization   a prediction about the distribution of a particular feature in a given group.

Subject   that part of the sentence about which something is being asserted.

Target population   the group about which the conclusion will be drawn.

Universal proposition   refers to all members of a designated class.

Validity   the conclusion follows of necessity from the premises; the form of the argument is correct.

CHAPTER 8

The Language of Argument—Style

Style is the dress of thought.

—SAMUEL WESLEY

Some may dismiss style as ornament, as the decorative frills of writing, or as something limited to matters of correct grammar and usage. A wiser definition of style would encompass more: choices of diction and word order that aim to strengthen our ideas and render them more precisely. An effective style chosen with your audience, your purpose, even your personal integrity in mind, can capture your reader's attention and possibly win the day for your argument. Style certainly includes a carefully proofread, grammatically correct final draft, but it also means well-crafted sentences that carry meaning gracefully to your readers, contributing to clear communication.

Sentence Length

How many times have you heard, "Keep it short, write short sentences?" Too many, probably. To be clear, direct, and concise, you do not always have to fall back on repetitive short sentences. As the discussion of logical joining in Chapters 3 and 4 and of appositives, parallel structures, and verbal modifiers to follow in this chapter suggests, you can extend the flow of your ideas and insert necessary information by expanding your repertoire of sentence structures.

Appositives—A Strategy for Defining and Identifying Terms Within the Sentence

As we illustrate in Chapter 5, abstract terms need defining so that our readers understand what we mean. One might agree in theory but question in practice how a writer defines terms without derailing the organization of the paper or paragraph. Often, the answer is to use **appositives**— noun phrases placed beside nouns to elaborate on their meaning (note the appositive here).

Here is Joan Didion, contemporary American essayist and noted stylist, giving us a vivid picture of the Los Angeles climate:

> In fact the climate is characterized by infrequent but violent extremes: *two periods of torrential subtropical rains* which continue for weeks and wash out the hills and send subdivisions sliding down toward the sea; *about twenty scattered days a year of the Santa Ana,* which, with its incendiary dryness, invariably means fire.

Didion has added details and combined ideas into one sentence by using appositives. In each case, the appositive (italics) modifies the noun "extremes," explains or defines what the extremes are, all within one sentence.

Appositives usually follow the nouns they modify, but some writers introduce a sentence with an appositive:

> *An expression of frustrated rage,* gangsta rap tries to be outrageous in order to provoke strong reactions.

The phrase, "an expression of frustrated rage" modifies "gangsta rap." Such additions allow a writer to include essential information or background details that may not warrant separate sentences. And as you pile up ideas, you can expand meaning even as you remain economical in sentence length. A series of appositional phrases often replaces a series of separate sentences expressing the same ideas. The effect is streamlined thought in fluent prose, as the following examples in Exercise 8A illustrate.

EXERCISE 8A

Recognizing Appositives

In the three passages that follow, identify the appositives and the nouns they modify by underlining the appositives and circling the nouns.

   1. A descriptive passage with examples

The Evertons are introduced to a second national peculiarity, one they will soon recognize on the streets of Ibarra and in towns and cities beyond. It is something they will see everywhere—a disregard for danger, a companionship with death. By the end of a year they will know it well: the antic bravado, the fatal games, the coffin shop beside the cantina, the sugar skulls on the frosted cake.

—HARRIET DOERR, STONES FOR IBARRA

2. Identification

Cotton Mather was an exception, one who so fully accepted and magnified the outlook of his locality that he has entered folklore as the archetypal Puritan, not only a villainous figure in the pages of Hawthorne, William Carlos Williams and Robert Lowell, but an object of parody even to his fellow townsmen in 18th-century Boston.

—LARZER ZIFF, THE NEW YORK TIMES BOOK REVIEW

3. Definition

As Baranczak points out, Milosz [Nobel Prize–winning poet] rejects symbols in favor of metonymy and synecdoche, those figures of speech which represent a whole by a thing allied to it or by a part of it.

—HELEN VENDLER IN THE NEW YORKER

Appositives and Argument

In arguments, appositives can be helpful, allowing you to expand and emphasize ideas and to show opposing points of view in the same sentence, as illustrated in the following example.

Unilateral disarmament, a policy that was considered dangerous and impractical by many, but one that was vigorously promoted by a number of hardline strategists, would require only one side to reduce its arms.

Two views on disarmament are juxtaposed in one strong sentence.

Punctuation of Appositives

Punctuation choices are simple and logical. In most cases, the appositive phrase is set off from the noun it modifies with commas. If you want greater emphasis, you can do as Harriet Doerr did and use a dash: "It is something they will see everywhere—a disregard for danger, a companionship with death."

Or choose a colon (appropriate only when the appositive ends a sentence) for an even sharper break as Joan Didion did:

In fact the climate is characterized by infrequent but violent extremes: two periods of torrential subtropical rains which continue for weeks and wash out the hills and send subdivisions sliding down toward the sea; about twenty scattered days a year of the Santa Ana, which, with its incendiary dryness, invariably means fire.

This passage also illustrates the way in which Didion varies punctuation to control all the information in this long sentence, providing logical markers for the reader: The colon sets off the appositive series; the semicolon marks the major division in the series, separating these points from the lesser pauses marked by commas.

For the vast array of punctuation rules and conventions in English, refer to a handbook. But as a start, think of punctuation as organizing patterns of thought and guiding the reader through the meaning of sentences. It is in this role that punctuation provides a vital service.

EXERCISE 8B

Creating Appositives

Most of you already use appositives to some extent in your writing whether you recognize them or not. But a little conscious practice may expand your knowledge of this useful device.

A. Combine the following sets of sentences by reducing one or more sentences to appositives. You may find more than one way to combine them.

> Example:
>
> Unilateral disarmament was considered dangerous and impractical. It was a policy that would require only one side to reduce its arms.
>
> becomes
>
> Unilateral disarmament, *a policy* that would require only one side to reduce its arms, was considered dangerous and impractical.
>
> or
>
> Unilateral disarmament, *a policy* that was *considered dangerous and* impractical, would require only one side to reduce its arms.

1. New York has long been the destination of America's adventurous young. It is a city of danger and opportunity.

2. Punk was a return to the roots of rock 'n' roll. It was a revolt against the predictability of disco.

3. People have very different ideas about the meaning of poverty. It is a condition that to some suggests insufficient income, to others laziness, and to still others a state of unwarranted discomfort.

4. Writing ability can have far-reaching effects on a college graduate's future accomplishments. Writing ability is the capacity to generate and organize relevant ideas, compose coherent sentences, choose precise diction, control mechanics.

5. They regarded the dictator with a mixture of fear and awe. These feelings were not conducive to an attitude of respect and trust toward their government.

6. According to the lieutenant's testimony during his court-martial, he was simply following orders as any military man is trained to do. These orders came from his commanding officers.

7. When the Soviets sent troops into Vilnius, Vytautas Landsbergis isolated himself and members of his government in a fortified parliament building. Vilnius is the capital of Lithuania and Landsbergis was the Lithuanian president.

8. Lisa read only spare modern novels. She liked ones with quirky characters, subtle structure, and ambiguous turns in plot, if they had plots at all.

9. Over time, psychiatrists have expanded the definition of the term "addiction." It is a word whose meaning has undergone revision to cover a broader range of compulsive behaviors. These compulsions now include sex, television viewing, designer clothes, shopping, computers . These extend to a whole spectrum of dependencies.

10. Concrete has spread over wider and wider areas of the American landscape. It has covered not just the weed patches, deserted lots, and infertile acres but whole pastures, hillsides, and portions of the sea and sky.

B. Finally, write a sentence about your major, your job, or another interest, being sure to include a related technical term. Then add an appositive that defines or illustrates the term.

C. Read the following passage:

James R. Johnson, general manager of the city zoo and a noted authority on reptiles and amphibians, died shortly after his morning run on Thursday, June 25. He was 47.

Mr. Johnson's body was found in his home, on Marsh Lane, a landmark craftsman house constructed by Johnson and his wife Marie out of unusual woods gathered all over the United States. Zoo staffers Jeffrey Kelley and Susan McMillan became concerned when Johnson failed to show up at the zoo and went to his house to investigate. James Kincaid, a spokesman for the zoo, notified authorities yesterday morning.

Mr. Johnson, manager of the zoo since 1992 and an expert on reptiles and amphibians since earning a PhD from Johns Hopkins University in 1980, was an avid runner and noted collector of books and manuscripts relating to his field. He was also well known for his personal collection of iguanas and rare lizards—particularly those found in Mexico, a favorite travel destination.

The coroner, Jacob Feinstein, reported that Johnson died suddenly of a cerebral hemorrhage. He was alone in the house at the time of his death.

Johnson is survived by his wife, Marie Coleman Johnson, daughter of Marvin Coleman, the district attorney from 1970 to 1998; his parents, Laura and Daniel Johnson of St. Louis; and three children: Beverly, Anna, and Robert, all residing at home. Funeral arrangements are pending.

Using this as a model, write an obituary for either a public figure or a fictional character you make up as you go along. Feel free to embroider upon the life of the person you choose for this assignment. Write as many appositives as you can think of and underline each of them. You will find it helpful to first identify the appositives in the passage above.

You may choose to do this exercise in small groups in class.

Parallelism

In previous chapters we have discussed strategies for increasing the coherent flow of ideas in your writing. **Parallel structures** used to organize items in a sentence, and even ideas in a paragraph, can contribute another element to coherence. The emphasis you achieve by harnessing your points into balanced grammatical structures increases the force of your written arguments.

The Structure of Parallelism

Parallel structure is simply a repetition of like grammatical units—a list of items if you will—often joined by conjunctions.

Look at the following two sentences:

I came, I saw, I conquered.
They plan to visit Rio, Madrid, and Bangkok.

Though different in content, they are similar in form: They both illustrate parallel structure. As stated above, parallel structure is simply repetition, usually of the same grammatical structures used in the same way, sometimes of the same word or phrase, often joined by the conjunctions *and, but, or, yet.*

Parallelism is a useful rhetorical device, providing a powerful means of emphasizing relationships by organizing ideas into predictable patterns. We hear a repetition and expect the pattern to continue. Read the two sentences above. Listen to the "ring" of the first sentence and the aid to attention and memory such a rhetorical device provides. Then note the logical organization and its contribution to meaning in the second sentence; the grammatical grouping underscores the implicit relationships between these cities: historical cities of diverse beauty, international centers representing distinct cultures, and interesting travel destinations for some, home for others.

When our expectations are thwarted, we may falter briefly in our reading or even lose the thread of the writer's thought. In most cases, our ear tells us when a series is wandering off the track, but sometimes it can be helpful to check the grammatical structure. Here is a strategy for examining your own sentences.

Think of parallel structures as lists, in the preceding case, a list of cities to visit. We can illustrate this list and the need for it to conform to the principles of parallelism by placing parallel lines at the beginning of the list:

> They plan to visit // Rio, Madrid, and Bangkok.

The conjunction "and" joins three proper nouns acting as direct objects of the verb "plan to visit."

We can do the same thing to more complicated sentences taken from writer Joan Didion's essay on Alcatraz, "Rock of Ages."

> It is not an unpleasant place to be, out there on Alcatraz with only // the *flowers* and the *wind* and a bell *buoy* moaning and the *tide* surging through the Golden Gate. . . . [a list of nouns as direct objects of the preposition "with"]
>
> Once a week the Harts take their boat to San Francisco to // *pick up* their mail and *shop* at the big Safeway in the Marina. . . . [a list of two infinitive phrases]
>
> Mr. Scott, whose interest in penology dates from the day his office acquired Alcatraz as a potential property, // *talked about* // *escapes* and *security routines* and *pointed out* the beach where Ma Barker's son Doc was killed trying to escape. [This sentence contains two lists, one within the other—two verbs for the subject "Mr. Scott"; and two nouns acting as direct objects of "talked about."]

Now read the next sentence (aloud if possible) and hear how the loss of expected balance or harmony offends the ear.

> When I should be studying, I will, instead, waste time by watching television or daydream.

The two verbs are not in the same form and are therefore not parallel. They can be made parallel by simply changing "daydream" to "daydreaming."

While it is important to listen for grammatical parallel structures in a series, English can be somewhat flexible when it comes to parallelism. For example, few readers would object to this sentence:

> The bus system is economical, but it is crowded, uncomfortable, and may not be depended on.

Here the third element, a phrase with a verb, does not conform to the grammatical structure of the first two, both adjectives, yet it is neither confusing nor harsh in its rhythm. All three elements serve as complements to *bus system*. We could easily revise the ending to read "undependable," but some writers might prefer the original. Careful writers make such decisions judiciously, generally preferring to maintain the grammatical and rhetorical integrity of a parallel series.

Before doing Exercise 8C, note the rhetorical effects of parallel structure on the following passage taken from *The Road from Coorain*, an autobiography by Jill Ker Conway, the first woman president of Smith College. Use our system of notation to mark off the different series or lists.

> Those night train journeys had their own mystery because of the clicking of the rails, the shafts of light pouring through the shutters of the sleeping compartment as we passed stations, and the slamming of doors when the train stopped to take on passengers. In the morning there was the odd sight of green landscape, trees, grass, banks of streams—an entirely different palette of colors, as though during the night we had journeyed to another country. Usually I slept soundly, registering the unaccustomed sounds and images only faintly. This time I lay awake and listened, opened the shutters and scanned unknown platforms, and wondered about the future.

This passage has several parallel lists. Did you find them all?

EXERCISE 8C

Supplying Parallel Elements

Complete these sentences with a parallel element.

1. Writing a good paper is a task that demands // hard work, patience, and . . .
2. She // rushed home, threw her assorted debris into a closet, and . . .
3. Fewer Americans are saving these days // not because they don't think it's wise to save, but . . .
4. The first lady is a woman who // has an open mind but . . .
5. The first lady is a woman who has // an open mind and . . .

In the following sentences, identify the misfits—the element of the sentence that is not parallel—and revise the sentence so that all the elements of the list are parallel. Putting slashes where each series starts will help you see where the sentence goes off track.

6. Many influences shape a child's development: family, church, peer groups, economic, social, and school.

7. Michelle lives in a neighborhood where knife wounds, killings, and people are raped are as common as the sun rising in the morning.

8. He helped to wash the car and with cleaning out the garage.

9. Free inquiry in the search for truth sometimes necessitates the abandonment of law and order but which always demands freedom of expression.

10. Pineapple juice is my favorite because it is a good source of energy, it isn't artificially sweetened, and because of its low cost.

11. The president launched a campaign against drunk driving and promoting the use of seat belts.

Now write three of your own sentences—one with three or more verbs sharing the same subject, one with three or more adjectives, and one with three or more nouns. Use as your subject a topic you are currently writing on for this or another class.

Logic of the Parallel Series

The items in a list, however, must not only be **grammatically** similar but also relate **logically** to one another. Sometimes faulty parallelism offends not only our ear but also our reason.

> People who have "book smarts" usually work in places like // *libraries* or *assistants* to attorneys.

Though the writer has joined two nouns (grammatically compatible elements, both nouns), an assistant of any kind cannot be a "place." He has lost control of the sentence because he has forgotten where the list begins. There is more than one way to fix this sentence, to make it logical and balanced. How would you correct it?

To understand further what we mean, look at the following sentence.

> We will have to look at the language used in the text for sexism, racism, and bias.

The list in this sentence is "sexism, racism, and bias." The list is *grammatically* parallel because all three words in the list are nouns, but not *logically* parallel since sexism, racism, and bias are presented as three separate and distinct categories when in fact sexism and racism are particular forms of bias; they are included in what we can call the class or group of *bias*, not separate from it. One way to correct this faulty logic would be to replace *bias* with *other forms of bias* and thus illustrate the logical and actual relationship that exists between the three terms.

EXERCISE 8D

Editing the Illogical Series

Revise the following sentences for logical parallel structure.

1. In their attempt to excel, our employees often work extra hours and work through many lunch hours.
2. I have seen city ordinances that do not allow smoking in restaurants popping up all over the place: in offices, in buildings.
3. I asked Linda if she had any materialistic aspirations such as living in a mansion, having a nice car, or being extremely wealthy.
4. The customers at the bank where I work are wealthy depositors, checking account holders, cooperative individuals, and those who are thoughtlessly rude to me.
5. For the most part, he is handsome, active, and well dressed, usually in expensive clothes or a suit and tie.

Emphasizing Ideas with Parallelism

As we mentioned above, parallelism can be a powerful rhetorical device. Beyond the sentence, parallelism can provide emphasis and organize major ideas in paragraphs, particularly in argument. Pamela Reynolds, an editor at the *The Boston Globe*, focuses her reader's attention on the pain and horror of a race riot in Los Angeles by closing an editorial with emphatic parallelism. In both paragraphs she relies on parallel structure at both the sentence and paragraph levels.

Read the following passage aloud for full effect and then mark examples of parallelism, both within sentences and running through the paragraphs.

At least half a dozen other stores within walking distance of my parents' home had disappeared in smoke and flames as well. The beauty supply store was gone. The liquor store was trashed and looted. My father sighed. Life wouldn't get any easier with fewer stores, fewer banks, fewer businesses in the area. I was sad that things like this were happening.

I was sad that a community would turn on itself, and destroy the banks, stores, supermarkets that are already so scarce in black neighborhoods. I was sad that innocent motorists had been bludgeoned on national television. I was sad that I, in Boston, couldn't protect my family, who had protected me while I was growing up in Los Angeles. I was sad because I never thought I would ever identify with the kind of bleak anger and dark frustration that drives a riot.

Sentence Focus—Techniques For Sharpening The Flow of Ideas

He draweth out the thread of his verbosity finer than the staple of his argument.

—SHAKESPEARE, *LOVE'S LABORS LOST*

We are all familiar with the confusion and obfuscation of much official prose today—political, bureaucratic, academic. Some of this muddled language may be deliberate, to conceal meaning, as we discuss above. But often it is inadvertent, a result of writers surrendering to the abstractness of language, of fuzzy language overwhelming complex ideas. We refer to such writing as "unfocused," in much the same way that fuzzy, confused thought is often unfocused. It may help you to understand our discussion of sentence **focus** to think in terms of focusing a camera. When you take a picture, you select and concentrate on a given image—you focus your camera to sharpen that image. An unfocused photograph is blurred. In much the same way, unfocused writing may be easy to write, but it is usually difficult to read.

The New Yorker magazine found this example of unfocused writing:

> Agreement on the overall objective of decision usefulness was a prerequisite to the establishment of a conceptual framework. Now, at least, we know where we are headed. (The Week in Review, newsletter of Deloitte Haskins & Sells)

After this, do we know where they are going?

Compare the following memo from the Internal Revenue Service and a possible revision.

> Advice has been requested concerning tax deductions for research expenses, including traveling expenses, incurred by college and university professors. (original)

> College and university professors have requested advice about tax deductions for their research expenses, including traveling expenses. (possible revision)

Which version is clearer, easier to read? We assume that the majority of readers will prefer the second. What are the differences? The possible revision is shorter by two words. But is this the only distinction? Make your evaluation before reading on.

Calvin and Hobbes

by Bill Watterson

Concrete Subjects

Look at the grammatical subjects in the two sentences on p. 215—"advice" in the first, "professors" in the second—and notice what kinds of nouns they are. One is an *abstract noun,* the other a *concrete noun.* Because the sentence subject tends to reflect what a passage is about, the subject is where the *focus* of a sentence usually sits. A concrete noun is capable of producing a visual picture and thus can also *focus* a reader's attention more closely. When that concrete noun is a person or people, readers can visualize an action and so more readily follow the precise progression of ideas in a sentence. Hence, "professors" as the subject of the second sentence is preferable to the "advice" of the original. The reader can see the "professor" but not the abstraction "advice."

Active and Passive Verbs

Now look at the verbs. In the original sentence on tax deduction, the verb is "has been requested" while in the revision the verb is "has requested." The first is **passive voice,** the second, **active voice.** The basic distinction is that

> with a passive verb, the subject is acted upon; the subject is not doing anything in the sentence—it is passive.

"Advice" is being requested, not, obviously, doing the requesting.

> When the verb is active, its subject is performing the action of the sentence,

and thus the reader can see a subject doing something. The "professors" are doing the requesting.

We must wade through the original IRS memo to understand the point, whereas in the possible revision we see from the beginning that professors are requesting advice, people are doing something. A possible confusion about who is doing the requesting is made clear. Bureaucrats, often writing about vague or abstract subjects in which they have little invested interest or feeling, can easily fall into the passive verb trap. They are rarely the ones actually *doing* anything they are writing about. Don't let your academic writing succumb to this danger.

Sentences written in the passive are easy to spot because they always follow a grammatical pattern:

> subject + a form of the verb "to be" (am, is, are, was, were) + the past participle of the verb (usually with an -*ed* ending) + an expressed or implied "by" phrase, which contains the agent of the verb.

(subject)	(to be)	(past participle)	(optional by phrase)
Mistakes	were	made	(by the chief of staff)

The following two sentences say essentially the same thing, but note how the change in the form of the sentence shifts the emphasis from the concrete subject, "J. Robert Oppenheimer," to the abstract, "elemental danger."

> *Active* J. Robert Oppenheimer, one of the creators of the atom bomb, *felt* the elemental danger loosed on the earth.
> *Passive* The elemental danger loosed on the earth *was felt* by J. Robert Oppenheimer, one of the creators of the atom bomb.

Which version do you prefer? Why?

Passive Verbs and Evasion

A less honorable use of the passive, however, one politicians have a tendency to rely on, is, to evade responsibility. William Safire in his *New York Times* column, "On Language," comments on this predilection, focusing on a former White House chief of staff, John Sununu, who, when asked at a press conference about the use of government funds for personal expenses, replied, "Obviously, some mistakes were made."

Safire notes that "The passive voice acknowledges the errors, but it avoids the blame entirely. . . . When deniability is impossible, dissociation is the way, and the [passive voice] allows the actor to separate himself from the act."

When the Passive Is Appropriate

Aiming for direct, assertive prose, careful writers usually prefer active verbs. But, on occasion, when one wants to emphasize someone or something not performing the action in a sentence, the passive is useful. Scientists and social scientists, for example, must often focus on the content of their research rather than on themselves as researchers. Under such circumstances, the passive serves a useful purpose.

> This research *was undertaken* with a grant from the National Science Foundation.
> rather than
> I *undertook* this research with a grant from the National Science Foundation.

In this case, the **focus**, the emphasis, of the sentence falls on *research* rather than on *I*. Thus *research should* be the grammatical sentence subject.

Not surprisingly, however, when you rely on concrete nouns as your sentence subject, you stand a better chance of automatically using an active verb. Concrete subjects, as we point out above, can *do* something whereas abstract nouns usually cannot.

More Ways to Sharpen Focus

Beyond the issues of concrete subjects and active verbs, we can note four additional features to be alert for when considering sharp focus:

1. **The logical progression of focus:**
   Central to good paragraph focus is the logical progression of ideas within a paragraph. Read the following paragraph closely to see how research physician and writer Lewis Thomas maintains consistent sentence subjects, emphasizing the topic of the paragraph— how we relate to the concept of death. Note how the grammatical subjects provide a coherent line of reasoning even though at the heart of the passage lies an abstract idea.

   We continue to share with our remotest ancestors the most tangled and evasive attitudes about death, despite the great distance **we** have come in understanding some of the profound aspects of biology. **We** have as much distaste for talking about personal death as for thinking about it; it is an indelicacy, like talking in mixed company about venereal disease or abortion in the old days. **Death** on a grand scale does not bother us in the same special way; **we** can sit around a dinner table and discuss war, involving 60 million volatilized human deaths, as though **we** were talking about bad weather; **we** can watch abrupt bloody death every day, in color, on films and television, without blinking back a tear. But when the numbers of dead are very small, and very close, **we** begin to think in scurrying circles. At the very center of the problem is the naked cold **deadness** of one's own self, the only reality in nature of which **we** can have absolute certainty, and **it** is unquestionable, unthinkable. **We** may be even less willing to face the issue at first hand than our predecessors because of a secret new hope that maybe **it** will go away. **We** like to think, hiding the thought, that with all the marvelous ways in which *we* seem now to lead nature around by the nose, perhaps *we* can avoid the central problem if **we** just become, next year, say, a bit smarter.

2. **The expletive "there is":**
   The expletive "there is" ("there are," "there were") is useful when a writer means that something exists:

   There are several reasons for recycling.
   There is every reason to believe that a third political party will grow stronger in the future.

   But when you can use a concrete noun paired with a more vigorous verb, the prose is tighter. If you are unconvinced on the "there" issue, read the following paragraph from an essay written for Writing Assignment 4 (Chapter 2).

Children and the ability to have them are equally important to the society of the Small People. *There is* only one word for sex in their language and it translates as "to plant a wise one." To me this implies the final product is more important than the act of "planting a wise one." *There is* also a great emphasis put on childhood. *There are* seven terms used to describe stages of life from birth to puberty. *There is* only one word describing life after puberty.

This paragraph conveys the existence of the terms but very little additional reasoning. Poor focus is combined with choppy prose and needless passive verbs. Note how easy it is to avoid vigorous, active prose once you let the "there disease" take over. Let's fix the focus in three of these sentences.

Original
There is also a great emphasis put on childhood. There are seven terms used to describe stages of life from birth to puberty. There is only one word describing life after childhood. (original)

Revision
They clearly emphasize childhood, using seven terms to describe stages of life from birth to puberty, with only one word describing life after childhood. (revision)

The revision is tighter and reveals the logical relationship between each point. When the sentences stood isolated with their "theres," that logic was less obvious.

3. **Over use of "to be"**

Beware of the verb "to be" (am, is, are, was, were). It is, of course, an important verb, but again, it states existence (being) only, and you often want your prose to be more expressive than that. Here's another reason to use passive verbs sparingly; they always, by definition, contain a form of the verb "to be." The same applies to "there are" sentences.

4. **Dangling modifiers**

Experienced writers often turn verbs into **verbal modifiers** (participles such as running, buying, avoiding). Such transformations increase sentence fluency and combine ideas to express logical relationships. Look at the examples below.

two choppy sentences
She *thought* critically about the issue. She *recognized* that her opponents had a good argument.

one revision
Thinking critically about the issue, she recognized that her opponents had a good argument.

another option
She thought critically about the issue, *recognizing* that her opponents had a good argument.

Such modifiers can enhance the fluency of your prose, but you need to be cautious about their logic. When you use a verbal as a modifier, the person or object serving as the sentence subject must usually also work logically as the agent of the modifier.

In the two revisions above, "she" is logical as the agent of "thinking" or "recognizing" as well as the grammatical subject of the actual verb in each variant of the sentence.

When the logical agent is missing from the sentence, the verbal modifier is said to dangle, hence the term **dangling modifier.** One newspaper columnist, a stickler for sound sentence structure, was disgusted with himself when he fell into the dangling modifier trap:

"Having used up all his frequent-flier miles to Paris to woo and win her, Attorney Joe Freitas and Douce Francois . . ."

Had he looked back, he would have noticed that it wasn't logical for both of them to have used his frequent flier miles in this context, and Douce was unlikely to have been wooing herself. As he wrote in a future correction, "right there I should have stopped and started over."

EXERCISE 8E

Repairing Dangling Modifiers

Many an experienced writer has lost track of the logic in her sentence. Identify the illogical dangling modifiers in these examples from published writers and recommend a remedy.

1. While writing today's piece, Gerald Nachman's column was lost in the computer. (Did his column write itself?)

2. After passing around pictures of Christopher, the couple's conversation returned to the latest Star Wars movie. (Can a conversation pass pictures around?)

3. Walking up the staircase to Joyce Carol Oates' office in the Creative Arts building, through the halls that smell of artists' paint, past the neat rows of studios and classrooms, the blood-stained story of her most recent book, "Angel of Light," seems a tale told on another planet. (Did her blood-stained story walk up the staircase?)

4. Speaking as an old friend, there has been a disturbing tendency in statements emanating from Beijing to question the good faith of our President on the issue of Taiwan. (Do you see how the "there" construction has led the "old friend" astray? Did a disturbing tendency speak as an old friend?)

Revising for sharp sentence and paragraph focus helps to maintain the clear, direct expression you and your readers demand, no matter what your academic or professional discipline. Keep in mind, however, that revising is often most effective as a late stage in the writing process. We may expect a first draft to have several poorly focused sentences and paragraphs. Look back at Chapter 1 to refresh your memory on the writing process.

EXERCISE 8F

Sharpening Sentence Focus for Clear Expression and Fluent Style

A. Revise the following sentences for good focus, combining where appropriate for a smooth, logical flow of ideas. Look back at the discussion of active and passive verbs, overuse of "there" and verb "to be" constructions. Think in terms of assertive sentences, ones that use strong verbs and say directly who is doing what.

> **Example:** It was while I was waiting in the registration line that the realization came to me of how complicated a university is.
>
> revision
>
> While I was waiting in the registration line, I came to realize (or I realized) how complicated a university is.

1. Fear of brutality from customers is a concern many prostitutes have.
2. When it is seen that a criminal act is being committed, a call should be placed to the police.
3. A strike is used when employees want things their employers are unwilling to provide.
4. The leaders have determined that the spiritual initiate has no need of worldly things, so only minimum wages are paid.
5. There is a much bigger emphasis placed on the role of the individual in this generation than in our parents' generation.
6. Teenagers are easily influenced by TV. Specific violent acts have been committed by teenagers after such acts have been shown on prime time.
7. The people of this tribe are literate, given that they have twenty terms for "book." There also may be several kinds of artwork they create, since they have nine words for "artist."
8. Having developed a complex social order, cultural patterns have been shown by the people of this tribe. These patterns are reflected in their arts and their theater.

B. Now try your hand at revising this student paragraph with the same strategies in mind. Note how difficult it is to follow the writer's reasoning in this poorly focused paragraph.

There are many ways to be a bad teacher. There are mistakes made by bad teachers that come in a variety of forms. Assignments are given unclearly so that when papers are graded it isn't known what students are graded on or what the grade means. Grading by the ineffective teacher is according to arbitrary standards, so students think their grades are unfair. There are problems with explanations given by bad teachers and understanding is hard to arrive at. This disorganization can be seen by students when the poor teacher fails to bring all materials to class. There are many explanations given, but the dissatisfaction of students is clearly not done away with. In such cases it is not clear who is responsible for a bad grade—the student or the teacher.

Wrap-up on writing style

1. Use parallel structure to increase coherence, organize lists, and emphasize relationships.

2. Focus your thoughts and your writing on precisely what you want to say. When logically possible, use concrete, consistent subjects. As you develop ideas through a paragraph, your sentence subjects develop and change, reflecting the new information introduced in the previous sentence.

3. Unless you have compelling reasons for preferring the passive voice, choose active verbs that allow for more direct, vigorous expression of your ideas.

4. Unless you intend to express the existence of something, avoid the over-used, empty phrases "there are" and "it is" and in the process look for more vigorous verbs.

5. To increase the flow of ideas, expand your sentence repertoire with appositives and verbal modifiers.

Caution: **Do not think about these writing strategies until you have completed a first draft. Content and organization must come first; then you can turn your attention to coherent, graceful sentences and the final proofread for spelling and other mechanical details.**

Revision

Throughout the text, we have discussed ways to both write and rewrite your papers. You may want to review Chapter 1 for the sections on audience and purpose and the writing process. In particular, the section on writing first drafts provides essential material when it comes to revising your papers. Assignments in Chapter 4 also offer ways in which longer written arguments can be written in stages, allowing you to separate the steps toward a successful finished paper. The sample essays in that chapter may help you think about the organization of your own papers. We offer suggestions for revising at the sentence level in several places throughout the text, particularly in this chapter, where we illustrate how you can polish for coherence, style, and fluency. In Chapter 9, you will find suggestions for selecting and researching your topic.

As a final step, you always need to proofread carefully for mechanical errors—typographical and spelling errors, omitted words—as well as for appropriate verb tenses, subject/verb agreement, and pronoun reference. After reading through your final draft with close attention to detail, try reading it aloud, slowly, perhaps to a critical friend or classmate. Reading pages in reverse order can help you find small technical mistakes easily overlooked when you read straight through for meaning.

WRITING ASSIGNMENT 18

Revising an Essay

Choose one of the assignments you completed earlier and revise it in light of material covered in this chapter particularly and in the book in general, and in response to suggestions from your instructor or possibly your class-mates. As you reread your work, consider whether you have changed your mind about the issues and whether you have discovered new material relevant to your topic. You may also want to look back to Chapter 6 to see if your arguments contain any logical fallacies and to Chapter 7 for reminders on logical thinking. Consider your word choice carefully in light of Chapter 5, The Language of Argument: Definition, and review the "Wrap-up on writing style" above for a refresher on polishing your prose. Read your own prose just as critically as you did the stories in Chapter 2 or in any other important academic work.

Going back to a paper after time has elapsed can give you a useful new perspective. Whichever assignment you choose, these skills and the passage of time will help you strengthen the draft you choose to work on.

SUMMARY

Style as well as correctness is an essential part of effective written argument.

Parallelism is a useful rhetorical device, providing a powerful means of emphasizing relationships by organizing ideas into predictable patterns.

For a vigorous and concise writing style, writers prefer concrete subjects and active verbs and use "there is" only to express existence.

Combining and expanding sentences with appositives and verbal modifiers increase the logical flow of ideas.

Revising a manuscript plays an important role in strengthening any writer's prose.

KEY TERMS

Active voice   a sentence construction in which the subject performs the action of the sentence. Example: The Supreme Court ruled on the constitutionality of the 1991 civil rights legislation.

Appositives   noun phrases placed beside nouns to elaborate on their meaning; useful for describing, identifying, and defining.

Dangling modifier   a verbal modifier that lacks a logical agent in the clause it modifies. Example: *Before resorting to violence,* all other means of resolution must be thoroughly investigated.

Focus   concrete, consistent sentence subjects that reflect the rhetorical subject of the writing.

Parallel structure   a repetition of like grammatical units, often joined by the conjunctions and, but, yet.

Passive voice   a sentence construction in which the subject is acted upon, not doing anything in the sentence. Example: The constitutionality of the 1991 civil rights legislation was ruled on by the Supreme Court.

Verbal modifier   participles—verb forms usually ending in *-ing*—used as sentence modifiers. Example: *Before resorting to violence,* we must thoroughly investigate all other means of resolution.

CHAPTER 9

Research and Documentation

Research

Think First

Before you rush to the library or your computer, topic in hand, to begin your research, consider the two important preliminary steps.

A. **First Step, the Topic:** In some instances your instructor may select your topic for you or assign a general subject area from a reader. Or, you may develop a topic of your own, either from a subject in which you are already interested or from a library search. Databases in your library or keyword searches on the Internet may prove helpful as you look for ideas. For example, let's say you are interested in Japan. You might start with a keyword search on the search engine, *Infoseek* (**<www.Infoseek.com>**) and, following their directions for "Tips/Quick reference," search for ideas by narrowing the scope: *Japan* and *"Samurai tradition"* or *Japan* and *"Mitsubishi production."* (For additional discussion of researching your topic on the Internet, see below under "How to Conduct Your Research" and the subheading "The Internet.") Your topic must be sufficiently narrow and focused, no matter where it comes from. Once you think you know your topic, you need to narrow it to a clear **question at issue** (see Chapter 4), a process that will help you to focus your research efforts. With only a general topic to guide you, you might become lost in an avalanche of material, taking voluminous notes, conducting fruitless computer searches, most of which would have no application to your final paper.

Look at the difference in scope between an issue and a related question at issue:

Issue: Protection of the environment
Question at issue: Should the environment be protected at the expense of jobs?
Or, even more refined
Question at issue: Should spotted owl habitat be protected at the expense of jobs in the lumber industry?

Imagine what it would be like to research the issue, and then imagine what it would be like to research one of the questions at issue. Which would be easier?

Sometimes you need to do further investigating in the library or on the Internet before you are able to arrive at a question at issue, just as you might have done when first deciding on a broader topic. Or you may be led to revise your question at issue as your research leads you in unexpected directions. But a well-focused question at issue is essential for ensuring that you know where you are going with your paper and what further research you need to do. Narrowing the focus of your research pays substantial dividends in time, energy, and the ultimate success of your paper, although it is also important to keep an open mind as you explore multiple sources in depth.

After you have narrowed your topic to a question at issue and done some research, you will be ready to take a stand on the question, your research providing the basis for your position. Expressing your opinion on the question at issue will help you craft a thesis. You may argue for or against a position or you may want to qualify it without taking a particular stance. No matter where you stand, you will eventually need to express the primary conclusion you have reached in a **thesis statement**, one or two sentences clearly stating the position you will argue in your paper. This thesis may be tentative, subject to revisions as you continue to explore your topic, but as your drafts begin to take shape you will need a thesis to help organize your ideas and guide you to a finished written argument.

As you prepare a research paper, you will find it useful to review strategies discussed under "Writing as a Process" in Chapter 1 and suggestions for narrowing an issue, writing a thesis, and shaping an argument in Chapter 4. If you have studied journalism, you are familiar with the useful questions Who? What? When? Where? Why? How? that journalists use to probe a topic.

It is often a good idea to check your topic and the question at issue with your instructor before you start off on an unproductive tangent. Try talking to others, inside and outside of class, and when possible, pursue a subject that relates to your own interests. But don't be afraid of exploring an issue that's new to you. That's how you expand your knowledge.

As a preliminary step, after you have established your question at issue, you may want to write a short **proposal or abstract** (for placement in your paper, see below). Doing so gives you a chance to express in writing just what your topic is, why you are exploring it, who your audience is (see "Audience and Purpose" in Chapter 1), and, when you are ready, what position you expect to take.

B. **Second Step, the Argument**. As well as establishing a question at issue at the outset of your research, you should construct an argument both for and against the question at issue. This argument will consist of premises in their roughest form—not developed, not supported, not yet refined. Such a framework or working outline will serve as a guide as you develop your paper.

You will already have some knowledge based on your experience, your reading, or your Internet searches. This knowledge may be general but it will be sufficient to enable you to construct a preliminary argument (see Assignment 9, Chapter 4).

The two advantages to this approach are as follows:

1. You are not overwhelmed by the opinions of experts, feeling as if they have left you nothing to say.

2. Your research has a focused, precise purpose as you look for support for your premises, discovering in the process gaps in your reasoning and counterarguments that had not occurred to you.

Don't be surprised if you find yourself changing direction as you gather more information. This stage can sometimes seem chaotic, but the process of exploring available material on your topic is essential to learning as you write. Research and writing about what you know and what you uncover will not only provide unexpected opportunities for discovering new material on your topic but may also lead you to take a different position. This is the point at which you may need to revise your question at issue and your working thesis. In the process, you will write a more convincing paper and also expand your own outlook. Being able to look at an issue from another perspective represents an important step in refining **critical thinking**.

How to Conduct Your Research

What follows is a condensed summary of strategies, sources, and documentation conventions necessary for writing a successful research paper. If you have not been assigned an additional guide to research you may find it useful to select one of the many excellent little books currently available. *The Essential Guide to Writing Research Papers* (Lester), and *Researching Online* (edited by Munger), are short and easy to use. *The Little, Brown Handbook*, available in both complete and compact editions, and *S F Writer* offer more in-depth guidance. The list will have changed by the time this book is published. The Modern Language Association (MLA) publishes helpful guides to conducting research and documenting sources: *The MLA Handbook for Writers of Research Papers* and *The MLA Style Manual and Guide to Scholarly Publishing*, the second designed for more advanced research needs. The **MLA** Web site: **<www.mla.org/>** keeps the technical details of documenting electronic sources up to date under the heading, *MLA Style.* Their handbooks can be ordered through this Web site. The American Psychological Association (**APA**), preferred in the social sciences, also publishes research information on the Web. Their home page does not offer documentation support, but currently two additional sites do: **<www.lib.ricks.edu/inet_apa.html>** provides excellent information on documentation of electronic sites. **<Http://humanities. byu.edu/linguistics/Henrichsen/APA/APA01.html>** offers thorough coverage of the APA approach to documenting sources and gives a broad range of examples. The APA also produces the *Publication Manual of the American Psychological Association.* Be warned that these sites have a way of disappearing as others emerge, so no list can be definitive. In addition, you may want to consult your instructor for specific research guidelines and investigate whether your campus offers courses in using the Internet. Your **reference librarians** are a valuable asset in suggesting useful bound indexes and online sources. We suggest you establish a working relationship with such a librarian as a guide to the many resources available in both print and electronic sources.

Reading Strategies

If you are limiting your research to a collection of preselected articles in an assigned reader, some of the work will have already been done for you. If, however, you are going farther afield and must survey a number of books, articles, and Web sites, you will have to use some methods of reading for main points without including every word. For example, learn to select **relevant** material by checking the table of contents, subtitles, abstracts of longer articles, topic sentences of paragraphs, and opening and concluding paragraphs. With a book, read the introduction and preface to be sure the book is what you think it is. Where possible, try to determine whether the author is a **credible source**. If you find one book or article useful, be alert for references to additional sources and bibliographies mentioned there.

Essential to your research in books and journals or in electronic sources is **critical judgment**. As you read, **think critically** about the author, the point of view, the quality of the argument, the date a piece was written, and the possible relevance of this date.

From the outset, start taking notes that highlight the important points. Small cards work well, because you can shuffle the sequence when you start writing the paper. Be careful to write down the complete bibliographical material you'll need later when you provide the necessary documentation of your sources. Formats for this follow. For a more in-depth treatment of the technicalities of attribution, consult one of the books mentioned above. With the proliferation of electronic sources, the mechanics of documenting sources has grown ever more complex.

When gathering material from sources, either quote exactly, paraphrase what an author says, or summarize the passage.

Direct quotation: A word-for-word transcription of what an author says, requiring quotation marks.

Paraphrase: A restatement of an idea in language that retains the meaning but changes the exact wording. Such references require documentation but not quotation marks.

Summary: A short restatement of the main points in a passage, an article, or a book. See "Summaries," Chapter 3. When summarizing the works of others, you need to document the source.

Printed Sources

Although a vast amount of information is now available on the computer, if you are looking up material dated before the last ten years, you need to be familiar with some of the print indexes available in your library. Of particular use: The *Readers' Guide to Periodical Literature* (your library may have this on a CD-Rom database) lists articles from a broad range of general magazines. You can find articles on more specific subject areas in, for example, the *Humanities Index, Social Science Index, Business Periodicals Index, Biological and Agricultural Index, Education Index, Applied Science and Technology Index.* For even more specialized searches, you could try sources such as the *Music Index* or *Philosopher's Index.* Newspapers such as *The Washington Post, The New York Times, The Wall Street Journal, The Los Angeles Times, The Chicago Tribune*, and possibly your own local newspaper are indexed for back issues not available on the Web. For biographical information on specific individuals, you will find a number of biographical resources on your library shelves. Ask a librarian to point you in their direction. When you are searching for a specific essay published in a larger collection, you can turn to the *Essay and General Literature Index*. With time and experience in your library, you will find many more useful sources of data.

The government publishes a vast number of pamphlets and other documents important for research purposes. More and more of these are becoming available on the Web, but once again, you may need to consult your reference librarian. The *Monthly Catalog of US Government Publications* and the *Congressional Record* are two useful sources. In some cases you may need to order a particular document directly from the Government Printing Office, Washington, DC, 20402.

Once you have located a specific citation for an article, you will be able to find the text on either microfilm or microfiche in your library, except for very early editions, which may still be bound. Your library will have an alphabetized list of publications available on your campus and identify the format.

The Internet is a seductive source of research information, but because of limitations discussed below, you will be wise to include books and journals, the traditional print media, as a solid basis for much of your research.

The Internet

The Internet and the World Wide Web, which attempts to gather up and organize the material on the Internet, have revolutionized research in the last ten years. Electronic resources vary from library to library, but most offer databases that list recent newspapers, magazines, journals, and speeches, in some cases providing texts of articles in full. Some of these databases can be accessed from your home computer; for others you must go to your library. Although some, such as Lexis-Nexis (law, newspapers, and business), may charge for their services, others are free to students, some free to all users. To access databases offered through your campus library from home, you need a modem attached to your computer, a telephone line connection, and software provided by your university. For direct Internet connection on your own computer, all you need is the modem with telephone connection and an Internet server, often offered through your college or university.

Electronic searches can be confusing—think of the Internet as a vast unindexed encyclopedia. Or, as someone said: Everybody is connected but nobody is in charge. The seemingly random nature of information on the Internet makes it difficult to find precisely what you want. The metaphors imbedded in the terms "Internet" and "Web" say a lot about the shape of this field of virtual knowledge—an endless sea of netting or webbing, every corner filled with facts and ideas waiting to be found, constantly ebbing and flowing, never stable or complete. Once again, we urge you to consult your research librarian or instructor for directions to specific sources.

The Internet has introduced an entirely new vocabulary, as you already know. Once you have the necessary equipment, you need three different levels of access for maximum information:

> An **Internet server** or **provider.** Technology is rapidly expanding, but your university, telephone company, cable company, and such commercial organizations as AOL, JUNO, and others link users to the Internet.
>
> Commercial **browsers,** such as Netscape Navigator or Microsoft Internet Explorer, take you to the World Wide Web.
>
> A constantly multiplying list of **search engines** helps you narrow your searches.

As new companies emerge and Internet use is refined, the character and names of these steps to successful interaction with the Internet will keep changing, with some trusted sites suddenly disappearing.

SEARCHING THE INTERNET   Material for your research paper may be scattered all over the Internet. Your best way to reach the Internet is through the World Wide Web, using one of the commercial browsers. Organizing the immense amount of random knowledge available, a growing number of **search engines** operate on the Web to help you find what you need. If you are still looking for a topic, you can begin with a **subject search**. Once you have settled on your topic and narrowed it to a specific question at issue, you will be ready to refine your search. First, you will want to experiment with **keywords**, which you type in as you try different search engines (see examples below). While you may be lucky if your keyword is precise enough, many such searches give you so many responses that you don't know where to begin. Usually, those that seem most relevant appear at the top of the list, but often the initial list is too long to be useful. To be more successful, you need to **refine your searches**, providing clusters of words rather than single terms. For example: *First Amendment* and *the Internet* rather than just the *First Amendment*. Most search engines now use techniques known as **Boolean** for phrase searches, but each search engine depends on variations of the method. You need to check the "Help" menus to find specific suggestions for what many call "advanced search." Here, for a start, are a few common Boolean search devices shared by most resources.

> Some search engines ask that you group more than one word as a single term by putting double quotation marks around the words; for example, *"nature versus nurture," "Dolly the sheep."* Proper names, *Abraham Lincoln* for example, do not need the quotations.
>
> The word *AND* indicates that you want all the terms to appear in your search; for example, *selling AND embryos.*

The word *NOT* indicates that you want to exclude irrelevant words; for example, *embryos NOT "adoption of."*

The word *OR* can widen your search to two or more terms; for example, *"indecent speech" OR "pornographic speech" OR "Cyberporn."*

On some databases, you group words in a phrase by placing parentheses around the words: (*embryos and selling*) not *adoption.*

On the search engine Yahoo!, for example, you can limit your search to the titles of articles: *t: harassment,* means the term must appear in a document's title only.

Proximity operators can also help in some instances: *adj.* (adjacent*), near, before, followed by.* Such terms can help limit the number of hits—the listing of sites you specify—to a manageable number.

Many sites have highlighted **links** that can connect you to related sites, some useful, others false leads. Links usually appear in blue and are underlined. Most of you are familiar by now with the feature called either a **bookmark** or a **favorite place** by which you can store a useful site in your own list. Given how tricky it sometimes can be to arrive at such a site, it makes sense to "save" it for future reference, especially if you are going to need the Web address for documenting your research.

Every year new **search engines** appear, helping to supply some form of order to the chaos of information on the Web. Each one has its own special features, so you should refer to the *hints* and *help* and *advanced search techniques* each provides. Here are a few from what is growing constantly into a long list:

Yahoo! http://www.yahoo.com/
   Very comprehensive in its coverage. Popular for casual browsing and for research. Subject directory and news sources are excellent.

Google http://www.google.com
   A recent, highly rated addition to the search engine list. A fast, clean homepage with no advertising and thoughtful searches make this site particularly easy to use.

Infoseek http://www.Infoseek.com/
   Large subject directory and list of services including travel information and maps. Foreign language available. Provides good documentation information.

Magellan Internet Guide http://www.mckinley.com/
   Annotated subject directory on opening page is helpful. Useful for magazine searches. Many peer-reviewed sites.

Excite http://www.excite.com/
   Broad reach but can be complicated to use. Provides a relevancy rating to the left of each result.

Northern Light http://www.northernlight.com
An excellent choice for serious research. Provides free article synopses, full texts for a fee.

HotBot http://www.hotbot.com/
Highly rated for fast, comprehensive searches.

AltaVista http://www.altavista.digital.com/
Useful for information about careers, entertainment, finance, health, news, travel.

Livelink Pinstripe http://pinstripe.opentext.com/
Designed for business users.

Lycos http://www.lycos.com/
Another business site. Larger database than Livelink. Foreign languages available. Material is stored in directory form.

"Go ask your search engine."

These are just an introduction. For long lists of additional search engines, you could consult **Best Search Engines** at **http://kresch.com/search/search.htm** or **Beaucoup** at **http://beaucoup.com/**, which lists search engines by category. For special subject areas such as medicine or scientific research, you need to consult your librarian. To find specific journals through a search engine, you can search by subject, such as *native american culture journals*, which should produce a list of relevant journals. Some search engines are more helpful than others for this type of search.

An early academic browser was **Gopher** at **gopher://veronica.psi.net:2347/7-tl**. This is helpful for methodical academic searches that move down from general lists to more and more specific levels.

For access to newsgroups that provide broad coverage of current events and allow you to participate in discussions, try **Usenet**, reached by keyword or, for a complete index of newsgroups, go to **http://www.liszt.com/news/**. Keep in mind that the reliability of Usenet sources varies enormously. No one is reviewing them in an orderly way. In addition to a wide range of newspapers, you can find even greater variety through the major news services, Associated Press and Reuters.

Sometimes you can print the results of your search or save them, either to a directory on your own computer or to a floppy disk, which may reduce the number of note cards you use in keeping track of your research before you actually write your paper. You should be particularly careful about saving information found in newsgroups. Such sites change rapidly and may not be reachable the next day. Always remember to make a note of the **Web address**, called a **URL** (Uniform Resource Locators), and the **date you used the site** (retrieval date) along with other data such as name of site, author, title of article (if relevant), and date of posting if available. As you will have noticed, Web addresses are divided into complex sequences of letters, numbers, and punctuation marks.

Http://www.mla.org/main__stl.htm
protocol   server   domain type   file name

Thinking Critically about the Material

It is easy to be overwhelmed by the volume of documents you find on the Internet. Part of your job as a researcher is to determine the **relevance** of sources. Does a given source relate directly to the question at issue to which you have narrowed a broader topic? Do you see how the material is going to fit into the paper you plan to write? For example, if you are going to write a paper on the environmental impact of acid rain on the forests of Pennsylvania, you will not want to do in-depth research on the environmental impact of smog on redwood forests, even though the two topics are related. Another issue is the level at which an article is written. Is it written at a level you can fully understand without being too simplistic? Although you may need technical data, you also want to be able to interpret it for your audience.

Evaluating Web Sites—A Warning

Now for the **cautions**. Unlike journals that are subject to peer review, magazines that are closely edited even if they have a particular bias, and books that undergo a lengthy editing process, the Internet provides open season for anyone who wants to post material on a Web site. The Web is only as good as the people who put material on it, sometimes excellent, sometimes uninformed, sometimes deliberately deceptive. In many cases, articles come from reputable sources, and sites provide information you can trust, but in plenty of instances, a reference from a reliable site can send you to something completely unreliable, or a search will turn up an undependable list of documents. No matter which search engine you use, you need to keep in mind that each one creates its own database without impartial, outside review or evaluation. And economic interests often play a role in the selection a search engine may feature. You must constantly be on guard against the potentially unreliable, often muddled information lurking everywhere. You don't want your paper to be as bewildering as the Web so often seems. Nowhere are your **critical reading skills** more urgently needed than in discriminating among sites on the Web.

Sprinkled throughout are pornographic sites that come up on your screen without your having knowingly asked for them. In 1999, controversy surrounded the Web address, www.wallstreet.com. One could assume that such an address would lead to some centralized site in the heart of New York's financial district. But, in fact, it was a small financial domain, run privately, which decided to sell its address, worth considerable money. One of the would-be buyers was a pornographer hoping to cash in on unsuspecting visitors to the site. The same is true of sites spewing hate speech. **Chat rooms** are particularly dubious as authoritative or trustworthy sources. They may be engaging, even productive for generating ideas, but it is impossible to verify information gleaned from such sources. The same skepticism is necessary when you use e-mail as a source. Names are easy to forge and no one is out there in cyberspace monitoring who is posting what. Keep in mind that accessing pornographic sites on campus computers can be a serious offense.

So, what do you do? How can you know if information on a site is **reliable**?

- Use reputable search engines (see above), although they don't always screen out questionable sources and can be linked to sites over which they have no control. Because search engines can sometimes be self-serving or unintentionally limiting, try more than one to avoid omissions or hidden biases. Try to compare some Internet findings with those available in more familiar print sources.

- Rely particulary on the "edu," "org," and "gov" domains, other than search engines, and know what each of these domain types signifies: *edu* stands for an educational institution like your college; *org* means a nonprofit organization; *gov* means a government site. Note that .*com* indicates a commercial site with all the perils to be found in self-serving commercial ventures.

- Try to find out something about the author or at least about the publication in which an article appears. Are you aware of any particular bias attached to a given source? For example, the weekly political journal, *The Nation*, is known to give a very liberal, if not sometimes a radical, view. *The National Review*, on the other hand, is recognized for its conservative perspective.

- Ask yourself, have you searched out opinions on both sides of the issue?

- Does the author reason well according to some of the principles discussed in *Writing Logically*? Does the author support assertions with strong evidence and address opposing views? (See "A Dialectical Approach to Argument," Chapter 4.)

- Be alert for inflammatory language and be prepared to qualify or explain sources that sound didactic and heavily one-sided.

- You will also want to note the date of an Internet posting. Often information has become out of date but looks current at first glance.

- Ultimately, you will begin to develop a critical sense of what looks reliable, what dubious.

All this is not to say that developing a sense of what is reliable in books, magazines, and journals isn't still important. Remaining alert to seriously slanted material, no matter what the source, is an extremely important feature of research.

Finding Your Own Data

Keep in mind that you can, and often should, conduct your own research in the field. You may want to survey a group of people, conduct an experiment, especially if you are working in the sciences, or interview people who can provide information for your paper or project. (For how to set up a survey, see Writing Assignment 17, Conducting a Survey: A Collaborative Project, in Chapter 7.) In addition to face-to-face interviews (still the best option), you can also interview someone over the phone; by e-mail (electronic mail sent over the Internet); in chat rooms, discussion groups, or newsgroups online (note caution above); or by various more complex synchronous communication arrangements over the Internet, by which you can communicate with individuals simultaneously. Your campus probably has a computer center where you can receive help in learning about these online sources and activities if you are not already familiar with them.

PEANUTS *Charles Schulz*

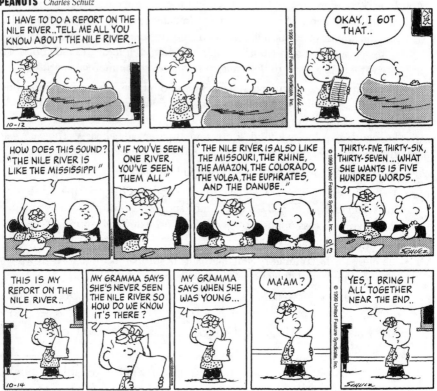

Documentation

What Information Should Be Documented?

1. All direct quotations.
2. All indirect quotations in which you summarize the thoughts of others without quoting them directly. For example:

   Semanticist S. I. Hayakawa notes that although poetry and advertising seem unrelated, they actually share many characteristics (162).

3. All facts and statistics that are not common knowledge. If we were to state that many modern marriages end in divorce, documentation

would not be necessary because the assertion reflects common knowledge. But if we state that one out of six women in this country has been raped, we must provide documentation; our readers would want to know the source of this exact conclusion to evaluate for themselves its reliability. When you cite numbers and percentages, your readers may be skeptical. Careful documentation of your sources contributes authority and thus strengthen your claims.

The key issue here is that you correctly attribute all the ideas and information you gather from outside sources. Plagiarizing the work of others is an extremely serious offense that can have grievous consequences. Once you have completed your research, remember that the paper is going to be yours, written in your own words, interpreting the information you have gathered, and expressing the opinions you have developed during the course of your research.

Incorporating the Ideas of Others into Your Own Writing

If you want your paper to read smoothly, you must take care to integrate direct quotations and paraphrases of other people's ideas into the grammatical flow of your sentences. Don't just "drop" them with a thud into a paragraph. Rely, rather, on a ready supply of introductory or signal phrases with which to slide them in gracefully, for example, "As Freud discovered," "Justice O'Connor notes," and "according to *The New York Times.*"

Sometimes, to make a quotation fit in smoothly with your own writing, you must add a word or words. Such additions are placed in brackets. For example:

Carson McCullers sets a strangely luminous night scene:

There was a party at the banquet table in the center, and green-white August moths had found their way in from the night and fluttered about the clear candle flames.

She seems to make a point of the "green-white August moths [that] had found their way in from the night . . . ."

As well as introducing quotations and paraphrases smoothly into the syntax of your sentence, you must also pay attention to semantics. Don't assume that the relevance of the quotation is self-evident. Make its relationship to your reasoning explicit. Is it an example? An appeal to authority? Premise support? A counterargument? Whatever the case, the purpose of the quotation—how it relates to the point you are making—should be made explicit.

Punctuation and Format of Quotations

Periods and commas are placed *inside* quotation marks unless the quotation is followed by a parenthetical citation, in which case the period follows the citation.

> "Writing, like life itself, is a voyage of discovery," said Henry Miller, author of *Tropic of Cancer.*
>
> "Thinking is the activity I love best, and writing to me is simply thinking through my fingers."
>
> —ISAAC ASIMOV
>
> "The true relationship between a leader and his people is often revealed through small, spontaneous gestures" (Friedman 106).

Colons and semicolons go outside quotation marks.

> Read Tamar Lewin's essay, "Schools Challenge Students' Internet Talk"; we'll discuss it at our next class meeting.

Use single quotation marks [' '] for quotations within quotations.

> "In coping with the violence of their city, Beirutis also seemed to disprove Hobbes's prediction that life in the 'state of nature' would be 'solitary.'"
>
> THOMAS FRIEDMAN, *FROM BEIRUT TO JERUSALEM*

If the prose quotation is more than four lines long, it should be indented, about 10 spaces for MLA, 5 for APA, and double spaced as in the rest of the text. No quotation marks are necessary.

Omitting Words from a Direct Quotation

Sometimes we don't want to include all of a quotation, but just certain sections of it that apply to the point we are making. In this case, we may eliminate a part or parts of the quotation by the use of *ellipsis* dots: three spaced periods that indicate the intentional omission of words. If the *ellipsis* concludes a sentence, add a final period.

1. Something left out at the beginning:
   " . . . a diploma from Harvard or Emory nearly guarantees a financially rewarding career," says columnist Cynthia Tucker of *The Atlanta Constitution.*
2. Something left out in the middle:
   Explaining the desperation of a writer, William Faulkner once said, "Everything goes by the board: honor, pride, decency . . . to get the book written. If a writer has to rob his mother, he will not hesitate; the 'Ode on a Grecian Urn' is worth any number of old ladies."

3. Something left out at the end:
   As Henry Lewis Gates says, "The features of the Black dialect of English have long been studied and found to be not an incorrect or slovenly form of Standard English but a completely grammatical and internally consistent version of the language . . . ."

How Should Information Be Documented?

Although each discipline has its preferred style of documentation, four standard styles prevail. The Modern Language Association (**MLA**), documented in the *MLA Handbook for Writers of Research Papers* and mentioned above, is the choice in English, foreign languages, and some other humanities. The American Psychological Association (**APA**), documented in the *Publication Manual of the American Psychological Association*, is preferred by psychology and other social sciences. History, art history, and philosophy tend to follow *The Chicago Manual of Style*. The sciences, including the health sciences, and mathematics rely on a system created by the Council of Science Editors (CSE) (formerly, the Council of Biology Editors, CBE), documented in *Scientific Style and Format: The CBE Manual for Authors, Editors, and Publishers*. The Chicago Manual of Style and the CBE use raised numerals in the text to refer to either footnotes or endnotes. The MLA and the APA have evolved a system of parenthetical references—author and page number cited in the text of the paper—with a list of cited works or electronic sources and all relevant publishing information at the end of the paper. Chances are, you will be following MLA style. If writing for a class that requires one of the other forms, consult your instructor about the preferred documentation.

In most cases, more important than the fine details of documentation is a sensible consistency. The major concern is that you provide accurate information from the sources you have used and insert that information into your paper in a reasonably standard way. We illustrate examples from the MLA style, offer the basic distinctions of the APA system, and introduce electronic documentation.

The MLA Style of Documentation for Printed Sources

When referring to a cited work, MLA style generally uses the present tense ("Gloria Feldt shows.") This is a distinction from the APA style.

CITATIONS WITHIN YOUR TEXT   In many cases, you can slide a reference into the text of your paper without disturbing the flow of your ideas. Introduce the material being cited with a signal phrase, usually the author's name, and use a parenthetical citation stating the page number of the sentence. Readers can then turn to the list of works cited at the end of the paper to discover the title and publishing information, which are listed under the author's or authors' last name.

1. A book by one author

> S.I. Hayakawa points out that advertising and poetry are alike in that "they both strive to give meaning to the data of everyday experience" (162).

When the author is not identified in the text—when there is no signal phrase—the author is identified in a parenthetical citation.

> Consumers want to identify with the happy, attractive people featured in advertisements (Hayakawa 164).

Note that there is no punctuation between the author's name and the page reference.

2. A magazine article

Once again, you may identify the work and/or author in a signal phrase, placing the page number in a parenthetical citation.

> In "Reinventing Baltimore," author Tony Hiss tells us, "A city [Baltimore] that was almost two-thirds white in 1960 is now almost three-fifths black" (41).

Or, in the absence of a signal phrase, you may identify both the author and page number in a parenthetical citation.

> Baltimore, "almost two-thirds white in 1960 is now almost three-fifths black" (Hiss 41).

3. More than one author

When the source is a book or a magazine with two or more authors, list all the last names in either the text or the parenthetical citation. If there are more than three authors, you may list all their last names (within reason) or cite one last name followed by *et al* and the page number. If an author has more than one work cited, you need to provide a shortened version of each title in the text reference, relying on the concluding list of works cited for the full title.

Sometimes you will be quoting a writer who is cited by another author you are reading. If you are unable to find the original source yourself, acknowledge both sources: original author in the body of your text, followed by (qtd. in Hiss 68). Note that MLA now suggests abbreviations in their parenthetical references.

Here is an example of multiple authors quoted from an essay from a collection:

The authors reason that "since gene selection is not limited to cloning, what we have to say about the demand for cloning may well have implications for other reproductive technologies" (Eric A. Posner and Richard A. Posner, "The Demand for Human Cloning," qtd. in Nussbaum and Sunstein 235).

Place your parenthetical citations close to the material quoted or referred to, sliding them in at the end of grammatical units in the sentence and thus making them as unobtrusive as possible.

Consumers want to identify with the happy, attractive people featured in advertisements (Hayakawa 164), and thus you will find that advertising models are forever young, healthy, and slender.

The idea in the first part of the sentence belongs to Hayakawa, the comment in the second half reflects the idea of the student writing the paper.

Although disciplines that follow the *Chicago Manual of Style* may still use traditional numbered footnotes at the bottom of the page or the end of a paper, this is rare in literature or the social sciences.

List of Works Cited: MLA

This list, to be titled "Works Cited," will be the final page of your paper and include all of the works cited in it, documented according to the examples that follow:

1. The information comes in three units—author, title, and publishing information—each separated by a period.
2. List, in alphabetical order, the authors by last name, with first names following. If more than one author, all *additional* authors are listed first name then last.
3. Capitalize the first word of a book's title and proper nouns.
4. For the publisher, write place or publication, colon, name of publisher, and date. Dates now follow the European form, day, month, year. Example: 29 April, 1999.
5. Where there is an editor, write *Ed.* and the editor's name before the title of the book, after the article or chapter taken from it.
6. Indent the second line five spaces under the first.

1. **Book by one author**
   Hayakawa, S.I. *Language in Thought and Action.* Orlando: Harcourt Brace Jovanovich, 1990.

You can find the publishing information on the reverse side of the title page of the book.

2. Excerpt from a collection or anthology

Posner, Eric A. and Richard A. Posner. "The Demand for Human Cloning." *Clones and Clones: Facts and Fantasies about Human Cloning.* Ed. Martha C. Nussbaum and Cass R. Sunstein. New York: Norton, 1998. 233–261.

3. Magazine article

Toufexis, Anastasia. "Seeking the Roots of Violence." *Time* 19 April, 1993: 53.

4. Professional or academic journal article—(same format as for a magazine article)

Reiss, David. "Genetic Influence on Family Systems: Implications for Development." *Journal of Marriage and the Family* August 1995: 547.

5. More than one author

Use the last then first name of the initial author followed by additional authors' names in reverse order—first name then last.

Specter, Michael, and Gina Kolata. "After Decades and Many Missteps, Cloning Success." *The New York Times* 3 March 1997: A1.

When a magazine article is unsigned, list the title of the article first, alphabetized by the first letter of the article, followed by the title of the magazine, appropriate dates, and the page number.

If an entry refers to an editorial or letter to the editor, cite the author, or if no author, title, followed by either "Editorial" or "Letter" set off by periods.

The APA Style of Documentation for Printed Sources

Because this book is intended primarily for classes in the humanities, we concentrate on MLA style, but for quick reference we include an introduction to the fundamentals of APA documentation.

CITATIONS WITHIN YOUR TEXT

1. Book by one author

Introduce the quotation using the author's name followed by the date of publication in parentheses. Place the page reference in parentheses at the end of the passage.

Semanticist S.I. Hayakawa (1990) points out that advertising and poetry are alike in that "they both strive to give meaning to the data of everyday experience" (p. 162).

2. Paraphrase

If paraphrasing rather than quoting directly, include the author's name in a signal phrase followed by the publication date in parentheses, similar to the example above. Or, if the author is not identified in a signal phrase, place his or her name and the publication data in parentheses at the end of the sentence. Note that a page number is not required for a paraphrase.

3. **Magazine article**
For a quotation taken from a magazine article, follow the same format required for a book by one author.

According to Toufexis (1993), the roots of violence are complex and diffuse.

LIST OF WORKS CITED: APA In APA style, the alphabetical list of works cited is entitled "References" and conforms to the following guidelines (you will note several distinctions between APA and MLA):

1. List the authors by last names, and use initials instead of first names.
2. Capitalize only the first word of a book's title and proper names.
3. When more than one author, separate their names with a comma and the symbol &.
4. Place publication date in parentheses after the author's name.
5. Omit quotation marks around title of an article.
6. Where there is an editor, place the name before the title of the book, write (Ed.) followed by a comma and the book's title, the pages in parentheses, location, and name of publisher.

1. **Book by one author**
Hayakawa, S. I. (1990). *Language in thought and action.* Orlando: Harcourt Brace Jovanovich.

2. **Book by more than one author**
Nelkin, D. & Lindee, S. (1996). The DNA mystique: The gene as a cultural icon. In P. Brown (Ed), *Perspectives in medical sociology* (pp. 415–433). New York: Waveland.

3. **For a magazine article**
Hiss, T. (1991, April 29). Annals of place: reinventing Baltimore. *The New Yorker,* pp. 40–73.

Electronic Sources

Precise information about author, date, and other source details is not always consistent on the Internet, but the Modern Language Association (**MLA**) and the American Psychological Association (**APA**) have established guidelines for documenting online sites. Web sites for these updates change, as we've said before, but at time of printing the following addresses for documenting electronic sources, introduced earlier in the chapter, can help. For MLA, try **<www.mla.org>**; for APA,

<www.lib.ricks.edu/inet_apa.html>, or for more complete research help, **<http://humanities.byu.edu/linguistics/Henrichsen/APA/APA01. html>**. If you have difficulty with these sites, consult your instructor. You will also find expanded coverage of documentation of electronic sources in *The MLA Handbook for Writers of Research Papers, The MLA Style Manual and Guide to Scholarly Publishing,* and the APA's *Publication Manual.* If your paper is intended for the sciences or social sciences, you should consult your instructor about preferred electronic documentation. When you are not able to find all the information desirable for complete documentation of electronic sources, provide as much as possible. The point is to provide easy Web access to your readers, acknowledging that address and sites change and information available on a given date may not be accessible later.

Under most circumstances, you need the following information from an Internet site:

1. Author (if one is named)
2. Name of the specific page(s), usually in quotation marks
3. Name of the main page, usually underlined or in italics. Sometimes this and the previous citation are the same.
4. Date of the page or the last update
5. URL in angle brackets
6. Date of access (preferably given in parentheses after the URL so as not to be confused with the date of the Internet page)

CITATION WITHIN YOUR TEXT   You may refer your reader directly to a Web site without including it in your list of works cited. The form follows the same guidelines for printed sources listed above, reflecting either MLA or APA style as appropriate.

> For a complete legal brief prepared by the National Legal Center, visit the Web site, <www.filteringfacts.org/ >.

LIST OF WORKS CITED: MLA   The author or first of several authors' last names come first with additional authors listed first names first, in the same form they appeared under List of Works Cited (MLA) (see above under MLA). Next comes the title in quotation marks, and then the **source and date** of publication or posting. This material is followed by the **date you accessed the site** and then the Web address or **URL** (Uniform Resource Locator). It is particularly important to make a note of the address before leaving the site because, if you wanted to recheck your documentation, you need that address. When a line break occurs in the middle of an address (some can be astonishingly long), make the break immediately following a punctuation mark, not between letters or numbers. Another way of safeguarding your own retrieval of material is to use the bookmarking or "favorite places" storage on your Internet server (see above), but that may not include the electronic address and could be unavailable when you try to return to it. Printing a hard copy from the Internet can also be helpful, especially if you want to quote a substantial passage. Again, list the documentation information; printed pages often omit it.

1. **Source directly from the Web**

   Beeson, Ann, Chris Hansen, and Barry Steinhardt. "Fahrenheit 451.2: Is Cyberspace Burning? How Rating and Blocking Proposals May Torch Free Speech on the Internet." ACLU Whitepaper 16 Jul. 1997. <http://www.aclu.org/ issues/cyber/ burning.html> (26 Aug. 1997).

2. **Article from the World Wide Web that has also been published in print magazines**
   Include that source before the electronic address.

   Morton, Oliver. "Overcoming Yuk." *Wired* Jan. 1998. <http:// www.wired.com/wired/ 6.01/Morton.html> (20 Mar. 1998).

   Wilmut, I, A. E. Schniek, J. McWhir, A. J. Kind, and K. H. S. Campbell. "Viable Offspring Derived from Fetal and Adult Mammalian Cells." *Nature* 27 Feb. 1997. <http://www.nature.com/Nature2/ serve?SID=90209795&CAT=NATGEN&PG=sheep/sheep3.html> (19 Jul. 1997).

3. **Article in a newspaper or from a newswire**

   Wade, Nicholas. "The Genome's Combative Entrepreneur." *The New York Times* 18 May 1999. <http://www.nytimes.com/library/national/ science/051899sci-genome-venter-html/> (19 May 1998).

LIST OF WORKS CITED: APA   Here is an example of an article from the Web to show distinctions between MLA and APA.

   Inada, K. (1995). "A buddhist response to the nature of human rights." *Journal of Buddhist Ethics 2*, 55–66. http://www.cac.psu;edu/jbel/twocont.html (visited 1996, July 23)

Sources on CD-ROM   Cite author, title, magazine or journal if applicable, and specific disk publication information.

Information Received through e-mail (electronic mail)   Give the name of the writer, describe the transmission with name of receiver, and give the date the e-mail was sent.

   Todd, Alexandra. E-mail re status of the human genome project sent to the authors, Cooper and Patton. 2 June 1998.

Formatting Your Paper

When you prepare the final draft of your paper, some matters of format will vary according to whether you are following MLA or APA guidelines. But in general, you should double space, have margins of at least 1" all around, and for APA allow 1 1/2" on the left. Beginning with the title page, number each page. If you are including an abstract, place it on a separate, introductory page.

For MLA, you have a choice of using a title page for your title, name, class name, and number, and date **or** of placing identifying material at the top left of page one with the title centered below it, immediately above the opening paragraph. In general, you will omit section headings within the paper unless called for in a technical subject.

For APA, put identifying material and title on a title page and place your name and a short version of the title at the top right-hand margin of every page. Scientific disciplines tend to be more demanding on specifics of format than the humanities, so when writing papers that require the APA style, consult your instructor about details of format.

Placement of Quotations

If a quotation runs over four typed lines of text, set it off with a five-space indent and continue to double space. You may choose to set off shorter quotations for clarity or emphasis. Drop the quotation marks when you indent. (This advice for quotations holds for almost any category of student paper or published article.)

Verb Tenses

Verb tenses in English are complex, but when writing in the humanities, it is customary to use the present tense when referring to matters discussed in the writings of others. This is a convention and not all disciplines follow it. Trusting your ear and depending on common sense will usually serve you well.

> An example of the *present tense* used in a paper about a book: "In *Zen and the Art of Motorcycle Maintenance,* Robert Pirsig *breaks down* the steps of motorcycle repair into logical components."

> An example of the *past tense* to express a contrast in time: "Richard Epstein, in his essay 'A Rush to Caution,' *warned* against a quick ban on all cloning, but today he might approve of cloning under some circumstances."

In Conclusion

This chapter contains a great deal of detailed information that we don't expect you to memorize. Before each paper that requires research, we suggest you look over the chapter to refresh your memory on the basic principles of generating ideas for a research project, finding material, and documenting sources. Once you have gathered your information and are ready to start writing, use the chapter as a reference, consulting Web sites and research handbooks for more complete technical support.

"*You've taught me how to think.*"

TEXT CREDITS

"A's Aren't That Easy," by Clifford Adelman, *The New York Times*, May 17, 1995. Copyright © 1995 by the New York Times Company. Reprinted with permission.

John Brunch, Letter To the Editor, response to "How Colleges Are Gouging You," *Time Magazine*.

"Five Good Reasons to Oppose the Vouchers Initiative" California Teachers Association/NEA, Coalition to Educate Against Vouchers, Revised 29.VII.93.

"Totleigh Riddles" by John Cotton from the *Times Literary Supplement*, July 24, 1981. Reprinted by permission of the author.

"Dispute Over Claims of Ibuprofen Dangers." Copyright © 1990 by United Press International. Reprinted by permission of United Press International.

A *Study in Scarlet* by Arthur Conan Doyle. Copyright © 1996 The Sir Arthur Conan Doyle Copyright Holders. Reprinted by kind permission of Jonathan Clowes Ltd., London, on behalf of Andrea Plunket, Administrator of the Sir Arthur Conan Doyle Copyrights.

Max Frankel, "The Facts of Media Life," *The New York Times Magazine*, Sept. 27, 1998. Copyright © 1998 by the New York Times Company. Reprinted with permission.

Ellen Goodman, "Boxed-In by Ethics 101?" *San Francisco Chronicle*, December 17, 1998. Copyright 1998, The Boston Globe Newspaper Co./Washington Post Writers Group. Reprinted with permission.

From Ellen Goodman, "The Straw Feminist," *The Boston Globe,* February 1, 1994. Copyright © 1994, The Boston Globe Newspaper Co./Washington Post Writers Group. Reprinted with permission.

Excerpt from *Language in Thought and Action,* Fourth Edition, by S. I. Hayakawa and Alan R. Hayakawa. Copyright © 1978 by Harcourt, Inc., reprinted by permission of the publisher.

Reprinted with permission of Scribner, a Division of Simon & Schuster, from *A Farewell to Arms* by Ernest Hemingway. Copyright © 1929 by Charles Scribner's Sons. Copyright renewed 1957 by Ernest Hemingway.

Reprinted with permission of Scribner, a Division of Simon & Schuster, from *Men Without Women* by Ernest Hemingway. Copyright © 1927 by Charles Scribner's Sons. Copyright renewed 1955 by Ernest Hemingway.

"Why U.S. Must Support the Arts" by Charleston Heston. From *The San Francisco Chronicle,* April 19, 1995.

James H. Jones, Letter To the Editor, *New York Times Book Review*, November 11, 1997.

From *Bird by Bird* by Anne Lamont. Copyright © 1994 by Anne Lamont. Reprinted by permission of Random House, Inc.

"Hostess" by Donald Magnum. Reprinted by permission. Copyright © 1987 Donald Magnum. Originally in *The New Yorker*.

Miss Manners reprinted by permission of United Feature Syndicate, Inc.

INDEX

Behavior Belongs in the Brain